PIMLICO

153

CAITLIN

Paul Ferris has written a number of novels and histories, most recently *Sex and the British*. Among his biographies is *Dylan Thomas*, the standard life; he also edited Thomas's *Collected Letters*. He is currently at work on a Life of Freud.

CAITLIN

The Life of Caitlin Thomas

PAUL FERRIS

PIMLICO

For Mary

PIMLICO
An imprint of Random House
20 Vauxhall Bridge Road, London SW1V 2SA

Random House Australia (Pty) Ltd
20 Alfred Street, Milsons Point, Sydney
New South Wales 2061, Australia

Random House New Zealand Ltd
18 Poland Road, Glenfield
Auckland 10, New Zealand

Random House South Africa (Pty) Ltd
PO Box 337, Bergvlei, South Africa

Random House UK Ltd Reg. No. 954009

First published by Hutchinson 1993
Pimlico edition, with a revised Author's Note, 1995

1 3 5 7 9 10 8 6 4 2

© Paul Ferris 1993, 1995

Printed and bound in Great Britain by
Clays Ltd, St Ives PLC

ISBN 0-7126-6290-1

CONTENTS

ILLUSTRATIONS

Author's Note

Caitlin's life was a fight to assert herself as a woman and an artist, and if she failed in what she sought, the attempt was full of fire. Before she gave up alcohol (more or less), she liked to call herself an 'Irish fighting drunk', but behind the belligerence was a deep sense of her own inadequacy. Marriage to Dylan Thomas when she was twenty-three gave her a career as 'the poet's wife' that she both wanted and hated. Her passionate nature could make life difficult for herself as well as for others. There was never anything half-hearted about her. After Dylan's death she became disenchanted with Britain, and especially with Laugharne, the little town in west Wales where they had lived. Eventually she stormed off to Italy, and lived there for the rest of her life.

As I describe towards the end of the book, I first met Caitlin in 1978, a year after my biography of Dylan Thomas was published, a work with which she declined to cooperate. She was no longer a hard drinker, and for that and other reasons – by then she was sixty-four – the violence one heard about had gone. I enjoyed her company more than I suspect I would have done twenty years earlier. But the reformed Caitlin never found tranquillity, or even the compromise between dreams and reality that keeps most people going. Her toughness of spirit was always admirable. In the end, though, her story is that of a disappointed woman.

She died in Sicily on 31 July 1994, after the hardback version of the book appeared. As unpredictable as ever, she indicated before she died that she wanted to be buried beside her husband at Laugharne. Her body was duly brought to Wales for interment ten days later. Peace reigned at last.

The book could not have been written without her cooperation, in the form of interviews and the right to quote from her letters and other writings. Our amicable agreement gave her the right to read the typescript and suggest changes, though I was not obliged to make them. In the event, by the time the book was written, in 1993, she was unwell. Her Italian son, Francesco Thomas Fazio, read it with her over a period of six weeks. Her comments were restricted to a dozen or so small points, some of which are incorporated in the text.

I am grateful to her immediate family for their help at different times – to Giuseppe Fazio, her companion of many years; to Silvia de Marcai (Silvana), their long-time housekeeper; but most of all to Francesco, Caitlin's son by Giuseppe, a Sicilian and an Anglophile.

I make grateful acknowledgement to the following for information and/or access to material:

Llewelyn Thomas and Aeronwy (Aeron) Thomas, two of Caitlin's three children by Dylan Thomas; Brigit Marnier, the sister closest to Caitlin, who died three weeks after her; the estate of the late Nicolette Devas, Caitlin's other sister, in the shape of Lady Monson, Prosper Devas and, especially, Esmond Devas; Ben Shephard; the Summers family – Vincent, Simon and Gabriel; Gwen Watkins, widow of the poet Vernon Watkins; Roger Lubbock, Caitlin's former publisher, who found an unpublished typescript by her; David Gardner (and his wife Fifi), who knew Caitlin in the 1950s and kept many letters; the Dylan Thomas trustees – Stuart Thomas, Michael Rush and Sir Kingsley Amis – who let me see certain Trust files.

I am grateful also to: Brenda Aherne, Barbara Arthur, Jim Blackwell, David Chambers, Richard Christopher (British Library), Gordon Claridge (Oxford University), Nest Cleverdon, Jane Dark, Walford Davies (University College of Wales, Aberystwyth), Roz Devore, Peter Diggory, Francis FitzGibbon, Nigel Gardner, Dan Garrihy, Noreen Garrihy, Tony Garrihy, David Gascoyne, Pamela Glendower, Sir William Glock, Colm Hayes, Michael Holroyd, Rebecca John, Lady Pansy Lamb, Lansdowne Reference Library (Bournemouth), Ken Layson (Mirror Group Newspapers), J.C. Wyn Lewis, Edgar Locke, Nesta Macdonald, Richard Mangan (Mander & Mitchenson Theatre Collection), Ralph Maud (Simon Fraser University, British Columbia), Bernard Merchant (former police superintendent), Jill Mindham, Naomi Mitchison, Sheila Morgan (Laugharne), Sheridan Morley, Michael de la Noy, Kate O'Brien, Gus O'Connor, Brendan

O'Regan, Peter Owen, Frances Partridge, David Vernon Phillips (former police sergeant), James Casalis de Pury, Gabriel Pustel, Neville W. Reed, Joan Rodker, Paddy Shannon, Bettina Shaw-Lawrence, Adam Sisman, Anthony Storr, Clem Thomas (Laugharne), Dai Thomas (Laugharne), Eve Thomas (Swansea), Jeff Towns (Dylans Book Store, Swansea), Susan Watson, Barry Wiles, Joan Wintercorn (Bernard Quaritch Ltd), the late David Wright.

Several people wrote to me about Caitlin's school at Bournemouth: Wally Driffield, Mary Knott, Marjorie Springman.

I thank the following for permission to quote material:

As owners of letters and other texts, chiefly by Caitlin Thomas: Special Collections, University of Delaware Library, Newark, Delaware (Emily Holmes Coleman Papers and John Malcolm Brinnin Papers); Houghton Library, Harvard University; Harry Ransom Humanities Research Center, University of Texas at Austin.

As copyright holders: Estate of Nicolette Devas (Nicolette Devas and Francis Macnamara copyright); Aeronwy Thomas (her letters); David Gascoyne (his *Collected Journals*); David Higham Associates (*Collected Poems* and *Collected Letters* of Dylan Thomas); Vivien John (Augustus John copyright); Edgar Locke (Cordelia Locke copyright); Ben Shephard (Rupert Shephard's unpublished journals); Trustees for the Copyrights of Dylan Thomas; Stuart Thomas (letters of Florence Thomas); Dr F. C. C. Todd (Ruthven Todd copyright); Charlotte Townsend-Gault (William Townsend journals copyright); Gwen Watkins (her *Portrait of a Friend* and Vernon Watkins's poem, 'To a Shell'); Susan Watson (Wyn Henderson copyright).

As publishers: Jonathan Cape Ltd (*The Seventh Child* by Romilly John); Century (*With Love* by Theodora FitzGibbon); J.M. Dent (*Dylan Thomas in America* by J.M. Brinnin); André Deutsch Ltd (*Time after Time* by Molly Keane); Faber & Faber Ltd (*Letters of Philip Larkin*); Hamish Hamilton Ltd (*A Personal History* by A.J.P. Taylor); William Heinemann (*Augustus John* by Michael Holroyd); Ticknor & Fields (*Their Ancient Glittering Eyes* by Donald Hall).

I

Under the Volcano

The family consists of four people: Mrs Thomas, the poet's widow, in her late seventies; Giuseppe Fazio, a dozen years younger, a Sicilian who used to be in the film business; Francesco, their grown-up son, and Silvana, a middle-aged Venetian cook and factotum. At the time of writing they live on the poet's royalties, administered by trustees – whose names are not spoken with affection – while the works remain in copyright. This will not be for much longer, the poet having been dead nearly forty years already. But until 2003 the cheques arrive monthly, and there is always the chance of giving copyrights a new lease of life by publishing 'revised' editions with hair-splitting changes. *Under Milk Wood* is on the list for this treatment.

A substantial income finds its way to the Thomas-Fazio household, which has come to rest – an inappropriate word – in suburban Catania, the grimy conurbation on the east coast of Sicily, which lies on the lava slopes of old disasters and exists by courtesy of Etna, smoking and sprinkling cinders over its snows ten thousand feet above.

As suburbs go, it is not very salubrious. From a corner on a thoroughfare, occupied by a post office and a few shops, a road wanders for half a mile, past run-down villas, blocks of flats and wasteland, before becoming a dirt-track with a rubbish-dump at the end of it. Smoke rises and a goat or two can be seen, surveying Catania and the distant Mediterranean from their rubbish-hill. Mrs Thomas's property, which is comfortable but modest, is in the last group of houses before the dump, and the way to it is barred by iron gates. They moved to Catania from Rome ten years ago. She regards it as a kind of prison, and perhaps it is.

'Nothing could be so far away from culture as we are,' she wrote to her daughter, Aeron, in London in 1983, 'and I do envy you your opportunities, now that I am sober. I have got heartily sick of always living in the midst of dumbcluck primitives, who I used to think once, when I was much younger, were oh so romantic!'

The idea of attaining wisdom and serenity after many misspent years appeals to Caitlin Thomas. She refers to herself sometimes as 'Santa Caterina', though she can hardly be serious. Wanting (she says) to withhold nothing in our conversations, she does hold back at times, on the grounds that the wild woman who used to drink immoderately has been succeeded by a 'different' Caitlin. But behind the uneasy quiescence of age and ill-health, it seems to be the same old Caitlin, her soul still at war with most of the rest of creation.

She enjoys mischief. I arrive from Britain on a spring day in 1991. We have known each other since 1978. I have two presents bought at Harrods, a tin of chocolate biscuits from her daughter, a wooden box of English tea-bags from me. The biscuits are dismissed at a glance. 'I *never* eat them. I get chocolate in my teeth. She should have known.' The tea-bags are examined with a pitying smile. In Catania, apparently, English tea-bags are as common as lemons. 'There is a boat comes from Malta,' says Francesco helpfully. In the following days, when Silvana, who often seems in a temper, is serving beverages, tea is never in sight. At every opportunity the chocolate biscuits are offered, and melt a bit more.

Caitlin's voice is soft, with a trace of something that might be Irish, indicating either the origins of her paternal family, the Macnamaras, in Co. Clare, or – just as likely – the listener's imagination, since she was born and brought up in England, and has rarely set foot in Ireland for half a century. An hour or two's talking tires her, some subjects being worse for her than others. These make her bite the ends of her fingers, and next day they are tipped with sticking plaster.

'Francis, my father, had big hips and big boobs.'

'And that worried him?'

'Yes, it did. I saw him for the first time go into the river at Ennistymon, and he really looked obscene.'

Earlier she expressed a lifelong distaste for men's naked bodies. Might the uninhibited Francis be the reason for this?

'It may have had a lot to do with it. He was always imitating Augustus John, you know. He wanted to look like him.'

As a rule she prefers to avoid the subject of Augustus John, with whom she had a prolonged love affair, and whose daughter she was once rumoured to be. Presently she will write me a note saying, 'I would very much like a more serious approach from you. I do not want a cheap gossipy book. You can make a clean cut of Augustus John for a start.'

As a further aid to biography, she suggests one morning that I read the latest revision of an autobiographical manuscript that she has been rewriting on and off for twenty years, *Double Drink Story*. The 1984 version was the last I had seen. I accept politely. This is a mistake. She says, 'If you like it, is it possible for me to ask for more money?'

We already have a contract, which took six months to negotiate, to cover her cooperation.

'You mean more money from me?'

'Yes.'

I say no. Giuseppe urges her to let me read it – she has been revising it with the help of Francesco, who is close to his mother – and of course she does.

Among the passages that weren't there in 1984 is one about fish. Fish-descriptions and fish-analogies appeal to her. She describes catching flat-fish in the estuary at Laugharne, the small seaside town in Wales where she spent nearly half her married life. The idea was to detect a dab or plaice in the mud with bare toes, trap it underfoot and throw it clear of the water. One day she found she was being followed by the infant Aeron, who was throwing back the dabs, in tears because she was sorry for them.

'Acting,' wrote Caitlin. 'She was not my daughter for nothing. I had play-acted all my life, and it was only in those rare precious moments alone that I was not. I knew that I was right, that my solitary enjoyment had been good, and that my daughter was wrong.'

She shouted, 'A fish can't feel, you fool,' though she later found this to be untrue, as she admitted, when she threw a live flat-fish into a pan of scalding oil, and it leapt out on to the floor. It went back in, still jerking, no match for Caitlin. 'It was still scalding hot and half raw as I tore into it in my impatience, but, I have got to say, I had never tasted anything so delicious in my whole lifetime! Such is the potency of devouring one's very own victim captured with the sole of one's very own foot.'

Returning the manuscript, I said the flat-fish story made me wince. 'It did?' she said. 'Oh, good.'

Aeron, now married and with children, lives in a London suburb, and is not a frequent visitor to Sicily. Llewelyn, Caitlin's first-born, had recently lived in Spain for a while and was now in Cork City; his mother sees even less of him. For filial visits she relies on Colm, the youngest of her children by Dylan. Francesco, their half-brother, is a devoted son, having abandoned or postponed a career as an architect in Rome, where he studied for years. His mother usually calls him 'Francis' or 'Chico'. From his quarters, a small damp building just within the iron gates from the lane, come the sober rhythms of modern but not too modern dance music. He spends hours in there practising ballroom-dancing steps, advancing and retreating with eyes half closed. He dreams of going to the international ballroom champion-ships at Blackpool.

Sixty years earlier, Caitlin had a similar passion for dancing, though not of the ballroom kind. When our conversation reached subjects that made her bite her fingers, she would say crossly that she preferred to remember the dancing.

'My father and Dylan were both people who went in for sex and drinking, things I tried to get fun out of, that now I despise. Talking about it pulls me down, it diminishes me. Sex wasn't enriching.'

'What would have been enriching?'

'If I'd had more opportunities for dancing. A life of dedication to dancing, or writing, or any of those things you feel you've got inside you.'

Francis comes in from the terrace in time to hear the word 'dancing', and says that after lunch he has a Vienna waltz lesson with his dancing master. 'Strange,' he ponders, 'that I got the chromosome of dance. Llewelyn could very well have got it, or Colm, or Aeron.'

Caitlin agrees, adding, with the usual hint that her family is not coming up to scratch, that she had had hopes of Aeron and the ballet. 'I was trying to explain,' she says, 'that the pleasure one gets from dancing doesn't diminish one, like the pleasure one's supposed to get from sex.'

'In dancing you're sure to get pleasure,' says Francis, leaning close to his mother and smiling into her face. 'Nothing can go wrong there, once you know your steps and have the timing right.'

'My whole idea of dancing was to have freedom from the coils,' says Caitlin.

Months earlier, when we were still haggling about the biography,

4

one of her letters talked about the 'cold dark prison' of her childhood in the Hampshire countryside. 'What an unbearable sadness when I came down in the icy mornings,' she wrote, 'and peered out of the misty windows to see the same old elms still starkly standing there and blankly staring back at me. What could I possibly do to banish the elms from my consciousness but dance? To keep on dancing until I fell, in a straggling heap of limbs, into unconsciousness. Which is roughly what I did.'

A mysteriousness about her early years had been an added inducement for me to go on haggling. Perhaps she suspected this, and wrote accordingly.

In Catania she takes a masochistic pleasure in talking about what she has missed in life. She hankers after places she turned her back on long ago. 'Somewhere,' she says, 'there is a place waiting that's right for me.' She talks about England in winter – buttered crumpets, fires blazing. 'Nostalgia,' says Francis kindly. They talk about streams and rivers; she is thinking of Hampshire and Co. Clare.

Thirsty for the fulfilment of art, she married a poet, a poor substitute in her view today; although at one time she felt differently. What suffered were her own artistic ambitions. She once wrote, 'I should have been black and white, carved-in-adamant marble,' adding that 'the proof of my pudding was in the hopping, clothed with a garment down to the foot.' Instead, the poet sapped her confidence. She hopped unnoticed. Now, for that and other reasons, he is reviled. She has said most of it before, but takes pleasure in twisting the knife. He was limp as a lover. What a bastard he was. Even his funny stories weren't funny.

Caitlin's blue eyes are sunk in moist saucers, as if water is seeping through the cheeks. 'People who are sentimental about Dylan would be horrified if they knew that this great love of his life is spitting in his eye.'

'You've spat in it already.'

There is an unkind paragraph in the dog-eared *Double Drink* typescript where she writes about their stay at a villa outside Florence in 1947, when a grant enabled Dylan Thomas and family to live in the sun for four months. She gloats over how miserable he was because no one was taking any notice of him in alien Tuscany, and says that she finds this 'a refreshing reversal of our roles'.

I murmur something about 'poor bugger', which doesn't go down well.

'For heaven's sake, he deserved to be punished for behaving so badly. He had all the cards and I had none. He traded on my lack of money.'

'I still think you're laying it on a bit – *I gloated and gloated to my heart's content.*'

'It's completely true.'

'It was forty-four years ago.'

'So what? It's still alive.'

'You're still remembering it with pleasure, gloating over poor old Dylan, who couldn't speak a word of Italian, who didn't know anybody, who was getting like a pickled beetroot in the sun.'

'He wasn't in the sun. He was in a bar, in the Giubbe Rosse.'

'Writing you pathetic letters on bits of paper, saying, You have left me, you have gone off on a tram.'

'Well, it was about time I did leave him.'

'You were having a wonderful time, having your bottom pinched by bambinos.'

'It's no good you taking his side. In a court of law that wouldn't mean a thing. I was the poor mother.'

The reference to Caitlin going off on a tram is from an unpublished letter by Dylan Thomas. I had seen it some days earlier, when Giuseppe – who has boxes of papers, most of them generated by the Thirty Years' War with the trustees – produced an old black wallet. This contained four letters written by the poet, three to Caitlin and the other to Aeron, together with two further fragments. These have remained unsold and unpublicised. The Florentine letter is in tiny handwriting on pages torn from a 1947 pocket diary, headed 'Cash Account'. It begins:

> Caitlin my dear dear dear, I am writing this useless letter to you at a table in the Giubbe Rosse, where, after I saw you go away in a tram, I went, sadder than anybody on the whole earth, to sit and wait.

It ends in much the same mood, demonstrating the elaborate self-abasement that colours most of his letters to his wife:

> I love you, Caitlin, I think you are holy. Perhaps that is why I am bad to you. I love you. I am holding you now and you are beautiful. Dylan. 10 o'clock, alone, in this place.

When the Thomas market for manuscripts was in good shape, the contents of the wallet might have fetched a thousand pounds. Caitlin was thought to have sold all her husband's letters years ago. In Catania she declares that she kept them through sentiment, not oversight.

After three weeks of conversations, interspersed by some unrelaxed sightseeing, I return to London. Among the papers Caitlin gives me to take back are a few of her poems, written in recent years. She doesn't ask what I think of them.

One is a 'Poem to Love', dated 1989, where she concludes that 'Sex is the knockout killer of True Love'. I find myself reading this reformed woman's poem on the deck of the car ferry from Palermo to Genoa. The island of Elba is in sight, where she had the sexual adventures that she wrote about in her book *Leftover Life to Kill*. The poem says that she encountered the real thing once, but then

> I drowned it in alcohol and sex
> Like a kitten in a sack
> With a stone in it
> Chucked in the river.

Her husband wrote about sexual jealousy in two or three of his own poems, without giving away much about their marriage. The unreformed Caitlin led him a dance, but he led her one, too. Forty years later she still doesn't know what to make of her feelings or their life. The poem offers cold comfort:

> Sooner or later the bell tolls
> Time's up!
> So a new fiddler must be found
> To tune up your fiddle.

I am reminded of her remarks about 'Santa Caterina' when I come across an old codicil to her will. Perhaps she is serious about her sainthood after all. She writes about the disposal of her body from the lakeside house they built in the Abruzzi mountains east of Rome:

I do not want to be put into a box at all, nor a hole.
    I want to be wrapped, tight as a cocoon, in fine white cotton cloth, like an old-fashioned newborn baby, with the arms and hands bound down,

flat against my sides; and only the head free. Almost mummified from feet to chin.

Then I want to be laid on a bier of vine leaves, profusely strewn with sweet-smelling mountain herbs, and covered with olive branches . . .

Then I want to be carried by ass or mule back supported by peasant hands, from Scanno, up the rocky path, to the disused church, except on special occasions, of San Esidio.

Then I want to be put down on a grassy mound, or a grassy hollow, nearby. Where an enormous bonfire has already been prepared underneath, with a large oak stake in the middle.

Then I want my bier placed at the foot of the stake, and my body lifted out and strapped, with strong cords, to the stake. In such a way that, when the bonfire is lit, the fumes of the burning bier will rise up, enveloping my body.

Then I want the whole construction set suddenly, explosively alight, into blazing cracking flame. So that, in a very short time, my bones are blasted to the four elements: to the music of nature.

If this funeral sounds symbolic of a martyred Saint at the stake: it is not only symbolic it is fact.

The Last Words are laced with her oddly endearing brand of plain-speaking. The instructions continue:

That is what I want. What I will get is another blacker story.

2

Fathers and Mothers

In the west of Ireland, the Falls Hotel, Co. Clare, overlooks the small market town of Ennistymon, and takes its name from a series of cascades where the River Cullenagh emerges below the town bridge, falling over wide ledges. The Atlantic coast is only four miles away, and there are salmon in the river (which then becomes the Inagh) below the cascades. The remains of babies born out of wedlock have been found there, too, in the backwaters.

The Falls, a two-storey Georgian house built on a small sharp hill, has been a hotel since 1936. Before that it was a derelict property-of-a-gentleman, with goats living in the hall and the young Caitlin Macnamara holding court in the stables round the back. During the 'Troubles' of the early Twenties it was shot at, and enthusiasts claim they can still find bullet marks in the walls; no great distinction in a country that has seen so many gunmen. Before the Troubles it was the home of a Protestant diehard, Caitlin's grandfather, 'Henry Vee'. Only echoes of that time survived into hers.

The house keeps its distance from the town. Such places can be found all over Ireland, left-overs from England's colonial rule. In her Irish novel *Time After Time*, Molly Keane invents a house which was 'built at the date when one of the marks of a gentleman's ownership, dividing his property from the vulgar public, was a long quietness of avenue'. The public, being Roman Catholic and peasant, was regarded as even more vulgar than it would have been in England. The Falls Hotel is separated from Ennistymon by such an avenue, tree-lined, with the roar of the cascades coming over the grass.

'Henry Vee' was Henry Valentine Macnamara, born on St

Valentine's Day, 1861, and brought up to be a staunch defender of the faith. The Macnamaras, an Irish family that must have sold out to the English religion in some earlier century rather than be dispossessed, owned land further north in Clare, and their seat was Doolin House, seven miles from Ennistymon, near the village of Fisher Street. Ennistymon House, built in the 1760s on the site of a castle that had belonged to the O'Briens, came to the Macnamaras by marriage in the nineteenth century. It was a finer house than Doolin, which stood in the middle of nowhere and faced the Atlantic (and is now a heap of stones). With it came the town at the end of the drive, raising its cap and paying rents to the Macnamaras.

Henry Vee, whose father died when he was a child, inherited a rich-man's income from the rents of around £10,000 a year; the figure was in an accounts book looted from Ennistymon House during the Troubles. For his time he was a considerate landlord as long as his interests were not interfered with, high-spirited, keen on country pursuits, married to an unpredictable woman of Australian descent. His eldest son, Francis – who became Caitlin's father – once told his wife-to-be that Henry Vee was born illegitimate, Henry's parents not having married till the child was two years old.*

Francis was born in 1884, six days after St Valentine's, a date for which Henry Vee may have been aiming, as a joke. He was a tall lanky youth, awkward physically and perhaps mentally as well, though he was clever enough. They sent him off to England to be educated at Harrow, as his father had been, grooming him for his future as another aloof occupant of Ennistymon and Doolin. But he had different ideas, which by luck or otherwise was far-sighted of him, since a career as landlord had a limited future. A romantic egoism led him towards poetry and a circle of artistic friends in London, while at the same time he irritated Henry Vee by his sympathy for the rising Irish nationalism of the Sinn Fein ('We Ourselves') variety; what that meant for landlords was more trouble with the peasants. By 1907, aged twenty-three, Francis was married, and two years later he published a book of verse, his first and last. Living in London on an allowance from Henry Vee, the young Macnamaras briskly produced a family, with Caitlin the last of four children, born 1913.

Henry Vee is a dead-end in the family story, eventually hounded out

* The recorded dates, e.g. in *Burke's Irish Family Records*, show no irregularity.

of the country; although Caitlin's generation – which had never known the pleasures of the big house, such as they were – came to terms easily enough with an Ireland he would have found unimaginable. In 1910 he had a taste of what was coming, when tenant farmers from Doolin, seeking attention for grievances over rents, turned loose hundreds of cattle from his land, and were sent to gaol. They sang a song about

> That so-called Macnamara from Ennistymon House,
> We swear before we're done with him he'll be muter than a mouse,

and ten years later, after the First World War, when rebellion was flaring up across the country, they came close to killing him in an ambush. Republican terrorists were beginning to murder and kidnap. Henry Vee's turn came on a December morning in 1919 when he and some friends went into the Burren, a stony district half an hour's drive from Ennistymon, intending to shoot rabbit and woodcock. They were in two cars. At a road-junction they found stones across the road, and as the cars stopped, shotguns and at least one rifle opened up on them. The terrorists, local men firing from behind a wall, shouted, 'Give us the guns! We will kill you all!'

The assailants wanted their weapons, not their blood, but the party chose to fight. They included a lieutenant in the British Army and a Lady Beatrice O'Brien; most of them were injured. A gamekeeper had the crown of his hat blown off and was nearly scalped. Henry Vee was wounded in the arm and face. But he shouted 'No surrender!' and they fired back, routing the gang.

Compensation was paid by the courts, Henry Vee living up to his reputation for jocularity when, during the inquiry into his arm injuries, he was asked by his lawyer, 'Did you ever find that you had to leave down an article which you had lifted?' 'Yes,' said Henry Vee, 'I had to leave down a decanter.' But Ennistymon was never the same. Police had to guard the house by day, soldiers by night. The authorities suggested it might be wiser if Macnamara left until the tension died down. In practice that could mean for ever. Henry Vee hung on. It was not until April 1922, when the Irish Republican Army's '1st Western Division' sent a letter ordering him to leave Ennistymon House, 'which with your entire property is confiscated', that he decided the game was up. The house at Doolin had already been destroyed. Henry

Vee retreated to London, to live in Kensington on an income that dwindled alarmingly when tenants asserted themselves, legally or otherwise, as Ireland began to drift free.

The inheritance that eventually came to Francis, when Henry Vee died three years later, was a fraction of what otherwise it would have been, affecting his plans, which were never less than ambitious, and helping to colour Caitlin's view of money, which was never less than demanding. (One of Francis's schemes had been to set up a 'republic of Macnamaraland'. No doubt it would have failed, even if the money had been available; all his schemes did.)

Marriage he judged to have been a mistake after seven or eight years of it. His bride, Mary Majolier (who preferred to be called Yvonne), twenty-one years old when they married, was a slight, pretty, lackadaisical woman, half Irish and half French; her mother was a Cooper from Limerick, another family of gentry (somewhat decayed) who lived in a Georgian house, her father a prosperous corn broker and lapsed Quaker from the south of France who had business in London. Mary and her siblings were expensively educated in England.

Between them she and Francis had allowances of just over three hundred a year, sufficient to live on but not enough to guarantee Yvonne the silk underclothes, first-class travel and daily hot bath that a young lady had a right to expect. Her family were not keen; they may have heard the story of Henry Vee's illegitimacy, and they would not have been happy to know (if they did) that Francis and Yvonne were lovers while still unmarried; at one time she feared she was pregnant. The Macnamaras liked women, and Francis found Yvonne physically enchanting. But her nature bothered him. There are stories of young Macnamara complaining that she was too matter-of-fact, and not as carnal as she might be.

They married at Paddington register office on 11 July 1907, amid family disapproval. At first they lived in south London, where their first child, John, was born, later moving to Hammersmith, by the Thames. Presently Francis fathered three daughters in quick succession. Nicolette was born in February 1911, Brigit in August 1912, Caitlin on 8 December 1913.

Whatever his defects, which worked their way steadily to the surface through his life, Francis had many assets, such as courage, vigour and intermittent charm. He was more than six feet tall and liked to wear blue to bring out the colour of his eyes. To Nicolette he 'carried himself like a conqueror'. She remembered his snatching her at dusk from the nursery, when she was an infant and they were staying at Ennistymon House, so she could hold an owl he had caught in the grounds, 'a miracle I would remember for the rest of my life'.

Nicolette's are the only personal memories of Francis as the father of small children. Sailing was one of his passions; once she was flung into the Thames at Hammersmith and nearly drowned when a yacht capsized. He used to leave her, aged two or three, stranded on a flat-topped buoy in the river while he sailed out of sight, so as to harden her spirit. Even Caitlin, whose feelings about her father combine loathing with fascination, once saw him as 'a lost hero', before perceptions of a different kind took over: 'straw man', 'bombastic gasbag', 'contemptible traitor'.

His slim book of poems, *Marionettes*, was published in 1909, before any daughters appeared. A sonnet addressed to his new-born son ('wailing diminutive of me') ends with a pleasing couplet,

> Some day you may forget I dragged you thence,
> Perhaps forgive the vast impertinence.

Five connected poems about Ennistymon, 'To a river, where it runs dark and slow beneath a cascade', suggest a man bracing himself for disagreeable but necessary action. Each concludes with a wish to be resolute, as in

> Oh, when such song is making in this marsh,
> Keep me from tenderness, make me as harsh!

and

> Oh, let me look at time as does this marsh,
> And be to individual hopes as harsh!

Ideas filled his head, literary to begin with, economic later on. It occurred to him that the best epic poem a man could write would not describe a war or episodes of history, but merely the events of an ordinary day. For a member of the land-owning gentry before the First World War, this was a promising thought, a decade earlier than James

13

Joyce put the same idea to work in *Ulysses*. But Macnamara was never to concentrate his considerable intellect. He had theories about education and the theatre, he wrote a play to illustrate the Irish mind, he hobnobbed with poets (and was friendly with Yeats), he thought to found a new religion, he wanted to build boats, he had plans for a puppet-theatre.

With money short and a wife who didn't entirely understand, he ploughed on optimistically with the writing career that refused to take off. He was away frequently, sailing or walking, usually in Ireland. Yvonne he wanted to think of as a lover. She thought too much about household accounts and servant-problems for his liking; her mind was caught in what he called 'the snare of matter'. As he once remarked, if he told her that the sight of white clouds blowing up from the sea made him think of the white frills of her underclothes, she would merely say it meant there was going to be rain.

A family on conventional lines was an encumbrance for an artist who was so keen that he answered 'Poet' when asked his profession. In London as a younger man he had encountered writers and painters, and brushed against the sticky allurements of bohemia. He knew Augustus John, perhaps since before his marriage, and told Yvonne that 'I love him above all men.' There was an element of hero-worship. The admiring Francis believed in sexual freedom, at least for men. John, notoriety already at his heels, was a paradigm of sexual ruthlessness. His complicated ménage was well established, and his sexual appetites seemed to spring from the same force of nature that produced the art. He was a dangerous model for a dilettante who relied on a tortuous intellect rather than on instinct.

There are traces of their relationship in Clare, where Francis entertained the painter, as well as other literary and family friends, around 1914 and 1915. Yvonne did her own entertaining, and slept with Augustus John, although the affair was brief, perhaps no more than a courtesy due to a famous man. She talked about it to her daughter Brigit, repository of family secrets. Perhaps her husband guessed at the time and was flattered.

Francis had the use of Doolin House, where he felt on close terms with the fishing families of the district – even if it was hard to stop the poor being obsequious – and he studied Gaelic, both at Doolin and on the nearby Aran Islands, already a place of pilgrimage for Celtic Revivalists; J.M. Synge's plays inspired by the islands were written and performed in the first decade of the century. None of this fraternising with the enemy went down well at Ennistymon House, where the butler was a Protestant, and Anglican servants who married local Catholics were dismissed. Francis was a frequent visitor to the cottages of Fisher Street (so was Augustus John, who entertained the locals by singing to them in Welsh). Stretched out on a bench by a turf fire, Francis ate bread with the salt butter for which he was unfailingly greedy, or tapped his feet to a tin whistle, or fell asleep listening to a story that was sometimes too long to be told at one session, and so became a serial.

Guests at Doolin enjoyed these glimpses of the primitive. Augustus John, always on the look-out for it, wrote thirty years later of the land where 'some forgotten people' had built their fortresses. 'The smoke of burning kelp rose from the shores. Women and girls in black shawls and red or saffron skirts stood or moved in groups with a kind of nun-like uniformity and decorum.' Francis, too, had an acute sense of place and the underlying history of stone and contour. But he was tempted to go too far, waffling on in philosophic terms that had his listeners looking at their watches. As well as being a Poet, he was now a Thinker.

A Macnamara family album has snapshots of the beach at Doolin, probably taken in the summer of 1915. In one, Augustus John, all beard and wide-brimmed hat, sits on a rock, confronting the photographer. A few yards away, Francis has his head in his hands, ostentatiously pensive. Another in the same sequence shows Francis on his rock – corduroyed legs spread and braced, hands folded – gazing intently past the camera to the sea. Beside him is a small figure, aged perhaps eighteen months, standing with her blonde head bowed, looking at his leg. The father's preoccupation eliminates her from the portrait. The child is Caitlin.

Yvonne was not as keen on Ireland as Francis would have liked. She preferred London. Doolin meant problems with the damp and the servants. A letter he wrote her in the summer of 1914 picked at the discontents. He was in Clare, she was in Hammersmith, and he wanted her to come over, leaving their nursemaid behind in favour of an Irishwoman –

there is old Mary Shannon I would love to have for a nurse. She would teach them splendid things, songs and stories, she would give them manners – but you would rather have them soaped every day. Is it nothing to you that you are the wife of a poet?

Francis's life as a family man was coming to an end by 1914. The marriage kept its outward form for a while longer, but he would speak of it, later on, as having lasted only seven years from their marriage in 1907. The war may have nudged him towards decisions. He was thirty when it began, young enough to enlist, had he chosen to. Like other Irishmen of the time, his loyalties ran in different directions. He sent a letter on the subject to Augustus John, 6 September 1914. His nationalist sympathies had come under suspicion:

> In the tension of these days (pardon me) I seemed to lose myself, or rather to realise that I had never found myself; expression was suspended – or must take the form of indecent exposure . . . I really don't know how I stand: [people] believed that I had taken service under the green flag, and I can't bring myself to explain that I only offered on the understanding that the volunteers were to be chartered by the govt.* That proposal is hung up owing to the divided feelings of the national army – not unnatural since all had been stirred to defiance of England by the Howth affair,† only a few Sundays before the European war broke out: now not wishing to bite England in the balls nor yet to disband, they remain simply a danger to the country in case of invasion, a band of francs-tireurs.

Francis wonders whether to enlist in the British Army for the war against Germany. In the Fisher Street cottages they 'believe that I have only to go to the war office, plank down a portion of my vast income, and be given a captaincy in France, more than one has begged me to take him as my servant'. A woman has written to Yvonne to say that 'there is no figure so magnificent as the warrior-poet', and vanity tempts him. But he suspects that 'I should only cut such a figure as Hamlet in the grave of Ophelia.' In any case, he doesn't want to die.

The letter was written after a visit to London, and 'I never was so glad to get away [. . .] into open fields; the grey stones of Burren were like a purge to my spirit.' Between the lines are uncertainties that go beyond the war. Francis writes of having

* An unofficial force of Irish National Volunteers came into being in 1913, a nationalist expedient as part of the campaign for Irish independence.
† The yacht *Asgard* smuggled nine hundred rifles for the Volunteers into Howth harbour. An associated demonstration in Dublin was fired on by British troops, causing three deaths.

an ideal study in the stable loft, in which I have just had windows put, and hope therein to work out some way to independence, God knows it's time, God also knows what way – and won't tell.

Letters from Augustus John to his wife Dorelia, about 1915, report the comings and goings of the Macnamaras and others. Gerald and Nora Summers, a wealthy English couple who painted and liked wandering about romantic landscapes, were encountered in Connemara, across Galway Bay. The writer and doctor Oliver St John Gogarty, who had a house in Connemara, was another good fellow. They all knew one another. Augustus kept a friendly eye on the Macnamaras. Yvonne and her sister Grace (another of the painter's conquests) were 'beyond praise', though the children screamed too much. As for Francis, he was 'a queer fish, not like a man at all. He's a devil for eating, and must have his tea [. . .] [He] is going to spend the winter in the wilds of Burren. This will finish him off. He dreams of the days when gentlemen addressed their wives as "Madam" and all was dignity and calm.'

Somewhere – in the converted loft at Doolin, or staying at a cottage in the wilds – Francis worked out his way to independence. He left his wife and children and went (it is said)* to live with an artist's model, the delectable Euphemia Lamb. According to Nicolette, who forgave her father everything, he abandoned them as a matter of principle, to demonstrate his belief in 'free love'. This phrase of the time sent a delicious shiver down middle-class spines, suggesting not just clandestine extra-marital sex but a bold assertion of the right to fornicate. H.G. Wells slipped it into novels, suitably packaged, and practised it enthusiastically in his private life. Augustus John did it because it came naturally. Francis Macnamara couldn't do it without making a fuss.

Some years later, writing a preface to Balzac's book about marriage, which he had translated, he read its message approvingly as 'Break with habit, break all adhesions, break, break, break all the time; or in one word DIVORCE.' Macnamara derided the dull Mr and Mrs Browns 'whose petty bickering, alternating with sentimental clinging, is often so embarrassing to visitors'. How much better, he wrote, was

* By Nicolette, who liked a romantic story, and was not always reliable when she came to tell one.

the freedom to separate: 'There is *design* in all that the husband does, he has attained to a position of free-will in regard to his wife, a position unknown to the drifting sentimentalist.'

Euphemia Lamb (1886?–1957) was the wife of the painter Henry Lamb, who had already given her up as lost. Augustus John attended their wedding in 1906 and was one of numerous lovers attracted by her long legs and husky voice. If she did have an affair with Francis, and there are doubts, she must have fitted him in between other liaisons with better-known (and richer) artists. She is unlikely to have been his first extra-marital mistress. There is even an echo of old gossip around Doolin, to be treated with caution, about the young blade who 'could do what he liked . . . girl friends in different parts . . . heard my mother say (God rest her) there were kids born within the parish, and sent off to America when they were old enough'. Landlords' sons, like royalty, attract tales of the misbegotten.

Yvonne was not well provided for, and she and her daughters lived where they could – the son was at boarding school, probably paid for by the Majoliers. Augustus John's house, Alderney Manor, in Dorset, near Poole, sheltered them for a while. So did the house in Chelsea of Nora and Gerald Summers. His family made steel. He had lived a quiet affluent life before the war and would continue to lead one afterwards. Now he had enlisted as a junior officer in the Royal Army Service Corps, so that he was away for much of the time that Yvonne and her brood were under his roof. Perhaps because of air raids in London, Nora lived in rented houses in or near Dorset, where she and her husband had gone to paint before 1914, and the Macnamara survivors went with her.

Nora liked photography, and there are innumerable shots of garden exteriors, including some at Alderney. Naked children feature prominently in anything to do with the Johns. Yvonne, full-faced and gentle, is occasionally glimpsed doing housework – she hangs out washing near a tree, or attends to mattresses laid out to air, probably at a holiday cottage. Nora, dark-haired, looks smarter, often in well cut slacks and silk shirt, smoking a cigarette or dipping her hands into her pockets; the mouth is both severe and sensual. Gerald (who appears now and then in uniform, lounging with a dog) would have taken the picture that shows them sitting shoulder to shoulder with arms around one another's backs, and Nora's head turned to smile into her friend's face. Mrs Summers was a stronger character than Mrs Macnmara, and she had lesbian tendencies that were awakened by her placid blonde companion.

Nora and Yvonne had been friendly for years. In the letter quoted earlier where Francis wanted his wife at Doolin for the summer, he said crossly that no doubt she and the nursemaid would be happier 'among the jerry-built villas of Lulworth'. Lulworth, in Dorset, was where the Summers had a cottage. It is conceivable that Yvonne, aware of increasing differences with her husband, was by 1914 already drifting towards an involvement with Mrs Summers.

By 1917 or 1918, Francis had gone, though not entirely, since he spent much of his time living near his wife, and kept up an energetic correspondence with her. Henry Vee had turned on him for deserting Yvonne, being especially horrified that his son kept insisting he had done it as a matter of principle. Francis is remembered for his monologues about how he had not really ended the marriage, but had assisted the two of them to rise above the banal confines of convention to some finer condition; Yvonne and the Majoliers thought this was humbug, but it took her until 1920 formally to ask for a divorce. She was only thirty-three and not ready for chastity (although as it turned out, she had Nora instead). Francis was asked to provide evidence of adultery. This was traditionally done by staying a night at a hotel with a woman, and sending a receipted bill, made out to 'Mr and Mrs', to the wife's solicitor. Ever resourceful, he proposed that his youngest sister Honor pretend to be the 'other woman'. The matter lapsed, and they went on being married until 1927.

Sometimes he sent Yvonne money; sometimes he borrowed money from her. Henry Vee's own income was threatened, and Francis can hardly have been a favourite son. Romilly John, Augustus's seventh child, approximately, remembered him at Alderney about 1920, standing gloomily on the edge of a pond, 'like a figure of superfluous thought'. Romilly found him 'a little larger than life' – praise indeed from someone with a father like Augustus – a man who was 'seldom at ease with his own body, which involuntarily tied itself into knots', tattered clothes hanging from his gawky frame. Macnamara tutored Romilly in poetry and philosophy, and at one time they lived together on a houseboat near Bournemouth, subsisting on onions and dried peas, while the master expounded the philosophical implications of Genesis, or floated economic theories that would change the world.

Charitable eyes saw Francis as an admirable figure, finding him an

idealist who refused to compromise. His rages were well known, and
so was a boastful, strutting quality that made him an exhibitionist who
could be entertaining as long as he wasn't too embarrassing. Caitlin
came to see all this as the behaviour of a fraud, too wrapped up in
himself to recognise his own failure. For the moment she was too
young to have much perception of him except as a missing person who
occasionally reappeared.

In Bournemouth, Francis was chairman and mainstay of the local
poetry society. Walter de la Mare, Edith Sitwell and Laurence
Housman came to lecture. Thomas Hardy accepted a portfolio of the
society's poems. Francis was still a practising poet, his tone as
awkwardly old-fashioned as ever, as in a sonnet to Bournemouth:

> What rises so material, where men tell
> Of cliffs remembered heather alone and pine?
> No natural growth! – 'twould seem, some Roman fine
> Had called for civilisation here pell-mell . . .

Others in the group did better. Trelawney Dayrell Reed was a bearded
farmer and archaeologist (he comes into the Caitlin story later), an
eccentric who found solace with other eccentrics in Augustus John's
household, and wrote poems that Francis printed in the *Wessex
Review*, a short-lived magazine that he edited from Wimborne. In
another of the poems to Bournemouth. Dayrell Reed bit the hand of
the genteel resort, expressing the dissidence that appealed to
Macnamara (even if the latter lacked the means to make it sound
memorable) in sharp stanzas that began

> Bournemouth! Respectability
> Stalks fig-leaved thro' your Square,
> Even the Flappers in your streets
> Lose their undaunted air

and ended

> So lulled you'll safely slumber on,
> Powerless for active sin,
> Too hogged with stale abundance
> For ideas to prick your skin;

> Till Lenin drive you to the Cliffs
> And Trotsky shove you in.

But the *Wessex Review* had higher aims. Francis pumped in articles about the future of Money and Transport, and wrote a strange 'Note on History' that represented civilisation as a line moving west from Egypt in 2000 BC, eventually reaching Paris 'in the millennium now drawing to a close', and due to pass 'right through the office of the *Wessex Review* in Wimborne'. Some of his work was signed with transparent anagrams, 'Marianna Camscarf' and 'African Mascarman'. But it was a serious magazine, which the London *Times* called 'fresh and imaginative'; its illustrators included Henry Lamb, Nora and Gerald Summers, and (with a drawing of 'A Domestic Scene') Stanley Spencer.

By 1923 – when Caitlin was ten, and Yvonne had found a modest but permanent home for them all on the edge of the New Forest – Francis was living in London, financed by a woman of means. Viewed from the outside he was a penniless poet and intellectual with something of the martyr about him, separated from his wife and half hoping to be taken back one day; a bit of a mystery, certainly to his men friends. But for a couple of years, the fog that surrounds his personal life disperses, to show a figure with a new dimension, violence. This is thanks to the woman of means, who wrote a novel about their relationship. She called it *Form of Diary*, and it appeared anonymously in 1939.

Her name was Erica Cotterill, which she changed later to Erica Saye. Her father was a socialist schoolmaster who wrote reforming books; her mother had money. Born about 1881, she was a neurotic with a difficult nature, a few years older than Francis, who poured her energy into writing and making the acquaintance of writers. Her most eccentric relationship, which existed only on paper, was with George Bernard Shaw, to whom she wrote impassioned letters after she saw a play of his in 1905, signing herself 'Miss Charmer' and provoking him into a correspondence that lasted for years. Rupert Brooke was also on her list. She wrote a serial autobiography, not very enlightening, of which Part One, published in 1916, was dedicated 'To Bernard Shaw'. Part Two, even less comprehensible, was 'To Bernard Shaw, whom I love'.

Form of Diary, which has 444 pages, is not easy to unravel, being written as an 'experimental' novel of the Thirties, with narrative and dialogue fused together; punctuation is unconventional and there are no quotation marks. Worst of all, the many characters are referred to by initials, usually a single initial. Copies have survived in the Macnamara family, its author unknown and its meaning forgotten, except that on a flyleaf at the end of one copy – it belonged to Nicolette – a pencilled list identifies sixteen of the initials. The writing is Francis Macnamara's: the first character identified is 'F.', who is himself. Others include Y. (Yvonne), E.L. (Euphemia Lamb) and L.J. (Lilian Johnson, another of his mistresses). C. is Cedric Morris, a minor painter. B. is Frieda Bloch, a Polish woman and former student at the Slade who had been one of Augustus John's nymphs. K.M. is the writer Katherine Mansfield. But the cast-list is a disappointment, since few of the names, if any, play a significant part in the story apart from Francis and the narrator.

Most of the novel is a claustrophobic account of the relationship between Francis and this narrator, who lets herself be identified as 'Erica', and who meets him on page 26. She has been reading his articles and poems in a magazine, no doubt the *Wessex Review*, and in no time she is offering him five pounds, thinking, 'Has all my life been to bring me to this person and has everyone and everything been a foreshadowing of this? Wait.'

Soon he is taking her money regularly and she is besotted with him, listening, often puzzled, to his monologues about the survival of the fittest or how to read novels or the nature of money. Their relationship is argumentative and, before long, violent. At the end of an evening (described with too many initials and not enough punctuation for clarity) Cotterill writes:

F. suddenly – Will you drink with me? I – *No*. F. up – gone. Im going to F. Wait. *No*. In and F. undressing . . . Into bed and I go and stand in front of him and still on F. still nothing then suddenly up and at me and he pulls down my body and beats it everywhere in frenzy then pushes it and throws it through the door. Lie still and wait. Back. F. up again and torrent of words – why did I not drink with him and if I come back now he wont answer for what will come and am I such a fool I cant see hes drunk and not master of a loathing in him of the whole of every part and particle of me? Feel nothing but that I must stand and wait. Suddenly again F. springs and at my throat and down and throttling then flings my body then violent shouting Go do you want me to go to the gallows for you, then again pushes and flings my body through the door.

Next morning the row continues when Erica returns to his room:

I – O take me in. F. – My bed isnt a cradle – pack off. I – O you dont understand. F. – I understand Ill have neither crying babies nor bitches in my bed – pack off. I – O I want to be comforted. F. – If you get in my bed youll be thrashed. I – O what is it crying out to you. F. – Its morbid lust – *be off*.

The violence recurs. '*Whenever* you ask for it again you shall have it,' he says. Called to the telephone while he is lighting a fire, F. is angry when he returns to find Erica lighting it herself – she was cold – and kicks her from behind. He likes to issue peremptory orders – 'Silence!' and 'Go!' and 'Hold your tongue!' On holiday in Paris he beats her in the hotel bedroom, the passage hinting that he is using something to beat her with. The masochistic Erica is happy 'in some way' but realises that if it goes on he may kill her. F. – 'panting more and white and lips back', and afterwards 'like an animal licking lips' – has a splendid time, announcing, 'I enjoyed that – yes I enjoyed it.' He also enjoys showing his contempt. 'Well,' he says in another scene, 'are we to go through the little ceremony of sleeping together again tonight?' He tells her he is going out for a bite to eat, after which he will read for an hour till 1.00 am, 'when I shall come in here and sleep with you'. Erica fumes but complies.

The real Erica Cotterill was a thin, nearly beautiful woman, eccentric but clever, who put up with Francis because she was in love with him. Susan Watson (daughter of the literary entrepreneur Wyn Henderson) was her friend in later years, when she still talked about him; by this time she had adopted two boys and changed her name to Saye. Her account of Francis in *Form of Diary* is authentic. Arland Ussher, a writer who was a friend of Francis, said that the book gave 'a full-length portrait of him, though a very nasty one'. Ussher saw Cotterill revenging herself in print. Her account showed 'how disagreeable he could be', caught, as he was, in difficult circumstances: 'in a bad position for getting tough with the lady (as her pensioner), and his consciousness of the fact no doubt helped to exasperate him'. *

* Ussher's typescript notes, dated 12 May 1963, are with Nicolette's papers. But in her family biography, *Two Flamboyant Fathers*, published in 1966, she avoided the subject of Erica and *Form of Diary*.

23

Francis's convoluted thinking, his bombast, his literary allusions, his interest in theories of money, are all recognisable in *Form of Diary*. F. is a translator, and Francis translated, from the French, not only Balzac's *Physiology of Marriage* but a volume of Brantôme's classic work of musty pornography, *The Lives of Gallant Ladies*. There are references to checkable names, as when F. talks of spending Christmas with E. at A., where 'E.' is Edie McNeill, sister of Dorelia John and thus Augustus's sister-in-law – whom Francis eventually married – and 'A.' is Alderney, the John house.

Erica seems to have brought out both his cruelty and his talent for obfuscation. F. loves to produce long-winded arguments to justify himself – 'imbecilities' and 'drivel', she concludes, and quotes a letter from F. where he says he is spending her money and using her flat, not because either is necessary to him but because she needs to prove that she loves him. 'O,' she groans, 'were there ever ever and will there ever be lies more despicable than F.'s lies.'

The affair falters when another of his lovers, L., arrives in London, and he carries on his affair with her while Erica is under the same roof. 'L.' was Lilian Johnson, a woman from the Aran Islands whose daughter, Pat, was acknowledged by Francis as his; the nearest island is an hour or two's hard rowing from Doolin. F. bullies and torments Erica, demanding that she give him her blessing, insulting and patronising her, shouting, while he brushes his teeth, 'Which am I to sleep with, Erica? L., which am I to sleep with?'

Near the end of the book, F. has left the scene, it being understood that he will marry E. when Y. has divorced him (which is what happened, Yvonne divorcing Francis in 1927, and Francis marrying Edith McNeill in the same year, a few weeks after the decree was made absolute). Erica and L. talk about their masterful friend, L. confessing how badly she wanted to marry him. 'But I never thought of F. as married,' she says, 'not really, I thought F. used his women as stepping stones to himself.'

Mrs Macnamara kept silent about her marriage, and there is no means of knowing whether her husband's angry cruelties were ever exercised in her direction. More likely she was handled with care, and the rough stuff kept for the inevitable failures who couldn't replace her; there are persistent stories that he tried in vain to persuade her to have him back.

Still, the dashing exterior of Francis Macnamara concealed some grisly features, and his sadistic tendencies can't have been entirely hidden from his family. Caitlin, who had a gift for detecting flaws in others, may have guessed at enough of her father's blacker side to make her shiver, and think twice about men.

3

Children of the Forest

The three Macnamara sisters (and their brother John, when he was not away at school) were brought up in what used to be called 'genteel poverty'. They were not poor in any serious sense. New Inn House, a former pub, bought for Yvonne with Majolier money, stood near the main road at Blashford, which was a location rather than a settlement, two miles from the market town of Ringwood. It had thirteen rooms and stone floors. The place would be primitive by today's standards, but it was no more spartan than a boarding school of the 1920s.

Fresh air and plain food supposedly went with good breeding; it would have been the same if they were rich. Mrs Macnamara didn't fuss over her daughters. She had other interests – tending her garden, reading Proust, being with Nora Summers. In the morning she doused them with cold water from a jug. Behind the house she kept goats, and their milk was poured daily down the girls' throats. It was supposed to make them hardy. For dresses they had loose cotton sacks, sewn up by Mrs Macnamara; they rarely went anywhere that required more. Beyond the fence was the New Forest country, a mixture of woods, heath and small valleys, places for them to run wild in. Education was spasmodic. Every so often a young woman came over from France, sent by the Majoliers, to teach the children French and learn English in exchange, and was given a hard time.

New Inn House had an air of self-sufficiency. What the neighbours thought didn't matter. They were inclined to be 'common', a word Yvonne used often. Farmers, shopkeepers, the people who passed on buses, came into the category, above which her daughters were expected to rise triumphantly, girls of good stock, with art and artists in the background. In due course they were sure to learn the wiles of well-bred women and catch wealthy men for husbands. She used to tell them so.

All were strapping, healthy girls. Brigit, the middle daughter, was the one who loved animals. She was shyer than the others, and rivalry didn't suit her nature. She kept in the background when cameras were about, and if her face did get into photographs, was apt to take a penknife and cut herself out of the album. Nicolette was more orthodox, full of life and ambition. She enjoyed the French connection that the Majoliers provided; she also made the most of the Augustus Johns, who were never far away, and their floating population of painters and writers. Caitlin, the youngest, had a simpler aim. She wished merely to make the most of herself.

When the Macnamaras first lodged with the Summers, the infant Caitlin with her golden hair was shared between the two women as if they were her joint parents. But when Lieutenant Summers came back from the war his wife was soon pregnant, and their child Vincent, born in 1919, displaced the five-year-old girl. Having done his duty, Gerald retreated into his own life of painting, woodwork and market-gardening, an amiable man who chose not to interfere in whatever it was that Nora did with Yvonne. In 1923 the Summers found a permanent home at Ferndown, just outside Bournemouth; it was the year the Macnamaras went to Blashford. The house, hemmed in by trees, was called Green Worlds. Often Nora drove the six miles to New Inn House for lunch, and in the afternoon she and Yvonne would retire to the bedroom and lock the door; or so Caitlin and Brigit remember. Yvonne sometimes stayed the night with Nora at Green Worlds, Vincent in his cot beside their bed, Gerald safely in his own quarters at the other end of the house.

In the 1920s the middle classes were just becoming aware that lesbianism existed. Later in the decade Radclyffe Hall's mildly written apologia for female homosexuality, *The Well of Loneliness*, was prosecuted and banned, as a result bringing the subject into the public domain. But it was generally regarded as so unspeakable that 'normal people', like Mrs Macnamara and Mrs Summers, would not have been suspected of it. Conceivably even Gerald thought their affection was platonic. Nora visited his bed once a week; otherwise he asked no questions. The details were told to Brigit once, as an adult, when she enquired of her mother, and over whisky and cigarettes heard the story of the long love-affair with Nora.

The Macnamara girls saw Nora as a witch and resented her. Later in life two of them exorcised her in their writing. Nicolette put her in a novel and killed her off with magic. Caitlin, trying to write a thinly disguised autobiography of her earlier years, *The Story of a Woman*,* called Nora 'Mrs Morgan', and saw her as an evil influence of childhood, 'blotting out the shape of her mother'. Nora was 'the sentinel of the house, with her bull's voice and her bull's mighty grip of the knees. When Ellen [the name Caitlin gave herself in the manuscript] was thus mauled and trapped, she felt the black jungle close over her head.'

Caitlin has several versions of her childhood, all of them concentrating on how she felt. Brigit has kept most of her memories to herself. Nicolette, in her family biography *Two Flamboyant Fathers* – which Caitlin both despised and envied – saw a childhood peopled with characters existing in their own right. She thought of herself as half adopted by the Augustus Johns, who, from 1927, lived at Fryern Court, half a dozen miles from Blashford, off the Salisbury road. Her intimacies irritated some of the Johns when the book came out. But Nicolette felt herself caught up in their vivid circle. Caitlin was largely untouched by it.

At her blackest, in old age, Caitlin came to see the New Forest childhood as 'a waste of our precious youth', a 'cold dark prison of isolation' whose 'deadly-dull background' left her with a 'paralysed inarticulateness'. This was the childhood of menacing elm trees, dripping in the mist. After revisiting New Inn House when she was in her fifties, and Brigit still lived there, she wrote to her sister that 'Blashford, my horrific ghost of the past, was not half so bad as it might have been.' But 'certain dusty grey shadows lugubriously lingered on'. The witch who tried to steal their mother was among them.

Caitlin's nature demanded more of whatever was going; even operations for appendicitis. Brigit (she says) was operated on at home by the local doctor, the country fashion in those days, and as part of her convalescence was pushed about in a wheelchair. As if this was not enough of a treat, every day Mrs Macnamara gave the child a small gift. 'My God,' says Caitlin, 'I was stiff with envy.' There was nothing

* Unpublished manuscript, probably written in London during or shortly after the Second World War. The account ends abruptly before she meets Dylan Thomas.

for it but to pretend to be ill herself. She mimicked her sister's symptoms, but at the last minute panicked, ran to the window and tried to jump out. 'Mad with rage', the doctor hauled her back, and stifled her cries with the anaesthetic. Afterwards, of course, there was no wheelchair and no daily present; self-punishment is the real point of the story, never mind that Brigit remembers it differently, without the drama.

Caitlin was prominent in Nicolette's writing, but not the other way round. Nicolette's account of her early life in *Two Flamboyant Fathers*, which is dominated by Francis Macnamara and Augustus John, glances uneasily in the direction of Caitlin, the 'chocolate-box beauty' with the 'underlying savagery' to whom danger was a challenge. Trespassing on a private estate, a keeper had trapped the three girls in a fork between a river and its tributary, when 'Caitlin whipped down her knickers, pulled up her skirts and waded across the stream with the water waist high'. Nicolette's fear of her volatile sister led her to take out libel insurance when the book was published in 1966.

Brought up, as were all the Johns and Macnamaras, to be relaxed about showing off their bodies, Caitlin was soon making the most of hers. A snapshot of 'Us 3 at Cannes, 1922', during a visit to the Majoliers, shows the sisters draped in bathing towels. Brigit, aged ten, is covered up. The towel around Nicolette, aged eleven, has fallen open, conceivably by accident. In Caitlin's case she is clearly parting the towel for maximum effect, her right foot bent back to touch the ground with her toes, eyes closed and a 'look at me being naughty' smile on her face. She was eight, already posing and arranging her limbs.

Four years later she can be seen in 'Caitlin and Vincent, 1926', taking no notice of the small boy with white-blond hair who is aiming a toy gun at the camera. Her stance is aggressive, left foot advanced and hands on hips, which swell below a long-sleeved sweater and pinstriped skirt; the camera is getting a nasty look. Nude Caitlins-in-adolescence are in other old albums, tastefully posed. Aged fifteen or sixteen, she stands on the dead branch of a tree, long-legged, arms behind her back, a roll of puppy-fat around her middle spoiling the effect. The photographer was sometimes Nora, who once posed the girl on a piece of agricultural machinery, half concealed by an armful of hay. Yvonne, too, came in for Nora's studies of the nude.

Caitlin once described herself in her youth as 'a pink pudding of undecided flesh'. Nicolette said that at eleven she was 'already precocious and physically attractive to men', at twelve 'a honey pot for men and boys', adding that her sister enjoyed the power this gave her.

Caitlin's own memories of childhood and early adolescence are rooted in her own physique and state of health, which in turn was bound up with her state of mind. They were all part of the same thing, the cast-iron stomach, the 'poster picture of rosy health', the feeling that she was 'aggression personified', that nothing could hold her back: leading her sisters on hectic pony rides that slashed their skins with bramble-tears, shouting in French at any clod-hopping farmers they happened to see, to keep them in their place.

Shut away in an Italian clinic long afterwards, Caitlin used her pony-riding memories to reach wider conclusions, suggesting that woman was a violent animal, less easily approached by a man than by a beast.* This is another of Caitlin's versions of childhood, the wild riding that carried suggestions of how she would take on life, 'bolting days of bolting recklessly down breakneck slopes: they had to be breakneck or they were not worth bolting down'. Her sisters fade from the story. She is alone with her animal. In the valley, the marshy ground makes them cautious, 'as though we had both read the same harrowing book about the disappearing pony and rider'. Then the facing hill has to be climbed 'in that mutual animal push of desire, the most important thing in the world then to both of us. Perhaps it was. I have not found anything more important, nor half so satisfactory, since.'

The member of the family closest to her was Brigit, 'Bronwen' in *Story of a Woman*, and it was to Brigit, stolid and undemonstrative, that she turned when Nora Summers became too overpowering. Brigit was 'usually to be found sitting with the goats, mute and insufferable. To Ellen's tale of hate she made no answer, but went on chewing her cabbage stalk, which she was sharing with the goat.'

The passages about Caitlin and Brigit have a glimmer of sexuality:

They were soon to be parted, as they walked through the marsh of marigolds, the mud oozing between their purple toes. Ellen tried to express her impatience and dissatisfaction. She was filled with an arduous thirst to drink to the depths of knowledge.

* In *Jug*, an unfinished and unpublished manuscript of sixty-nine pages, written 1958.

30

They arrived at the river bank, Bronwen pulled out the strings tying her together, and with one leap hurled her tremendous body into the icy current. She was carried away spouting and rollicking while Ellen shouted her ambitions across the water. Round the bend she rose resplendent with silver minnows and weeds caught in her scarlet breasts. On the way back they played their favourite shameful game of grown-up dolls. So impassioned did these scenes sometimes become that they dared not look up for the trembling in all their limbs.* They discovered a disused hen-coop, which they decked up with old coats and sacks. Here on hot afternoons they would retire and breathe the feathered air among nesting boxes and perches.

These days of burning innocence were suddenly broken by Ellen's passionate wish to go to school and learn how to be corrupt.

Caitlin's story has always been that her father was unwilling (and too poor) to have his daughters educated, believing that education only interfered with their growing-up. But as part of the divorce settlement – by which time he had inherited what was left of the Ennistymon estates – he put six hundred pounds in trust for his daughters' education. This is how the money was found to send Caitlin to Groveley Manor, a boarding school in Bournemouth, where she went in autumn 1928, aged fourteen. Writing in *Story of a Woman*, ten or fifteen years later, Caitlin said she was disappointed not to find glamorous uniforms and mysterious intrigues with mistresses. She got off to a bad start by weeping over a sardine on toast at breakfast the first morning. Shame and ostracism followed. Eventually a girl called Heather took pity on her. 'Her breast was like a moon where Ellen rocked and tossed on billowing mounds. Her back was covered in a soft close down, and Ellen wondered if tiny horns were hidden in her tufted hair.'

Caitlin always liked to hint at wickedness, if only to tease those who were apt to be shocked, and Heather's tiny horns may be in this category. Caitlin was two years at Groveley, until summer 1930. Three surviving letters to her mother describe lacrosse matches, confess to bad marks and ask for sweets. Nudity is mentioned in two of them: a doctor strips her 'completely naked', and a visiting lecturer

---

* Nicolette, who also played sometimes, remembered them as 'serial fantasies' about 'a world of doll-sized people'. She likened the Macnamaras' childhood to the Brontës', isolated and imaginative. Why the fantasies were shameful she didn't know.

on Italian art, 'a divine man', displays 'lots of Giotto's, Botticelli's, Fra Angelico's etc etc etc (I can't remember any more names) pictures including some nudes, which the school hardly dared look at, and were very careful not to mention afterwards'.

Nicolette (by 1929 in London at the Slade School of Art, a budding painter) said she was at Blashford the day Caitlin came home after her first term, dressed in a hideous brown uniform, looking down her nose at the house, saying, 'I didn't remember how awful it was.' When she left Groveley Manor, according to Nicolette, the headmistress, who had begun by calling her 'my little New Forest pony', advised her to 'paddle her canoe between the rapids of Men, Scandal and Poverty'. Caitlin's version in old age was that school had been a ghastly mistake, a sojourn among pudding-faced sheep which gave her 'my first smell of misery'. Too unorthodox to be welcome (she said), she was in demand only when she had chocolates. So she came to envy the popular girls, the 'unattainable goddesses', and longed 'heartrendingly' to be like them. The story, like many of Caitlin's, manufactures despair. She was 'sent to Coventry': no one would talk to her, and this banishment, she came to believe, was a foretaste of things to come in later life. 'Only alcohol, I discovered soon after, could alleviate this sense of being apart, out of things, on the outside, and it was I think my primary motive for starting to drink.'

Whether or not this is a plausible explanation, drink was on the horizon by the time she left school; men had loomed up already, in the shape of Augustus John's son Caspar, with whom Caitlin fell in love. Caspar, the second son, was nearly eleven years older than Caitlin. A strait-laced boy by his father's standards, he went off to be a naval cadet, and during the 1920s was a rising young officer (one of the few who thought aircraft-carriers were going to be more important than battleships), and was often abroad. Handsome but remote, he caused twitterings among the girls who encountered him at Alderney Manor and then Fryern Court.

It is not clear when Caitlin was ensnared. According to Nicolette, who liked to enlarge on family romances, it was before Caitlin went to school, when she was only thirteen or fourteen. This passion is supposed to have dominated her life for years. Caitlin's best connection with the Johns was Vivien, one of Augustus's daughters, who became a close friend. A year younger, she was vividly pretty and sophisticated, making Caitlin aware of her own 'mushroom thoughts'

In the later *Story of a Woman*, where Caspar appears as 'Galiad', the two girls organise a midnight picnic, and a small crowd, including Johns and Macnamaras, go out with food and rugs on a summer night. At a convenient moment, Ellen hurls herself at Galiad. '[She] pulled him, rolling on top of him, down the well of her desire.' They land in 'a spiky ditch of heather', but 'Ellen did not notice the spikes, she was riding on God's horses through the heavens'. The writing seems to be recapturing schoolgirl romance rather than reporting teenage lust, though one could be wrong:

> Bedraggled, earth-smeared, her neck wobbling to and fro like a ventriloquist's doll with a silly grin on its face, she thought that here was the beginning and end of experience.

Nothing more is reported of the midnight frolic. Ellen and Galiad have a further encounter when he calls at the school to take her out for a half-day, while the other girls hover 'like famished cattle at the smell of a bull'. She refuses to accompany him because of his 'stinging slight', but this is not explained; perhaps it was Caspar's lack of passion during the midnight picnic. Ellen spends the afternoon alone, biting 'deep into the quick of her nails, tearing at the frayed flesh till blood spurted on to her fingers'. She is 'an unwilling prisoner in her barbed wire character'.

In a more exciting version, not included in *Story of a Woman*, Caitlin has said that she meant Caspar to be the first man she gave herself to, and he rejected her. While staying the night at Fryern Court, she got into his bed wearing a pretty négligé, 'all dolled up and ready', and hoped he would respond as men were supposed to. He did not, a failure that left her 'enormously wounded'. Is this a fabrication based on rolling down a bank and exchanging kisses in the bracken? Her sisters believed the négligé story. A sub-plot has Mrs Macnamara frowning on the gap in their ages, writing to Caspar, who reciprocates Caitlin's passion, to warn him off. According to Caitlin, her mother also alleged a relationship between Caspar and Trelawney Dayrell Reed, the poet-farmer, who was homosexual. There is no evidence for this beyond Caitlin's cheerful reminiscence. In the same casual way, she could be heard, sixty years later, saying that Caspar had been made to pay for hurting her by losing his legs, a mishap that led her to deduce it must be 'God punishing him'.*

Caspar John (whose biographer, his daughter, says that in the 1930s he had no time for matrimony) was under no obligation to woo Caitlin. There is, however, an odd parallel with Brigit, who, later in the decade, was herself involved with Caspar. They seem to have been engaged. In Brigit's account, she was in bed with him at the home of one of his sisters when, two days before the wedding, he told her he couldn't or wouldn't marry her. In a letter that Dorelia John wrote to her husband, Augustus, in 1938 or 1939, she asks why the marriage has been postponed indefinitely, and sympathises with Brigit. Like Caitlin, Brigit was Augustus John's lover as well as Caspar's.

In 1927 and again in 1928–9 Caspar was abroad, serving on the China Station, finally returning to Britain in autumn 1929. The négligé incident could have happened before, between or after. A letter that Caspar wrote to his father in the spring of 1930, when he was based at Gosport, thirty miles away, spoke of 'an excellent party at the Summers's the other night and a farewell to John Macnamara [also in the Navy] who is off to China. We've also had some marvellous rides, about a dozen at a time, in the forest and on the downs.' There would have been opportunities for the schoolgirl to develop her feelings for the lieutenant.

The Macnamaras came under observation that summer, 1930, when a young painter, William Townsend, appeared on the scene. Townsend kept a journal. He was among a party of students at the Slade who were invited by Nicolette to stay in and around Blashford for a painting holiday. When he arrived, Caitlin, whom he knew only by repute, had not yet returned from school, and he thought her name was 'Kathleen'. He observed the seventeen-year-old Brigit, 'a masculine young woman' who 'spends her life among the animals', riding a horse off-handedly with a cigarette hanging from her lips, or rescuing a foal caught in barbed wire, treating its wounds matter-of-factly and expressing no 'futile sentiments'. In church she still wore her riding clothes. 'I found the place in the prayer book for her, and tried to sing

---

* If so, the punishment was long delayed. Admiral of the Fleet Sir Caspar John, as he then was, had his legs amputated as a result of vascular problems in 1978. He had married at the age of forty-one, and fathered three children: far too normal to please Caitlin, who preferred to believe he 'couldn't face doing it with a woman'.

one of the hymns. She remained quite dumb and counted the congregation.'

The unseen Caitlin was already causing disturbances. One of the visiting painters was a Spanish Colombian, Gabriel Lopez, who had met her, presumably on an earlier visit to Blashford, and fallen in love. Lopez, three years older than Caitlin, was talented but unstable. He once showed a black and yellow abstract to Henry Tonks, principal of the Slade, with the assurance that 'This is a great work of art'. Tonks told him, 'Better take care, young man, or you'll kill yourself.'

Townsend and Lopez were friends. Townsend disapproved of the unhealthy passion for Caitlin, which left Lopez 'wretched' as he waited for her to arrive. 'He has told Nicolette that he will commit suicide if his affair with Kathleen is a failure, and he is thoroughly fed up because she is not impressed by the idea.' When she did appear, on 29 July, she brought a friend from school, whose home in Jersey they were to visit in a week's time. Lopez, who was on the small side and lacked the manly air that Caitlin favoured, followed her about as the gang visited village shows and played tennis with the Summers. Vivien John arrived from Ireland, flown back by her brother Caspar, who had just bought himself a little biplane. Caspar began to appear at gymkhanas and games of tennis. Perhaps it was on his account that Caitlin was being whisked away to the Channel Islands. Townsend, who knew nothing of the Caspar business, wondered, to begin with, why his friend Gabriel was so enchanted with her, finding her 'still very girlish and flushed', with

a kind of high-school excitement and lack of seriousness about her – which perhaps is only superficial. But she has lovely, pale ashen-gold hair, curling loosely and abundantly: finer than Brigit's, which is much straighter, though finer in colour; and her features have not yet the firmness of her two sisters'. I was, but only at first, rather surprised that this was the girl Gabriel was so madly in love with, without whom he would not have bothered to come down here at all.

Presently Caitlin and friend left for Jersey, and it was not until the autumn that Townsend (and Gabriel) saw her again; by that time she was in London, beginning what was supposed to be her career.

She and Vivien John wanted to be dancers. They were both small-built. Caitlin's puppy-fat would soon disappear, and although her legs were on the short side, her figure was firm, shapely and elastic. She liked swimming and exercising, and to dance on a stage for the world to see seemed to her a natural extension of her physical talents into a medium where she would be effortlessly at home. She envisaged something more than high-kicking as a chorus girl. But her starting-point was a desire to be noticed. In later years she cursed the lack of a proper education, perhaps feeling that because she was not en-couraged to find intellectual outlets, she had to make the best of what she had, a useful body and a sense of rhythm. Whatever the process, dancing was singled out to justify her conviction that she was different from others – 'set apart', she wrote later, 'ardently and passionately *believing* in I knew not what'. Since she was always self-conscious about dancing in public, to choose dance as a lifelong medium of expression was asking for trouble. But asking for trouble was one of her characteristics.

The first thing was to get to London. She and Vivien ran away that summer, taking a bus to Salisbury and then a train, and landing on the doorstep of Vivien's maternal aunt, Ethel Nettleship, a kindly 'cellist. A telegram was sent home saying DON'T WORRY, WITH RELIABLE FEMALE, though Aunt Ethel had already reported their arrival. Their plan to approach the impresario C.B. Cochran, who knew Augustus John, failed because he was away, and Augustus took them back in his car two days later. But the gesture worked. The families arranged for them to attend dancing school and live in London, where they stayed, to begin with, at a hostel for 'business girls' near Paddington Station. Here they shared a poky room, its walls plastered with photographs of film stars, playing *I'm Blue Again* on a clockwork gramophone and scattering their clothes on the floor.

Caspar was still Caitlin's hero. In a letter to Nicolette in 1965 she wrote that 'I think I froze him off with my London caprices.' In *Story of a Woman* she said the same, that Galiad was alarmed to see Ellen becoming 'a headstrong, averse, deliberately annihilating young woman', who went out of her way to make him angry. She made one last attempt:

[Ellen] wrote humbly, asking his forgiveness. She was at breakfast when his answer came, looking forward to flaccid scrambled eggs. She swallowed a mouthful, it stuck, and tears started from her eyes – his answer was 'No'. The eggs went sorrowfully down. Her life over, as far as

Ellen was concerned, she tried hard to concentrate on death – visions of bread and butter rose provokingly to mock her, and she could not be satisfied without cutting a large slice off the loaf on the table, with which to resume her meditations.

Once she was in London, other men were after her. In 1930 one of them was Gabriel. When she and Vivien caught the bus at Paddington in the mornings to go into the West End, he was already on board, waiting for her. To have the glamorous Vivien, brother of the unattainable Caspar, know that such an unpromising specimen was in love with her was shaming. In general Caitlin was indifferent to what people thought, but not when it came to her desirability.

Caitlin and Vivien mixed with the Slade set, and so reappear in William Townsend's journal. At the end of October she refused to see any more of Gabriel. Townsend was not surprised that his friend wouldn't accept this, Caitlin having 'allowed him to spend money on her, send flowers and take her out'. Over the next few days the Colombian drank heavily, brandished a knife, announced that 'If she won't have me, I cannot leave her to another man, we will both die', and slashed all his paintings except one of Caitlin – 'immense bosomed in a scarlet shift, gold haired and with a face hectically crimsoned on the cheeks'.

One night he began rushing at the gas stove in his room, shouting 'Let's all die together!' and writing illegible notes to Caitlin; between times his friend read to him from the Book of Ruth. Eventually Townsend took one of the illegible notes round to the hostel:

> She was just going to bed when I called but came down, looking more beautiful than I have ever seen her, and talked in the gloomy hostel dining room, with its square tables laid for breakfast. She is worried about what he will do with himself, but not only does not care for him, but despises him and wishes never to see him again; so I know her position authentically.

For the moment Gabriel went off the boil. Townsend noted one or two further encounters with Caitlin. She and Vivien were at a 'tea and talk party' at Nicolette's room in Earls Court. They arrived late – 'Deliberately, I fear,' said Townsend, adding that:

young as they are they are old in wile, and know too well how ornamental they are. But they were delightfully gay and childishly exuberant, and made us stretch and bend our bodies and legs to imitate the movements they are learning in their acrobatic dancing.

The Gabriel business came to a climax on 6 December, when Caitlin gave a party, to which he was not invited, two days before her seventeenth birthday. The venue was changed at the last minute to the studio of Augustus John's house in Mallord Street, built for him in 1914. The studio, with two fires burning at opposite corners, was a striking place. Michael Holroyd wrote that it 'conveyed a sense of hemmed-in space, like the exercise yard of a prison'. The party passed off quietly enough. Augustus John came and went, keeping an eye on his daughter Vivien; perhaps on Caitlin as well. Caspar was there, too.

Townsend took a cool view of the Mallord Street guests, finding the men mainly 'worn-out profligates', the women 'of the easy-virtued demi-mondaine, intolerably blasé, with a noticeable little group of Lesbians'. He claimed to have heard someone say, 'Don't go into the lavatory. Don't be tactless. Two men are having an affair in there.'

Unknown to Townsend and his Slade friends until some days later, Gabriel gassed himself in his room at home on the night of the party, and was found dead by his parents, in whose house he lived. Caitlin did not attend the funeral. Her muddled recollection in old age was of an irritating little Italian who shot himself. She had felt 'absolutely no pity' because he was 'such an awful nuisance'.

Her feelings at the time may have been more complicated, her apparent cruelty self-protective; while the unfortunate Gabriel can be conveniently disposed of as the victim of his own hysteria, which awaited a suitable creature to trigger his response. Still, the creature happened to be Caitlin. She was beginning to have repercussions.

4

Encounters with Artists

An early event in Caitlin's experience of worlds beyond Blashford was her seduction by Augustus John, and her subsequent elevation to the status of long-standing model and lover. To be slept with by John was no great distinction. His appetite for women was strong and persisted into old age. Michael Holroyd in his biography suggested that John, when painting, relied on 'some extreme instinctive relationship' between himself and his subject. When he painted women, this was 'almost impossible to achieve if his concentration was constantly fretted by unsatisfied physical desire'. Holroyd quoted a letter from John to one of his mistresses: 'The dirty little girl I meet in the lane has a secret for me – communicable in no language, estimable at no price, momentous beyond knowledge, though it concern but her and me.' His desires thus became, conveniently, an artistic imperative.

Some of the liaisons were brief, while others became established in acquaintances that could be renewed as required. His relations with Caitlin were spasmodic, but they extended over a period of years, and presumably he felt some affection for her. What she felt for him can only be inferred, not least from the probable length of the relationship, though no one is sure when it started. Caitlin's *Story of a Woman* has only general references to John ('Antonio' in the manuscript). He appears at a fireworks party given by Nora Summers, where his hosts, 'like mice inviting a tom cat to the banquet, sought to placate his oppressive presence'. Caitlin has never been keen to acknowledge any sympathy for John or to concede that she was more than the victim of his lust, who was raped. Her story, told more than once in recent years, presents John as a 'hairy monster', an 'old beast', an 'old goat' who disgusted her and to whom she succumbed only because she was young and he was famous.

In a letter to Nicolette in 1965, where (not long after Augustus had died) she was scorning the John family for 'fussing about their moral reputations, like maiden aunts', she declared that 'Augustus was a disgusting old man who fucked [everyone], including the beasts of the field'. She then fussed about her own reputation, declaring herself 'mortally offended to have it said that I could have had a passion for such a repulsive old billy goat: who stopped me coming for years'.

Indisputably the painter's sexual manners could be gross. Nicolette, who, unlike her sisters, refused to take her clothes off to sit for him, once remarked that it was all very well for admirers to see something 'wonderful and pagan' in his approach, but it could involve his 'diving at women, even in company, and plunging his hand under their skirts'. Pamela Glendower, who saw him in action, said that one of his fancies was to 'try and grab the pubic hair through one's clothes'. Nevertheless, in 1936–37, at least six years after the likely date when Augustus first 'pounced', in Caitlin's phrase, they remained on intimate terms, and he was calling her 'my little seraph' in a letter he sent her, while emphasising (a nice unromantic touch) the need for sexual hygiene. One surviving witness from John's circle, who prefers not to be named, says that to begin with, it was Caitlin who led him on.

The initial pouncing may have been at Fryern Court, as Caitlin believes, or just possibly at Mallord Street. She says it took place when she first sat for him. She didn't reach sixteen, the legal age of consent, until December 1929, but it is unlikely that this would have deterred John. There are nude drawings of her but the dates are uncertain; at least one of them depicts a thick-waisted girl who might be a plump adolescent of fifteen or sixteen. What is probably the first finished painting shows her in a striped cardigan, hands on hips and head turned to half-profile, staring superciliously over the painter's shoulder. The gallery that sold the picture in 1934 dated it to 'around 1930'. In that year she lived first at Blashford and then in London. This could be the portrait she was sitting for when he struck.

John reached fifty in 1928, by which time he had a problem with drink and was beginning to age. A photograph of Nicolette's wedding in 1931, when she married a fellow painter from the Slade, Anthony Devas, shows a stout, elderly-looking gentleman, his features confined to a narrow strip between the brim of his hat and the twin growths of beard and moustache. The 'awful beard' was the bit that Caitlin found most distasteful, together with the fact that here was this old beast intruding on her romantic vision of his son. The beard crops up in an account, by a woman called Chiquita, of her seduction by John in 1921; she was sixteen at the time. Chiquita, who bore his child as a result, also recalled whisky-and-tobacco smells, but 'no words, just grunting and snorting'.

It is hard to make sense, from Caitlin's old-age accounts, of the sequence of events. Augustus and Caspar pop in and out of her memories like figures in a fairy-tale, the villain and the prince. According to the unnamed witness's private account, Caitlin, having failed with Caspar, turned her attention to Augustus.

> As to her 'Rape' – I doubt if it was one, as she was going out with men when she was at the dancing school. I think what *happened* was during the time Caspar was in China, and Caitlin was being extremely flirtatious with men in general, including Augustus! I suppose she was around 15 or 16! I happen to know this, and she encouraged Augustus, but of course it was extremely reprehensible of him to take advantage of such a young girl. I think when Caspar returned, she had changed, and this plus Yvonne's letter or words of warning would have caused the break-up. I do know Caitlin was devastated, and became embittered, but she was not the girl [Caspar] left behind when he went to China. Three years is a long time.

In the end Caitlin was stuck with the father who had ravished her, rather than the son who might have redeemed her in her own eyes. This might suggest a shrewd opportunism on her part. Augustus had compensations; he was famous and spent money on her over the years, and it is easy to see the young Caitlin as capable, precocious and calculating beyond her years. Yet the idea of innocence corrupted – or, in less dramatic terms, of unhappiness exploited – hovers on the edge of Caitlin's life.

It was her nature to make demands, and as the youngest sister she probably fought for affection. Her father was absent. Her mother, an undemonstrative woman at the best of times, was apt to disappear behind locked doors with Nora. Did the sad Caitlin who longed to be noticed join forces with the ruthless Caitlin who had understood her own charms even in childhood? It is a more charitable view of her precocity. It also agrees with the hints scattered through her life, that the real reward of sex was less its physical pleasure than its usefulness in making men interested, obedient and even loving. Caitlin survived as best she could. Caspar's coldness was one lesson she learned; Augustus's crude embraces were another.

The story that Caitlin was Augustus John's daughter is incidental but needs to be disposed of. It has persisted for years and is sometimes presented as incontrovertible fact. Although Yvonne Macnamara slept with John, there is no family story that he made her pregnant. Traits in Caitlin that she and others identified as coming from Francis can be cited as evidence that he must have been her father. 'I keep finding new horrible similarities with that man' was to be a constant refrain in Caitlin's letters; although they were imprecise characteristics, such as bombast and exhibitionism.

Constantine FitzGibbon, in his biography of Dylan Thomas (1965), referred briefly to Caitlin's affair with John, adding that 'he sometimes became confused and thought she was his daughter as well'. The story was already old when FitzGibbon hinted at it. Might Francis Macnamara himself, with his keenness on 'free love' and his admiration for John, have encouraged the scandalous tale?

More probably, John's exuberant taste for female flesh led those who knew the family to endow the old pagan with even more heathenish qualities. Someone may have livened up a dinner table by hinting that the succulent Miss Macnamara who had been sacrificed for Augustus's pleasure was closer to him than people realised. John's intensely inward-looking family provided a suitable setting for such tales. A son-in-law once described him as 'like an old stag, with his herd of women and children round him. Interlopers were beaten off.' Holroyd describes John at eighty-four, within months of death, groping his way into the bed of a natural daughter, putting his arms around her and muttering, 'Can't seem to do it now.' Congress with Caitlin would not have been ruled out, whatever their blood relationship. It is unlikely that one existed, if only because the story didn't take root within the family, where rumours about other carnal episodes abound. But it lingers on.

The liaison with Augustus led nowhere, except to more paintings and more pouncing, with a pound to be earned for each sitting. The dancing career progressed slowly, unobserved by Townsend, who was so upset by the death of Gabriel that he temporarily abandoned his journal. Caitlin and Vivien tried again with C.B. Cochran when they heard he was recruiting another intake of leggy showgirls, the so-called 'Cochran's Young Ladies', for a new revue. Their only hope was the Augustus John connection, Cochran having commissioned the painter, not long before, to do the sets for a production of Sean O'Casey's *The Silver Tassie*. Caitlin described the audition in *Story of a Woman*:

A vast confusion of legs, trunks, brassières and mouths bunched in professional boredom made Ellen feel more countrified and mock-rustic than ever in her spotted frills. They were lined up, a dozen at a time, and two or three selected from each batch to perform. Valentine [Vivien] and another swooning beauty were asked to move forward. The rest, Ellen stolidly among them, were told to go, but at a whisper of Antonio's name from Valentine, Ellen was reluctantly recalled. Watching the stale identical routines she waited impatiently to wake up the torpid reactions in the stalls. Her turn came. 'Can you sing?' 'No.' 'Can you do the Two Step?' Timidly inefficient, she jiggered towards the footlights. Her name was put on a list, they were dismissed. Even Antonio's name could not supply the deficiencies. They heard no more.

Caitlin found occasional work at clubs, in and around London – late-night entertainment as part of a cabaret act, throwing herself about a little stage. One of her French uncles recommended her to a London store, Peter Robinson, where she advertised rubber corsets by doing acrobatics in them for the passing trade. Vigorous routines made her feel better. The more she leapt and twisted, the quicker she could throw off her self-consciousness. A sudden display of cartwheels in public meant she was ill at ease.

It was as though she burned with energy that she would have been happy to convert into serious dancing, but was content to use frivolously if she couldn't. Her sisters had often accused her of being ostentatious, a charge to which she had no problem pleading guilty in due course. Since the career in dancing was slow to take fire, some of the energy took the path of least resistance and stoked her up as an object of desire. One of Caitlin's complaints against Gabriel was that he had been 'a dead loss to my desired reputation of a Fabulous Courtesan'. But it was the romance of enrapturing men that attracted her. Brigit has no doubt that this was Caitlin's sexual dynamic.

What survives is an impression of vitality and sex, of someone whose bones were made of rubber, who tormented men with her tongue, whose handbag was stuffed with love letters. After the hostel she moved on to a flat where her peripatetic father was living at the time, in Regent Square, where Bloomsbury begins to decline towards the railway stations. Francis's marriage to Edie McNeill was short-lived, and she was already giving way to Iris O'Callaghan, a stormy young Irishwoman who had been with Nicolette at the same finishing school in Paris.

Quarrels between Caitlin and her father were commonplace. She taunted him; it was in his nature to pose a threat to women, and she enjoyed being a threat to men. Nicolette felt menaced by her father, with his airy conviction that a woman was a blank slate for men to write on. It was the philosophy that Erica Cotterill recorded in *Form of Diary*, where she has him point to his wife as his ideal of womanhood. Yvonne is 'like the sea – universal [. . .] always in good health, always at one with life [. . .] accepting things as they are [. . .] the symbolic average – like a doll'. Francis saw nothing wrong with being cruel and overbearing to his women. Nicolette forgave the hero, the giant, but even she had her moments of hatred. In the Aran Islands with her father when she was a teenager, she found herself standing behind him at the prehistoric fort of Dun Aengus, on the edge of Inishmore – and Europe – where immense cliffs fall to the sea. She was 'swept by an urge to push him over', explaining this to the reader, not too convincingly, as a moment of 'primitive savagery' brought on by the surroundings.

Caitlin, unable to see her father as a hero for long, and determined not to be a blank slate for anybody, tried to fight him with derision. He was, she wrote, 'the only person who could unfailingly trigger off my rage [. . .] I thought he was a crueller sadist than Hitler!' Something festered between them. She said he could always probe her tenderest spots; she did her best to probe his. He found her disquieting, and came to think that 'Caitlin' was an unfortunate name to have given her; perhaps because its diminutive was 'Cat'.

When Francis lived in Bournemouth, she once telephoned in a disguised voice, pretending to be a young admirer, and managed to make a fool of him. In the Regent Square flat, a tall partition in the kitchen concealed the bath. It was one of Caitlin's tricks to stand on the table so she could see over the top, and make scathing remarks about the bather for the benefit of those eating breakfast. Francis was her favourite target. But if she could annoy him, he could reduce her to tears.

Caitlin continued to toy with a career on the stage. At Christmas 1931 she danced in pantomime, *Aladdin* at the Lyric, Hammersmith, produced by Nigel Playfair; she was just eighteen, listed in the programme as an extra, disguising herself as 'Tessa Macnamara'. For a while she was in a chorus line, doing three shows a day at an unidentified theatre. Popular entertainment still looked back to the music-hall era, and 'non-stop variety' drew customers off the streets, principally men, to spend an hour admiring women's legs through the cigarette smoke and guffawing at stand-up comedians. Caitlin soon learned the clockwork routines of high-kicking, except that on occasion she was confused about which leg to kick with. In old age she explained this by suggesting that she must have been drunk, since she was too unrelaxed to dance properly when she was sober. In the last period of her life, though, drink was retrospectively blamed for everything. In *Story of a Woman* the stage manager merely sacked her for answering back.

In 1932 or 1933, Caitlin gave up trying to be a showgirl and retreated to Ireland for a prolonged visit or visits that are still faintly – here and there, sharply – remembered. By this time her father was in Dublin, and he sent her the boat fare and let her stay at his house. *Story of a Woman* presents him as 'Father Godolphin, her mother's lifelong friend', a heavier disguise than anyone else receives. She stays with him for two weeks to become acquainted with 'Dublin society' – port-drinking solicitors, Godolphin's stately, plump brothers, some visits to the theatre – before being 'despatched to the West to take charge of his old crumbling mansion house'.

In later years she talked nostalgically about this journey to Co. Clare and the period of exile that it began. She travelled in a lorry that was taking furniture to the house, together with a caretaker and his family. Francis's life was entering an Irish phase. As his daughter she was a figure to be regarded in Ennistymon, even if she did nothing but bathe in the river or ride on a rattly bicycle to Fisher Street.

The town was content to have the Macnamaras back, now that their powers had waned. Whatever acrimony there may have been towards Henry Vee, none of it was left. He had died in London in 1925, leaving the remnants of the estate to Francis and other children. His ambushers, whoever they were, were never convicted. These days the English could drive about the Burren as often as they chose, and no one would aim a rifle over a wall.

The house at Doolin had gone, burnt in one of the unremembered incidents of the early Twenties, its slate roof stripped for pigsties, sour grass replacing the flower-beds, the socket where the brass sundial had stood now overgrown in the kitchen garden. Ennistymon House had been luckier. Republicans occupied it first; then the police used it as barracks for a while. The caretaker, not overworked, kept goats in the entrance hall, and charged for the services of the billy.

The town itself had suffered while the British forces were still in control in 1920. They burnt houses and threw a man into his own flames to die. In the Thirties the place was peaceable but not over-prosperous. Caitlin blew in as an object of almost solicitous concern, a new generation of Macnamaras, the fallen kings. She was not expected to be an ordinary young woman. When she was camping upstairs in the house, or occupying a makeshift bedroom above the stables round the back, they enjoyed glimpses of her. If she bathed nude in the river, it was no more than her popular father did. If a young lad who did jobs around the house was said to go swimming with her in the same condition after dark, it was only a rumour.

When she went dancing in the cottages, as she did at every opportunity, that only proved she had the right blood in her. These were the neighbourly dances, the 'ceilidhs', crammed into whatever smoky space was available, which could last all night to the tune of a melodeon, a flute or a screaming fiddle. Set patterns of dancers, four pairs at a time, stamped the stone floor, lit by the turf fire and a few candles. They could keep going till dawn, with tea and cake for refreshment, backed up with something stronger.

Her constant companion was Kitty O'Brien, the daughter of Francis's drinking friend in Fisher Street, a big red-faced fisherman with a wandering eye known as 'Cuckoo' for his skill at getting into beds that didn't belong to him. Caitlin and Kitty were always in demand; it was the women who were invited to a ceilidh, so that the men would follow. Caitlin was a good catch, with her soft skin, gold hair and flaring blue eyes. Her clothes, too, had shop-made colours to relieve the muted wools and flannels. An Englishman who was in love with her, and saw her in the Doolin cottages two or three years later, said she was 'a bird of paradise among sparrows'. An evening at Cuckoo O'Brien's, half a mile from the sea, was described in *Story of a Woman*. First his wife took Caitlin into an inner room, produced a small bottle from a clothes chest, and poured her a whiskey.

She was then allowed to make a formal entrance into the living room. The sons were ranged rigidly on the wooden settle, while the daughters were crouching inside the cavernous fireplace with their naked feet in the ashes. The Cuckoo himself was sitting on the flags mending his nets and spitting tobacco juice; his wife immediately shooed them all outside, along with the stray hens and ducks; then she put down the tea and turned the loaf on the grid, baking among the peat embers.

When the fiddling got under way, 'Ellen watched entranced the blind bovine expressions', relishing her power. She went to many dances. Describing her travels around the countryside, Caitlin sounds excited and triumphant.

As [the men] grew familiar with the eccentric girl, they followed her domineering commands with grave submission. If she chose some reluctant beau, already attached, he was for the evening.

The tribal name of Macnamara hinted at nobility. This degenerated lineage was to echo in Caitlin's imagination, so that years later she came to see herself as a cross between peasant and aristocrat. Her experience at the ceilidhs, often held in her honour, encouraged the 'aristocratic' side.

There were stories about Caitlin at the dances; there still are, around Ennistymon. 'The dance had finished and she went tumbling over the floor, doing the cartwheel. One of the old ladies crossed herself' (a woman). 'It is a fact that Caitlin did not wear knickers or stockings under her skirt. There was a fellow at a dance laid his hand on her leg, and she hit him across the room' (a man). He gave the names of Co. Clare lads, who, it was a near certainty, had courted her, a P., an O., a W., a T. and another P. Some of them were still alive and it might not do to make enquiries. But in his kitchen twenty miles away, T. (who had been in England for much of his life) didn't mind volunteering that Caitlin was a great dancer, a great swimmer, a great lover. He could vouch for it.

Story describes Ellen walking out on the river bank with a young man, a tailor she calls 'de Valera', when they see two policemen carrying the corpse of a newly born child whose mother has drowned herself.

The poignant episode seemed to wipe away the proud erections that Ellen and de Valera had set up; he came in the early dusk with always a few needles stuck under his collar, or a long piece of thread wriggling from his cuffs: the betrayers of his cramped trade.

Dates are hard to come by. One of Nicolette's albums has photographs of Caitlin and Kitty with the house behind them, dated 1934. Weeds are invading the path, but creepers on the wall are under control. Kitty, dark-haired and not quite at ease, is almost a head taller than Caitlin, whose face is still plump and juvenile. Sometimes the two shared a room at Ennistymon, in a bed upstairs salvaged from the wreckage. Caitlin could do as she pleased. Cuckoo and his son were persuaded to row them from Doolin Point, miles across the dangerous sound to the Aran Islands, in a fragile-looking currach. Keeping Kitty between her and the men, who had their backs to her anyway, she stripped and lay stretched out over the prow. There had been a death on the island and they were taken to see the corpse. 'The pitted eyes were propped open with matchsticks, the sagging mouth sucking at a stump of wax, and rags filled the cavities where once her bosom had been.'

Primitive Ireland was not a bad choice for a woman who had found London harder to take by storm than she expected. Caitlin's 'peasant' self thought slowly and said little. What she chose to remember of her visits later was a dream-country she could refer back to for the rest of her life, compressing the year or two she spent there into a handful of impressions. It was a wilderness, a state of mind, 'a road leading into the sky'. When she first saw the house it was empty, falling into ruin. She heard the crashing of the cascades. On the lawn a crimson-leafed beech tree rustled in the wind, but with none of the melancholy of the elm trees at Blashford. Excited by such beauty, 'my heart was bursting in my body and I could not believe it'.

This doesn't sound much like Caitlin, whose talent is to find the worm at the core of every apple. Sure enough, the letter she was writing (in 1991) continued, 'Into the best descriptions of perfection always comes the frightful flaw. In my case it was the appalling sight of my father, who never told me he would be there, mooching around all the rooms in the house.'

Francis was taking an interest in Ennistymon; otherwise there would have been no furniture or caretaker. He had plans to turn it into a hotel. Caitlin must have known he was coming, and that his visits were only temporary. But he bothered her. What she remembers is being ordered to make him an Irish stew in a saucepan meant for boiling eggs; to humiliate her, she thinks.

Nicolette has described how her father, when she was with him in Ireland, wanted to be closer to her, 'to take possession by storm', and how she resisted. Among his idiosyncrasies was to enjoy flirting with women in front of his daughters. Nicolette shrank from him when he 'did his great show-off act for my benefit, the great landlord, the feudal master loved (and this was true) by his people'. He was too explicit for her liking. 'Francis, slapping the barmaid's bottom, turned me green.' Caitlin felt the same.

Francis embarrassed them in boats, where he spent much of his time. His favourite craft were black-hulled Galway hookers, fat little vessels with open holds, and eccentric rigging that he said was a relic of Tudor times. His own boat, the *Mary Ann*, was a converted hooker, fitted with a deck. At Galway, across the bay from Co. Clare, he was a familiar figure around the quays. He traded to the Aran Islands or along the Connemara coast with salt and flour, like an itinerant grocer, irritating local seamen when they had to break off fishing and pilot him through the dangerous channels beyond Slyne Head. Sometimes a daughter or two lived on board when he was in harbour. Caitlin and Brigit were there when he and Iris O'Callaghan were sharing the best cabin. The girls slept in the fo'csle but they could hear what was going on. Caitlin says that as well as 'yelling and bawling when he was on top of her', he would shout 'Ship ahoy!' at the critical moment.

Caitlin's resistance to her father was fiercer than Nicolette's. In an unpublished manuscript (written about 1956)* she wrote savagely about Francis and how they clashed at Ennistymon. He was

that double-decker, blunder buster, swash huckster; pot bellied, ham handed, bull frog egoist of bluff: which characteristics, incidentally, he passed on very kindly and perfectly intact to me; and I am persecuted by them to this very day, not rid of them yet; with the haunted blue as blue eyes crying murder from their deep set captivity in the ravaged face. And he was always about to solve the problem of the universe, to write a great

* The ten-page manuscript is headed 'Finito (the Cuckoo)'. It was probably intended for her book *Leftover Life to Kill*.

book, to make a fortune: what a long time we waited for that fortune, never quite losing faith in it [. . .]

What remains to me is an irritating picture of him eating a boiled egg; gulping and guzzling over the three minute slop in a prolonged sucking mouthful; then looking up at me, through his concentrated appetite, with the loathing that only a parent can feel for a child that has betrayed him into understanding him. And me leaving the room quickly not to see any more of my young bestialities made obscenely manifest through him; grossly lying in store to maraud me, in the hoarily avid future. But was he satisfied with that: my tactful retirement; not him; not till he got me back again, called me unsocial, ungracious, 'surly' was his favourite word for me; insulted me as only those too near, who know too well, can; and was not content till I was all a blubber [. . .]

I went to my attic room and wrote – 'I solemnly swear merciless vengeance on my father, by the blood of my mother. However long it will be, Caitlin Macnamara, the Avenger of wrongs and injustice, will not forget, she will see Justice done.' And I pushed the document reverently in a secret hiding place reserved for threats and imprecations, vows and resolutions; then I looked down at the dress that had filled my day with the silky promise of femininity, that was subtly softly clinging, suggesting that world beyond the sea of sophistication that I yearned for with such an unseemly, and unsuitable, desire [. . .] And I saw my hands hanging, like square claws at the bottom; and they were his hands; and I knew, with a despair I put away for later, that they would always be there.

It seems a lot of fuss to make about an egg. But Caitlin had a physical loathing of Francis. His tongue was cruel, and she must have sensed (and perhaps even glimpsed) his taste for violence. Caitlin was to share these tendencies, both verbal and physical. Over the years she learned how to use her fists, and more than once she was on the receiving end of violence from men, without much protest. As a young woman, she found her own 'bestialities', which were 'obscenely manifest' in her father, disquieting. Was there in this some sexual ingredient, a coarse appetite in him that she suspected ran in her own blood? Seeing Francis, she feared herself.

Caitlin's regime of ceilidhs and peasants suited something in her nature. The bare strands and stony fields of the Atlantic coastline represented a silence that her angrier self always had to disrupt, but that she was always driven to respect. All her life she would curse the primitive places where she found herself. But she spent too many years in them to say it was invariably the fault of someone else. Her exile in Co. Clare – her 'outpost colony', she called it – left her ready for civilisation, though not for indulgence. A newer, primmer Caitlin emerged, talking of aesthetic principles. She wrote to her mother early in 1935 from Dublin, a half-way house between Co. Clare and London, to say that 'this re-educating oneself business' was painful, 'especially when one is not sure whether one wouldn't rather remain a boor!!! – but I can't all the same'.

In Dublin she shared a basement flat with Brigit in their father's house, and told her mother that she was less articulate now than her sister (who was famous for being silent). *Story of a Woman* describes them living frugally on a pound a week (Caitlin always thought 'a pound a week' sounded virtuous), though willing to creep upstairs from their 'chaste dungeon' to relieve Francis of the disgustingly rich left-overs from his parties.

Caitlin found a focus for her reformed ambitions in a dancing teacher then at work in Dublin, an Austrian woman, Vera Gribben, who claimed acquaintance with Isadora Duncan, or at least with her sister Irma and the Isadora school of expressive dancing. Mrs Gribben gave private lessons. Duncan, an American of Irish origin, had died in 1927. Her style of barefoot dancing to classical music, lightly clad and sinuous, was underpinned by a philosophy that talked about 'divine expression of the human spirit'. Her methods could be less electrifying in other performers. Caitlin was a serious convert; for a year or more, Duncan's was the purifying art she aspired to.

Spiritual matters had not counted for much in Caitlin's upbringing. Now she liked the sense of being caught up in higher things, and was prepared to waive her reservations. To look at, Mrs Gribben was not light and airy; she was well built, as Caitlin described her in *Story*, wearing 'a long purple tunic which hung upon her ponderous haunches as she swayed abundantly to the music, her arms suspended in mid air like zeppelins straining at their moorings'. Lacking a sense of the ridiculous, Caitlin didn't laugh. Instead she sought to make her own strong body disclose insights into the soul, a new word for her vocabulary.

They danced Palestrina and old Gregorian chants, wherein they portrayed the passion of the saints, the turmoil of good and evil, and Christ's beatitude; interspersed with angels of destruction and peace [. . .] Ellen, delving ever more arduously, showed the twelve Disciples' individual characters, devoting an entire Rachmaninoff tirade to the conflict and agony of Judas. To illustrate the healing miracles she convulsed herself upon the floor in a tortured position, representing a paralytic, and with painful staccato jerks one at a time unloosed her limbs, rising at last radiant to her feet. Devils were cast out of her; she was radiantly reclaimed from the dead.

'I will stay here until the "Gribbone" is through with me,' she told her mother, 'and that will not be, I'm sure, for quite a bit.' The teacher wanted her to dance at her next 'soirée', and 'shows great pleasure *when* I capture her spirit & method – à la Isadora par excellence – I hope to God I won't mess up her dance, it is a great responsibility for me as timid as I now am.' When the time came, Caitlin 'gyrated senselessly' and was not a success. Writing twenty years later she described the problem:

> According to my new boundless aspirations no music was undanceable, too long or too difficult: symphonies, operas, cavernous male chants, screeching drumming voices from the buried far-away nations [. . .] I had almost reached the abstract perfection of dismissing the music as a superfluity. This worked very well in private, where I experienced ecstasies of religious and harmonic fervour, with and without music; but when I was confronted by the all-seeing enemy, eyes, my concentration vanished. I lost my nerve, and before I could stop myself, my tragic Judas was doing cartwheels, and my passionate Magdalene succumbed in the splits.

At the time she tried hard to overcome the difficulties. The dancing was part of the business of changing her life. 'I do intend,' she told her mother, 'to settle down to a specific plan of work, and [. . .] *refrain* from going off at a tangent!!!'

> Ellen vowed to devote her life to aesthetic principles; never again to be tempted to over-eat; never again to be drawn by vanity into false company; and to crush the tail of lust for ever, with the blade of celibacy.

Mrs Gribben had plans for a Grand Tour of Europe, dancing their way from Paris to Vienna via Rome. Meanwhile they went to London – there was a Mr Gribben as well, an unsuccessful painter from Belfast – and Caitlin's education was improved with visits to art galleries and the British Museum. She sounds like a schoolgirl, deferring to her teacher; there is a sentence in *Story* about 'a constant struggle between her desire to be subdued and her will to assert'. From London they went to stay at Blashford, where they danced on the lawn at Fryern Court, one mild evening, for the Augustus Johns and their friends. Schubert was supplied by gramophone. Caitlin thought of Caspar, invisible in the darkness among the scoffers, watching Mrs Gribben exercise her 'vast thighs', and was reminded of the 'terror' of his reign. It must have been about this time that Nora Summers photographed her by the River Avon, clothed in what look like transparent pyjamas, striking poses against reeds and thistles on the bank. Before they left, Caitlin recruited Brigit to help her hawk portraits by Mr Gribben around the neighbourhood, telling everyone he was a protégé of Augustus John.

Caitlin was useful to the Gribbone. They began to perform in London for small audiences, a prelude to the tour. At the progressive Group Theatre, T.S. Eliot was seen in the audience, looking embarrassed at the writhings on stage. After one performance, at an obscure venue on an upper floor in Soho, a member of the audience introduced herself as Euphemia Lamb, the artist's model who was said to have been Francis Macnamara's mistress. Mischievously, she made it her business to seek a husband for Caitlin, who was not looking for one. *Story of a Woman* is half-hearted about the episode: 'Various beer lords were suggested, but Ellen was singularly lacking in the coquettish graces incumbent to tickle the jaded fancy of these gentlemen.'

Ellen goes to Paris, where the Gribbens are already living. Her mother is financing her (a pound a week again). She decides, after all, that chastity is not for her.

> Ellen felt herself changed into the heroine of an enchanting farce, where the men had eyes for her alone, and sweet babbling poured from their lips. Her hard resolutions were gently wafted away by a rosy breath, and her dried heart broke its cellar doors and soared, crying from its long constriction.

By now the narrative is faltering. Mrs Gribben becomes indistinct. More is heard about men, in a confused fashion. Caitlin finds herself in a bistro.

At one table the usual bedroom couple were languorously absorbed in each other; at another, a worm-tinctured individual fixed his rat-slits on Ellen's person. Sidling, with webbed steps, beside her, he emitted the sour gust of intestinal sewers: 'Tu viens avec moi, ma petite?' he said with precise articulation. Ellen sped for the world of light, but whenever she looked back he was standing, in a timeless attitude, watching her.

Reaching the hotel by roundabout dodging, she quickly lowered the blind on the prying sunlight, and picked up Jacob Boeme* as an afternoon soporific. Vacillating in the marshlands between reality and sleep, she was slowly resuscitated by moist hands grappling at the neck of her dress, but, so far had her mind strayed into the labyrinthine maze of the past, that the figure bending over her bed had no relation with an actual event.

She gets rid of the 'cringing viper' with 'fierce blows'. We aren't told his identity, and are left to assume it was either the man with the sewer-breath or a dream.

A few pages later she meets a group of artists, among them a 'shabbily invisible Russian Pole' called Legas, a painter. Walking the streets by herself at dawn, she takes the Metro, and day-dreams that she is rescuing a child from a river; perhaps the drowned baby at Ennistymon again. Then,

'Quel joli chapeau tu portes, Mademoiselle.' Ellen, unrecognising, looked through her story at the face of Legas. She let him take her to his mouse-nest, tuck her into his cotton blankets, and lie his chicken-boned skeleton by her side.

There the autobiography breaks off.

Caitlin remained in Paris for a while, living with the painter. When Brigit joined her for a holiday, the three of them shared the bed. She lost interest in the Gribbone, who in later years became a figure of fun, with the episode dismissed as 'my Isadora crank period'. It was 1936 before she returned to Britain. Her 'dried heart' was still suffering from its 'long constriction'. She was ready for more encounters with artists.

* Jacob Boehme (1575–1624), Silesian cobbler and mystic, who sought to explain evil as part of Creation. No doubt Mrs Gribben put him on Caitlin's reading list.

5

The Poet from Wales

Caitlin Macnamara met Dylan Thomas on one of his trips to London in February, March or early April 1936, not long after she returned from Paris. The meeting was in a pub, perhaps the Wheatsheaf in Rathbone Place, and Augustus John was either there at the time, or had previously mentioned Thomas's name to her as a new curiosity on the London scene.

Caitlin was still sleeping with John from time to time, and continued to do so after she was introduced to Thomas and, so she says, fell into bed with him. But presently she and Dylan were to be seriously attracted to one another; creating for themselves that self-enclosing community of two which sets itself against the dirty devices of the world outside. Part of the process was a private fantasy, at least on Thomas's part, of how unworldly, how *innocent* they were. It was a good game while it lasted.

Thomas was a fantasist with a sense of humour. He was also gloomily obsessed with death and physical horrors, had no income, and could afford only short visits to London, in between which he lived where he had lived all his life so far, at his parents' three-bedroomed house in the South Wales seaport of Swansea.

His origins could not have been less like Caitlin's. His father, David John, was a severe and disappointed man who had dreamt of a professorship at Oxford, and ended up teaching English at the local grammar school. To compensate for this he crammed poetry into the head of his infant son, and drank too much. Both D.J. Thomas and his wife Florence came from Welsh-speaking country districts, but their children were brought up in the anglicised gentility of the Uplands, a

55

suburb of the town. There were only two children, Nancy, born 1906, and Dylan, born October 1914. The boy's name, selected by his father from one of the early Welsh romances, seemed wilfully eccentric at the time.

By the age of sixteen he was filling notebooks with poems, which in a year or two began to develop vivid, morbid tendencies. Dwelling on the body in general and his own in particular, they were a young man's celebration of the senses and their ghostly relationship with the flesh, expressed in fine, sonorous language that had the authority of a new voice. A collection was published at Christmas 1934, soon after his twentieth birthday, and although the printing was a modest 250 copies, the book, *Eighteen Poems*, made his name.

Dylan Thomas is famous, not only for being a poet but for wanting to be one. In Swansea, where he spent a year and a half on the evening newspaper reporting church fêtes and writing articles about local literary figures, he was determined to be unconventional. This was not difficult in a manufacturing town where bourgeois respectability was enhanced by the Welsh factor: a religious abhorrence of drink and sexual immorality.

The last great religious revival in Wales, which began in a village near the town when a young coal miner saw the devil's face in a hedge, had occurred only thirty years earlier. Christ was seen to walk on a viaduct. Heavenly choirs were heard from the clouds. It was true that beer bottles were found under the pews and that free-thinkers alleged a sharp rise in the illegitimate birth-rate. But the chapels were potent, and remained so. Although the Thomases were not chapel-goers, D.J.'s ancestors were rural ministers of religion. One of his aunts was married to a Bible-thumping minister in the town; he was heard to say that 'the boy ought to be in a madhouse'.

The boy's defiance consisted of gaudy shirts, tall tales and ostentatious beer drinking. Sixty years later it sounds harmless enough, but for a nicely-brought-up adolescent it was enough to give him a reputation in a small social circle. In London he had to be drunker and wilder to achieve the same effects. Since he earned little from his writing, he sponged ruthlessly on acquaintances; it was what penniless poets were expected to do. When in Swansea he stole small sums from anyone who left money lying around the house.

In general he was unreliable and not a youth to whom thoughtful parents would entrust their daughters. But he was entertaining and affable, a Fool who could pretend one minute to be a dog and go round biting people's legs, then satirise the company with a verse or a sketch the next. There were plenty of unknown poets in corduroy trousers haunting the pubs of Chelsea and Bloomsbury in the mid-Thirties. But none of them had an *Eighteen Poems* to show for it.

His looks were unprepossessing, and Caitlin often complained about them later, especially when he grew fleshy. In 1936 he was a slightly built figure of middle height with large eyes and curly hair. A former girl friend, Pamela Hansford Johnson, called him 'darling old fish-face' in her diary. Johnson was no longer on the scene, having faded out after 1935 when the going got too rough and she found herself in competition with 'Comrade Bottle'. A poet herself, to begin with, who wisely decided to try novels instead, she had met Thomas's parents, and would have married him, had he asked her. As late as December 1935, a few months before Caitlin appeared before him wearing a flowered dress that she borrowed from Nicolette, he was writing to Pamela as 'my rose, my own', and telling her he loved her. But neither of them believed it by then. He was more at home with shopgirls and art students to whom he need promise nothing.

The district around the Wheatsheaf was still important in those days to writers, painters and other artistic riff-raff. Its invented title of 'Fitzrovia', after a once-popular pub called the Fitzroy Tavern, made it sound like a tourist attraction, and was not in everyday use. The area was no more than a dozen or two streets in the angle between Oxford Street and the Tottenham Court Road, a spilling-over to the west of Bloomsbury, home of serious culture since the nineteenth century. Six or seven pubs, and at least as many restaurants and cafés, could be found there.

The Wheatsheaf itself was brightly lit, with red linoleum on the floor, and had recently been modernised by the brewers, Youngers, into what was known as a 'Scotch Ale' house. This meant mock-Tudor panelling, decorated with the tartans of Scottish clans. George Orwell is said to have popularised the place. The idiosyncrasies of pubs were lost on someone like Caitlin, who was too aloof to enter into the noisy exchanges of saloon bars. Women were still out of place in pubs, unless they were 'arty' or 'loose' or both, and Caitlin's nature resisted the idea of being lumped in with the rest. She was to complain all her life about the pubs that Dylan dragged her into; though she needed no introduction to drinking.

To begin with, their relationship was uncertain. Having slept together almost at once (as Caitlin asserts), neither saw this as binding them to anything. Her story is that they ate at the Eiffel Tower Hotel, next door to the Wheatsheaf, and used one of its dingy bedrooms, charging the bill to Augustus John; he had an account there, and the proprietor knew Caitlin by sight. The story neatly suggests her revenging herself on John. It may be that a quick fling with a young artist, at the expense of an old artist who took her for granted, was how she saw her liaison with Thomas at the time.

Soon they had separated, Caitlin returning to Blashford and more idleness, Thomas to his other life of living on air and writing poetry. In April 1936, which may have been immediately after their first encounter, he went to stay in Cornwall, near Land's End, where he lived happily for a month or two, and left no record of hankering for her.

Something about Thomas persuaded people that he needed looking after, and he had no false modesty about accepting offers of assistance. At the end of 1935 he is thought to have caught 'a dose of the clap', gonorrhoea, in a London bed. In the aftermath of this, friends thought he needed a holiday. His trip to Cornwall, with charitable notions of fresh air and square meals, was organised by a poet and advertising copywriter, Norman Cameron. Thomas could always find a bed with the Camerons in Hammersmith, and they may have tired of his demands on their hospitality; Cameron later wrote an irascible poem about 'That insolent little ruffian, that crapulous lout'. He introduced Thomas to Wyn Henderson, an imposing auburn-haired woman with artistic leanings who had divorced a philistine husband, and now, aged nearly forty, made a career out of associating with artists, both helping and being helped by them. She had the use of a cottage at Porthcurno, in Cornwall. Thomas travelled down with her by train, and slipped happily into the role of the delinquent boy who needs mothering.

Mrs Henderson, who had been psychoanalysed and was said to be unshockable, cleaned up the bed when he soiled it after a drinking session. She encouraged him to work on the fantasy-stories he was writing, and the poems he was assembling for a new collection that Dent & Co. were going to publish. She also took him as a lover, being keen on sex herself and knowledgeable about it. Havelock Ellis was a friend, and she told stories, which interested Thomas, about Ellis's odd sexual habits. Later, in another life, she and Caitlin would be as close as sisters.

While in Cornwall, Thomas had a second affair, with a Veronica Sibthorp, whose husband had been one of Mrs Henderson's lovers. Mrs Sibthorp had a house in Cornwall, too, Oriental Cottage at Lamorna Cove, a place favoured by painters. It all sounds agreeably self-indulgent. But Thomas was also a working writer, in touch with a literary editor asking for books to review; with T.S. Eliot, offering his story 'The Orchards', and seeking instant payment when it was accepted; with Richard Church at Dent about the poems that Church couldn't understand but was brave enough to say he would publish; with his Swansea friend Vernon Watkins, poet and bank clerk, confiding his fears that already the creative energy of adolescence was ebbing.

Life in Cornwall, where he remained until the middle of May, appealed to him for domestic as well as sexual reasons. In London, his sleeping arrangements can't have been up to much. Here, he was in a cottage that he described as being 'in a field, with a garden full of ferrets and bees', but it was stocked with essentials and had a woman about the place to supply comforts. The location that appealed to him most was the fishing village of Mousehole, not far from Lamorna Cove. He fancied living there, he told Elfriede Cameron, 'not with our Wyn but cosy and cheaply with something dumb and lovely of my own choice, with a woman who hasn't been psychoanalysed or rodgered by celebrities'. He didn't elaborate.

After Cornwall, there was more Swansea and more London. The publishers proposed *Poems in Progress* as a title for his new collection, due out in the autumn, and he told them it must be *30 Poems*, or however many it was. In July, there was more Caitlin.

Thomas heard that she and Augustus John were going to stay in Laugharne, a large village in West Wales that is technically a town because it has remained an ancient corporation with a charter. He made arrangements to go there himself. His grandparents and a small army of uncles and aunts came from the countryside close to Laugharne, and he would have known about the place from childhood. It was remote; trunk roads missed it by miles. Two years earlier he was describing its cocklewomen, sands, sails, wrecks and herons to Pamela Hansford Johnson, and calling it 'the strangest town in Wales'.

His plan turned on an exhibition of paintings at Fishguard, in

Pembrokeshire, farther along the coast. Augustus John, who was born and brought up in the anglicised south of that county, had let himself be invited down from London, a distinguished son, to do the judging. This was his ostensible reason for being in Laugharne, where he and Caitlin were to be the guests of Richard Hughes, the novelist. Thomas, too, had an ostensible reason. A boyhood friend, the painter Fred Janes, was exhibiting at Fishguard. Fred's father, a greengrocer in Swansea, owned a car. Fred would borrow the car and they would visit the exhibition. On the way they could call at Laugharne, where the novelist lived in a castle.

Caitlin remembers little. Perhaps she and Dylan planned his visit. In a letter to a magazine editor, written the morning he left for the Laugharne expedition, Thomas referred to the 'few bolted drinks with Betty Boop' at their recent meeting in London. Later on, the editor would conclude that 'Betty Boop', the silent young woman who had been with them, must have been Caitlin. The real Boop was a blonde in a film cartoon; Caitlin would not have enjoyed the analogy. But in those days she said little in company. Did Dylan see her, to begin with, as the someone who would be 'dumb and lovely'?

Thomas and Janes arrived in the greengrocer's car in midweek, 15 July 1936, two struggling artists knocking at the gates of the famous. From the nineteenth century, Laugharne had attracted discriminating strangers who wanted somewhere remote to settle. The natives were poor, inbred and fond of fights; the strangers lived in a handful of gentlemen's residences, withdrawn. Richard Hughes's Castle was high up at the end of the town, where the main street dropped down to the strand and the cockle factory. He had been living there for two years, after knocking about the world as an itinerant author. In 1929 he became famous and well-off with his unsentimental novel about children captured by pirates, *A High Wind in Jamaica*, after which he bought a house in Morocco for two donkey-loads of silver, before setting himself up in Wales at the age of thirty-four.

The residential part of the Castle was a Georgian house amid the ruins, itself in a bad state until Hughes had it seen to by the architect Clough Williams-Ellis. Born in Surrey of English parents, and educated at Charterhouse and Oxford, Hughes claimed Welsh ancestry on a grand scale; his family tree was not a matter of a Welsh grandmother somewhere, but, if one believed him and the genealogists, a line extending back two thousand years to Beli Mawr,

Beli the Great, a semi-mythical chieftain who was King of the Britons at the time of Julius Caesar. Add to this Hughes's distinguished appearance, his wine-cellar, his summerhouse above a look-out tower on the walls (surrounded by haunted shrubbery) where he retired each day to write, and he became the kind of literary person, and Welshman, with whom Dylan Thomas was not at ease.

Augustus John, fifty-eight years old, was an even more dominant figure. Towards Caitlin he was protective and still lustful. Hughes recalled 'much giggling and kissing' between them in the house. According to Caitlin, Hughes stayed behind to prepare dinner while she and the other three men went off to Fishguard. There was a Mrs Richard Hughes, but she played no part in the story.

On the expedition, drink was taken in quantity. To begin with they were in two cars. On the way back Janes's modest vehicle broke down. He waited with it for help to come while Thomas transferred to John's powerful motor, and cuddled Caitlin in the back; John is supposed to have looked in his rear mirror and been enraged by their antics. Since Thomas had no head for drink, it is reasonable to assume he was the drunkest of them all.

Before returning to Laugharne, the three went drinking in Carmarthen, a town of innumerable pubs. There was an altercation between the two men, a scuffle in the car park – Thomas could be belligerent when drunk, but had no idea how to strike a blow – and the car drove off with Caitlin, leaving Thomas on the ground. When the painter staggered into Laugharne Castle, Hughes noted that Caitlin looked 'like a cat that's been fed on cream'. Her recollection is of John being 'on top of me' that night, the story carrying the obligatory aside that she 'wasn't at all happy' with this state of affairs.

Next morning Thomas turned up at Laugharne, and there was some melodramatic posturing. In the short term he must have found it a painful business. It was not embroidered into one of his anecdotes, though it had all the ingredients, but was seen as best forgotten. In the long term it was probably the real start of the affair.

The following month Caitlin was mentioned for the first time in one of his letters, when he wrote from Swansea to another contact at a literary magazine, Desmond Hawkins, of *Purpose*, depressed at his lack of money to spend on 'flashy clothes and cunt and gramophone records and white wine and doctors and white wine again and a very vague young Irish woman whom I love in a grand, real way'. Earlier in the month, he said, he had been in London over the August Bank Holiday, staying 'in Chelsea with my Ireland'. But he was afraid he would have to lose her because of 'money money money money'.

His first recorded letter to her was a card two months later, October 1936, to say he loved her, and 'we'll always keep each other alive'. As usual he was back in Swansea. His courtship was dogged by his absences. In theory he could have scraped a living of some sort in England. But that would have threatened his writing, and perhaps a need for security that lay behind the posturing. Until he had a free or affordable roof over his head, he clung to the home comforts of 5 Cwmdonkin Drive, where his mother would find him ink and paper, have clean shirts ready, and slip hot-water bottles into his bed.

Caitlin was still an uncertainty. Poems he would write in the next year or two suggested a deep-seated sexual jealousy on his part. When he wrote the next surviving letter, undated but probably in November, she was in the Royal Free Hospital, being treated, she says, for gonorrhoea, acquired from someone now forgotten. An enthusiastic love letter, it saw their condition as 'a sort of sweet madness' that cut them off from the world of 'the Nasties and the Meanies'. But it ended unsurely – 'You're not empty, empty still now, are you? Have you got love to send me?'*

Not long after this, Caitlin decided it was time to disappear from the scene, again choosing Ireland as the place to escape to. She wrote about the move to an admirer who wasn't a lover, a young painter called Rupert Shephard. A student at the Slade when Nicolette was there, Shephard met Caitlin on a summer visit to Blashford, probably the one in 1930 described by William Townsend in his journal. Shephard painted Caitlin there and came under her spell. Later he saw her dance at the Group Theatre with Mrs Gribben, while Brigit worked the gramophone.

Shephard now had a studio in London, and was in love with Caitlin in a hopeless sort of way. Patient and good-natured, he was someone she could be cruel to with impunity. 'She was able,' he wrote, 'to stir up my feelings for her with a flick of her little finger.'

Caitlin had been in touch with him when she returned from Paris,

* 'Empty, empty', presumably a phrase she had used, might suggest an abortion. There is no other indication. But she was careless about contraception, and a number of her marital pregnancies were terminated.

because she needed him to store a painting by 'Legas' that she meant to sell for him, but never did. Shephard was someone who came in useful. In December 1936, just after her twenty-third birthday (and not long after the gonorrhoea), she wrote to him from Blashford, addressing him as 'Dear friend Rupert,' and, in case there should be any doubt, 'Dear best special friend.' He was thanked for unspecified services and asked to 'collect me and the picture' as a preliminary to her visiting Ireland –

> please dear, as I ought to go sooner than ever now, for internal doctrinal reasons – Uncle Ruggles* you know of course that I'm smitten with love in a big way – Hence my erratic behaviour – Patience tho, I'll eradicate that bugbear from my system – but it's a handicap being so serious; a great handicap – How I wish I was flippant!
>
> I've written what I consider satisfactory poems. I'll show them you, I will [. . .] Your contrary Caitlin. Love & kisses.

'Internal doctrinal' reasons could be the infection or the love affair or both. She was floating out of Thomas's reach while she made up her mind. 'I nearly forgot him,' she once said, although she added, 'I was a bit worried . . . I thought maybe he'd forget about me.'

Caitlin made for Ennistymon. This time she can have been in no doubt that her father would be there, because he had fulfilled his plan to convert the house into a hotel, the Falls.

It was another attempt by Francis to make a name for himself. Now aged fifty-two, he dreamt of presiding over a centre of culture and conviviality in the west. A few years earlier the writer St John Gogarty had done something similar at Renvyle, in Connemara. The idea of poetry at the feast went down well in Ireland.

To pay for the renovations Francis took eight thousand pounds from Iris O'Callaghan, who had inherited it from an aunt. A good housekeeper and a better cook (although drink sapped her talents), Iris would marry Francis to become Mrs Macnamara No. 3 in 1937, Edie having died. Her capital was needed not only for the builders but for the wine-cellar, which Francis wanted to be, and briefly may have been, the best in Ireland. There was no shortage of conviviality, and

---

* Ruggles (and his wife Gladys) were comic suburban characters in a popular *Daily Mirror* strip cartoon, first seen in 1935.

Francis thought that here at last he would find himself, as an intellectual and an Irishman. The guests contained a preponderance of drinking buddies and may have lacked those well-heeled thinkers who would pay for the fine wines. But miserly calculations were not allowed to enter in. The rafters were meant to ring.

Some of the buddies were from England. Mrs R., a big beautiful woman whose family was in manufacturing, arrived in a Mercedes and was presently in bed with Francis. Iris, who happened to be naked at the time, discovered them and rushed into the grounds, where she was stung by nettles. The legend goes that Mrs R. was not presented with a bill. Or there was the titled woman who hurried down to Reception to report that 'some animal with whiskers is upstairs on my bed'. It turned out to be Cuckoo O'Brien, sleeping off a few pints of porter. From time to time the Cuckoo was summoned to Ennistymon for drinking purposes; Francis would send a taxi to bring him from Fisher Street. 'We can't move him,' Francis told the titled woman. 'He's the guest of the house.'

Caitlin, arriving on this scene, fitted in well enough. She served drinks in the inconveniently narrow bar down one side of the hotel, and occupied herself with painting in water-colours and writing poetry. But Francis continued to plague her. She must have been very fond of Ireland, or have needed its solace badly, to put up with him. She wrote to Rupert in January:

> My father's not man but monster – he horrifies every pore in my body. I hold myself apart, & meditate in silence – This place is totally beautiful – and *corrupt* – yes – God will guide me.

These short letters to Rupert Shephard – he kept four of them – are all that survives of her correspondence as a young woman, apart from the three schoolgirl letters to her mother. Shephard also kept a few lines of her poetry, sent to him with a letter she wrote, in French, on 3 February, looking forward to a visit he intended to make in the spring ('Je me réjouis à l'idée que tu vienne pour le printemps – nous irons pour un séjour aux Isles de Aran – tu veux?').

Caitlin was serious about her poetry. In the 'Finito' fragment of 1956 she said:

> 'What is this magic that pervades the air?' I wrote in my first immortal

poem, and nothing would persuade me that it was not immortal; I could feel the authentic throb and tingle running down my spine as I chanted it . . .

By 1937 she had moved on from magic-pervaded air. The first of the poems she sent to Shephard inclined towards the Imagists:

> Angelically the landscape chanted,
> As she twinkled her gilded slippers,
> And paraded her taffeta train
> Of snow, over the brackish marshes;
> Where rank stalks, protesting, thrust upward
> Noses, in stately disapproval
> At her feathering, pristine kisses.

Page 2 is more interesting. The verses are set out as three separate poems, but cling together as one. They have a touch of Thirties brutality, though the 'womb/tomb' rhyme hints at Dylan Thomas.

> From the bowels of horse dung,
> From cowpats and manure,
> Slumber is in the womb.
>
> From the suck of red squelch
> From blue-dipped, scrunch pebbles
> Dead lead is in the tomb.
>
> Lunatic gulls, black crows,
> Share that exaltation!

The last and longest letter that Shephard kept was dated 20 March, a week before Easter:

Forgive me, I was busy or busyish or preoccupied or something. However I have booked a room for you in town for the few days over easter, and afterwards it will be OK in the house for you – with blessings and welcomes and odd jobs . . . (plenty of decorating for you to do). Then we might do our painting adventure in Aran.

To give you an idea of the morality here, I will tell you a short story – Two joking policemen came sauntering down the river path, carrying a box between them. They asked me – 'Would I like to see a dead baby?' 'I would,' I said vaguely – so they took away some straw and showed it to me

– I had an awful shock as I hadn't believed them at all, and laughing they told me that an unmarried girl had been down the night before in a storm, had the baby on a bank and thrown it in a mud hole – wrapped in her knickers, and drowned it – so now she would be tried for murder and probably get gaol – but in any case no house would let her in as she was unmarried . . . and the boy of course would have no blame laid on him –

So you see there are still a few barbaric traces left – a noble survival.*

I'm in a strange mood these days, lackadaisical and silly – and a bit looney. What of yourself – as dynamic as ever?

By the way, we will meet you in Ennis – so don't get lost.

For Caitlin, these were the last weeks she would spend under the same roof as Francis. She would effectively break with him, and with Ireland, when she returned to literary London – as though the father and the place were two sides of the same coin, an experience it was time to turn her back on.

Shephard described the Falls Hotel in his unpublished memoirs. The chef had a white hat, an apron and a rifle to shoot the rats that infested the kitchens, after so many years of being empty. Caitlin painted her water-colours from memory in the bar, making herself strange alcoholic mixtures and pressing free drinks on Rupert. This was the rule of the house, since Francis, unable to resist the role of benevolent host, himself drank continually and handed out drinks to the numerous spongers. Economies were attempted and abandoned. When a lunchtime rhum-baba displeased him because it was short of rum, he strode to the bar and returned with a bottle, which he poured over the pudding.

Because it was Easter, there were more drinkers than ever. The barman was drunk, duplicating orders at no further charge. Francis lost his temper and sacked him, at which he retaliated by accusing his employer of improper advances to his wife. ' 'Twas a chaste kiss I gave her!' shouted Francis, and the bar listened with interest as they argued about when a chaste kiss became a sensual one.

Rupert Shephard busied himself around the place, painting and sketching. He found the Irish 'not colourful figures as Augustus John & Jack Yeats had seen & painted them but as a lot of querulous little men in rough tweeds & cloth caps – not unlike the Cockneys I had left

---

* This must be the same incident described years later in *Story of a Woman*, when she was out walking with the tailor (page 47), although in that version the woman had drowned as well.

behind in my London paintings'. Caitlin was among his subjects. She, her brother John and Rupert slept in makeshift bedrooms above the old stables at the back. The derelict rooms were still there in 1992, traces of a green design that had been painted on a wall just visible through the damp. Caitlin was idle, a gift to artists, sitting with a book or nothing, being decorative. Rupert found it 'tremendously romantic' to be painting her:

> Her life was largely a physical one of day and late-night dancing and drinking, alternating with long periods of sleep. She was as usual restless; she quarrelled with Francis much of the time & ignored her job as barmaid [. . .] I had no ruthless streak in my character to cope with her arrogance; her kiss was hard and so unlike the loving, gentle ones that I got from Irish girls, and I was unprepared to be the full-time drinking companion she required.

The 'painting adventure on Aran' didn't come off. Early in April they returned together to the British mainland, catching the night ferry from Dun Laoghaire to Holyhead. Caitlin ignored the segregation of bunks into Male and Female sections, and crawled under a rug near Shephard. As he wrote, 'It was her apparent total disregard of conventions coupled with her wonderful appearance, that drew me to her. But I knew that I could never deal with such a force of nature.' That was left to Dylan Thomas.

6

Warring Absences

While Caitlin Macnamara served drinks at the Falls Hotel and danced in the Doolin cottages, Dylan Thomas was pursuing the round of provincial life, broken up with sorties to London. While there, he was seeing the writer Emily Holmes Coleman, one of the American émigrés who stirred up literary Paris in the 1920s – her circle included Djuna Barnes and Peggy Guggenheim – and who had been in London since 1929. Wyn Henderson knew her, and may have introduced her to Thomas.

Coleman's autobiographical novel *The Shutter of Snow*, published 1930, described a woman's madness and incarceration after childbirth. Madness attracted Thomas. It was a subject he returned to in stories. His friendship with Vernon Watkins may have owed something to a psychotic breakdown that Watkins suffered as a young man. Thomas's own mental state – in which his obsession with words and their meaning could leave him in a state of suspended reality, as though, he said, he was unable to distinguish between the word and the thing it meant – may have verged at times on the psychotic.*

Three letters he wrote to Coleman at the time were affectionate and made references to bed, but were hardly 'love letters', if only because he was careful to bring Caitlin into two of them. The first was written on 28 and 29 January 1937. Much of it was taken up with a discussion of their literary pals, among them Norman Cameron, Antonia White – another writer who had had episodes of madness – and the poet David

* See, for example, his letter to Pamela Hansford Johnson of May 1934, where he described a day in Laugharne and speculated about the 'torture in words'.

Gascoyne, whose surrealist verse Thomas disliked. The letter said he thought he loved her. But it was written in response to a telegram she had sent him, chiding him for being back in Wales a week and not writing to her. Now he seemed to be putting on the brakes. He turned abruptly to Caitlin:

> I don't really know about Caitlin. I don't know how tough my Caitlin is, how powerful her vagueness is, whether the sweet oblivion in which she moves about is proof against the little tiny hurts that can eat through a mountain while the big hurts just batter against it. I know she hasn't got much feeling about *physical* pain: she once wanted to boil a lobster but hadn't got a saucepan big enough, so she found a small saucepan and boiled the thing bit by bit while it screamed like a frog or a baby and drove us howling out. I know she's done away with most of the natural sense of surprise; nothing, I think, can shock her except squeamishness; and she can blush like a naked schoolgirl too. Of course I shall sleep with her; she's bound up with me, just as you are; one day I shall marry her very much – (no money, quite drunk, no future, no faithfulness) – and that'll be a funny thing.

Thomas's next letter to Coleman, brief but friendly, was written early in February, and arranged a London meeting after he gave a lecture in Cambridge; Dent had published *Twenty-five Poems* the previous September, and his reputation was advancing. Finally he wrote at Easter, a longer letter, from the house on the outskirts of Swansea to which his parents had just moved, D.J. Thomas having left the grammar school and begun an angry retirement. This sent his love but slipped in the information that Caitlin had knitted him a sweater.

Nor was he forgotten by Caitlin. Ireland had not eradicated 'that bugbear' from her system – if she had ever meant it to. On 13 April, a week or two after Easter, and her chaste ferry-crossing with Rupert Shephard, she was with him in London. David Gascoyne, aged twenty to Thomas's twenty-two, met them on their way to a cinema in Villiers Street to see *The Golem*, the 1936 remake of an earlier German film about a clay monster brought to life, which prefigured Hollywood's series of *Frankenstein* movies. They were in Piccadilly Circus, and Gascoyne accompanied them some of the way. In Leicester Square Thomas got grit in his eye and went into a chemist's for an eyebath. 'Really rather repulsive,' wrote Gascoyne in his journal, 'as he sat there with his inflamed eye and ugly nose, his face thrown back, the boracic dripping between his corduroyed knees; but one did not feel repulsed, all the same.'

It was the first time Gascoyne had met Caitlin, but he was well up with the gossip:

> He apparently intends to marry Caitlin M. in a few days' time. She is small – florid in miniature, with an incipient Roman nose – blonde, *almost* fluffy, wearing a brick-red coat and skirt. My first impression was of a hard innocence, obtuse, hermetic, with a concealed but very precise knowledge of how to deal with anyone she might want to deal with. (This may be all wrong; I have never pretended to be a good judge of character, and am often very unfair to people on first impressions.)
>
> Until quite recently, Dylan has been living with Emily Coleman who was 'in love' with him. Yesterday or the day before, he confronted her with Caitlin M., whom he announced his intention of marrying almost at once – to put it baldly.

Gascoyne's view of Caitlin, modestly expressed, came close to an aspect of her, and her relationship with Thomas, of which Gascoyne can have known nothing. Behind the exterior that was almost that of 'a bit of fluff' – a Betty Boop-like character – he perceived a different Caitlin; he saw the machinery inside the innocence. Thomas, though, saw what he wanted to see. Her youthfulness helped the illusion. She appeared much younger than twenty-two, and Thomas had no idea that she was older than him by ten months. The idea of 'innocence' was important to him, and provided the context for the love affair. Her vagueness, her silences and her striking looks combined to make her seem untouched by the world. His 1936 letter to her in hospital, already quoted, is full of such fantasy about being 'young and unwise together', and an innocence that 'goes awfully deep'.

A few weeks after the meeting recorded by Gascoyne, Thomas was telling the same tale in another letter. The 'marrying almost at once' had not come off. They were separated again; she was probably at Blashford, he was in London, allegedly with bronchitis, writing from the address of Veronica Sibthorp, his lover in Cornwall, before returning to Wales for more coddling. The letter emphasised his illness and weakness, a habitual theme, then drew her into his magic circle, where they are united in 'a hairy, golden, more-or-less unintelligible haze of daftness'.

Childhood, innocence and disability were important elements in

Thomas's view of himself. He was small and frail, he coughed, he was impractical, he was an artist living in poverty: his early letters are full of such propositions. They were beliefs it suited him to hold, and Caitlin's willingness to go along with them must have been part of her attraction; perhaps the crucial part. In later years she took a harsher view, of that as of everything else. If asked why she had married Dylan, the answer was likely to mock her own naïveté: 'I was a wild Irish rose, taken with the romantic idea of marrying a penniless poet. I had some half-baked ideas, my God!'

But it was a conspiracy, like most love affairs. They wanted to look innocent precisely because they weren't. That, again, only hints at the truth. Caitlin would cooperate with his fantasy of happy young things, defying the world with their unworldliness. No doubt Thomas knew perfectly well, at another level, that the truth about her was more complicated. He can hardly not have had his suspicions about Augustus John, however unforthcoming Caitlin was on the subject. Her hard-headed practicality can't have escaped him. But he was arranging reality to suit his purpose, which was to preserve himself intact as a working poet, able to survive against the odds.

Thomas knew that the truth about himself was more complicated, too. Desiring to be a poet above all else, he was prepared to sacrifice everything to that end. He would scrounge, steal and exploit without conscience. The American poet, Donald Hall, has suggested that Thomas, with generations of nonconformist blood in his veins, saw the business of poetry as sinful, and himself as damned for it, his soul mortgaged to the Devil in return for his gift. Certainly vampires and ghouls, or the idea of them, haunted him. Faced with the reality of what he had to do in order to survive, the trick was to hide himself in a safe, childlike state where the world couldn't get at him, clinging and being clung to. It was this game that Caitlin, from the start, agreed to play; though the rules changed often before it was over, sixteen years later. At the deepest level, she suited him. He, in turn, a poet who needed looking after, fitted her requirements; she liked and needed men to depend on her.

As a preliminary to marriage, Thomas took her to Cornwall, to the scene where he had been happy the previous summer, and in June and July they lived at the Sibthorp cottage, minus Sibthorps, in Lamorna Cove. He wrote to his parents, who were upset at the news. His father understood that Caitlin was 'the niece of Augustus John', a story which may have come from Caitlin herself, aimed at soothing Dylan's suspicions of the painter; it could even explain the 'daughter of Augustus' tale.

John himself was still hovering. A letter from him to Caitlin (already quoted from on page 40) mentions having 'assisted at your revered father's wedding the other day' – Francis had married his third wife, Iris, on 9 June 1937. The letter, which began 'Dearest Caitlin', said that

> I spent some time combing out the London Pubs in hopes of finding you & getting you back for a bit to finish that pink picture* which I rather bank on. If I came down soon would you come back with me do you think? I could do Dylan's drawing† at the same time. You will be seeing Vivien I expect as she is going to Cornwall.

They had no money at Lamorna Cove, but Wyn Henderson was only a few miles away, at Mousehole, running a restaurant and guesthouse called the Lobster Pot, which she had begun with a thousand pounds from one of her lovers, or ex-lovers, Alexander Keiller, the marmalade tycoon. It was Henderson who organised the wedding, first having them to stay at the Lobster Pot, then paying for a special licence for the marriage at the nearest register office, in Penzance, on 11 July 1937. She sought to exercise a kind of female *droit du seigneur* by going to bed with them both, in Caitlin's words 'asking if she could be the mattress underneath us when we were doing what we had to do'. Caitlin was agreeable; Dylan was shocked; it didn't happen.

For a while they stayed on in Cornwall, renting a studio overlooking the harbour at Newlyn; Thomas's father had sent him five pounds, and in general the marriage made cadging easier. They had friends there, writers and painters, and spent their time walking, lounging, drinking in pubs. By September they were in Swansea, having free bed and board with the Thomases. 'My wife is Irish and French,' Dylan wrote from there to Desmond Hawkins, 'she is two months younger than I am [the year was still missing from her age], has seas of golden hair, two blue eyes, two brown arms, two dancing legs, is untidy and

---

* Probably the painting reproduced between pages 182 and 183 of this book, finished after Caitlin married Dylan.
† Thomas wrote to David Higham on 9 February 1937 about a Welsh travel book he was planning to write (but never did), to say that Augustus John would paint his portrait as a frontispiece.

vague and un-reclamatory. I am lost in love and poverty.' Later in the
year they were with Caitlin's mother at Blashford, and Thomas was
telling Vernon Watkins how they rode (presumably on bicycles) into
the New Forest every day, 'into Bluebell Wood or onto Cuckoo Hill
[. . .] we are quiet and small and cigarette-stained and very young'. The
phrase is poised between irony and matter-of-factness.

To begin with, Caitlin went unremarked by most people. She was
still withdrawn in company, except when drink livened her up. If she
wrote letters, no one was bothering to keep them. She was the artist's
wife, not the artist. Thomas worked slowly at poems and stories that
never earned him more than a pound or two each, and sometimes
nothing. But he was in touch with editors and critics, a figure in his
own right. Her poems were either concealed from him or brushed
aside. Her dancing was an eccentricity to be tolerated. If she had seen
these things as a pastime, it would not have mattered. Instead, she still
thought of herself as having a destiny. The fact that she had slender
grounds for this made no difference. Anger at being overlooked
burned away, below the surface, unknowingly fuelled by Dylan's pals.
There was the old pal Norman Cameron, for one, 'a kind of poet who
was in advertising', always engaged in 'little private jokes' with Dylan.
Caitlin in her seventies hadn't forgotten him. 'He treated me like an
utter idiot. I must have been very submerged. I think I'd kill him if he
treated me like that now.'

In some moods Caitlin looks back on herself as a simple case of
young love, happy and self-centred. They scraped a living, and money
worried her only 'when I could not get a new dress I desperately
wanted to satisfy my rapacious vanity. Whereas Dylan worried
constantly about money'. He was 'very endearing and sweet', saying
he adored her, and would never, never look at anyone else. She says
she believed all this, seeing him, 'from the start', as 'a good, chosen,
special-for-me person, and incidentally a poet. He had to be a poet. No
less would have done.' She had a superstitious fear of interfering with
his work, of tampering with the secret process.

The winter of 1937–8 they spent at Blashford, where the
acquiescent Mrs Macnamara fitted them in around her country-
woman's life. Thomas didn't care for her, though she claimed to have
found him 'a most lovable character, in spite of his faults'. In the spring
of 1938 they fetched up with the Thomases again, where Caitlin was
amused at being expected to dust the furniture. In an unloving mood

she once recalled her indignation when his mother gave Dylan double helpings of food and put him to sit in the best armchair.

She hated what she saw as provincial, cosy, hypocritical. Although there was never any drink in the house, Dylan's father would arrive back worse for wear after 'going for a walk', with nothing said to suggest that anyone knew where he had been. 'Daddy never touches a drop,' Florence would say. Appearances were all. This was not Caitlin's style, though it occurred to her sometimes that in his heart, under the layers of acquired bohemianism, it might be Dylan's.

Presently they were off again, this time to Laugharne, where they rented a workman's cottage called Eros. Thomas felt at ease in Laugharne. Neighbours gave them vegetables and fish, though Caitlin offended one or two middle-class residents, who didn't like her habit of popping out in a purple housecoat – purple was her favourite colour – with hair uncombed and fingernails bitten till they bled. Also, Mrs Thomas's bare breasts were inclined to burst into view. Others found the young couple entertaining. Youths peeped through the un-curtained windows at night and gave lurid accounts of what they saw.

In July they moved to Sea View, a house higher up in the town. She was three months' pregnant, coping with coal fires and candlelight, and just enough furniture for eating and sleeping. Cooking bored her. Boiled cockles were a staple, scraped up free from the sand. Stews bubbled in an iron pot with two handles, resting on red coals. Dylan always praised Caitlin's stew, which she called 'bone broth' to make it sound more distinctive. She would throw in old crusts and rinds to see if he noticed, but he never did. That summer he was engrossed in writing the stories about his childhood and adolescence that became *Portrait of the Artist as a Young Dog*. Visitors came to stay, among them Augustus John, who spent four nights there, and wrote to his wife complaining of 'frightful squalor and hideousness . . . The Dylans are impossible to stand for long.' One wonders what detained him. Thomas, no love lost on his side either, remarked that '[Augustus's] varnish was cracking visibly'.

Life in Laugharne took on a pattern. Dylan wrote; Caitlin chafed. The bitten fingers were to last a lifetime. Her pleasures were often solitary. Bathing alone in the estuary – he rarely went near the water – she would emerge from the tide with her uncapped hair glittering, red-gold and prismatic, to impress the curious. Or she walked for miles, over Sir John's hill, along the shore. If she was happy at times,

74

she was never content. Contentment eluded her. Looking back, she recognised it in him, behind the 'Rabelaisian appetites and indecencies' that he paraded in public, 'a core of content, a peace, an untaught wisdom'. There were (she wrote) rhythms that she found tedious, to which he could adjust, drawing sustenance out of surroundings that to her were barren. 'If you tethered him in a field all day like a lonely donkey he would summon company out of the invisibly crowded atmosphere, and soon be surrounded with the cries and hoots and pipings of his misty kingdom.'

It annoyed her that he was like most men in wanting a woman who was 'jolly, dumb nursemaid, prim secretary, darkly wanton at night only behind blinds'. She still hankered ('in my idiotic girl's head') after some 'powerful maestro' who would 'subdue me to his will', a Caspar John with ideas – a wish that was irreconcilable with the other, probably deeper wish, to have a man who would be lost without her. Dylan was a long way from any dreams of physical perfection. He was clumsy in their intimacies (but so were all men, in her sad retrospection). Orgasms eluded her, to be found alone with a gramophone, pretending to be Isadora Duncan, when dancing would make her come. Thomas had other deficiencies. He 'killed the romance stone dead', she wrote, 'by introducing a comic element', which sounds like the truth, if exaggerated. Caitlin had little sense of humour; a cruel wit, directed, to be fair, at herself as much as at others, was the nearest she came to laughter. Dylan, part clown, included sex as part of the joke. What Caitlin thought she wanted was earth-trembling fornication with a tall dark stranger and a straight face. What she got, which suited her better, was something less threatening: a rather flabby young man, on the short side, with sexual equipment of modest dimensions, who was unromantic and apt to see the ludicrous side of things, but who loved her and wanted to be mothered. She was strong and energetic, and if she persuaded him to join her on a walk, and they came to a stream, she would carry him over it; lacking pride, in her eyes, he fell easily into the role of dependant.

Now and then they were in Swansea, being introduced to her husband's old haunts. She was no more at home there than anywhere else. Caitlin never belonged in the place where she happened to be – not Blashford of the elms, or Laugharne with its sweeping tides, or Chelsea, or later Elba, or Rome, or Catania. Perhaps only Ireland would have been home, and then it would have been an Ireland that was no longer there, or had never existed.

In Swansea there were obligatory visits to Dylan's friends, in particular to Vernon Watkins (Dan Jones, the composer, the closest of all, was abroad much of the time). Watkins, eight years older than Thomas, worked at Lloyds Bank in the town; his first book of verse was not published until 1941. Unmarried in the 1930s, and still in the shadow of his earlier psychotic breakdown, he lived with his parents on the Gower peninsula, beyond the town, in a house on the cliffs at Pennard. His manner, intense and naïve in many ways, and his apparent lack of interest in women, made the Thomases think he might be homosexual. When he stayed a night at Eros, the three of them slept in a double bed, allegedly at Dylan's suggestion. Nothing improper happened, though Watkins heard Caitlin giggling in the dark.

At Pennard there was sand for bathing, and a garden to play games in. A photograph taken there in July 1938, the month they moved to Sea View, shows them wielding mallets for croquet. They both look about twenty. Caitlin's breasts are unsupported under her floral dress, and the short, stubby hands she was ashamed of contrast with Dylan's slender fingers. Ethel Ross, who knew Thomas in his amateur-dramatics days before he left Swansea, met her at Pennard, and thought that she 'never seemed fully present. One would have said she didn't understand English.' Caitlin would have made little of the comedy that coloured Dylan's relationship with Vernon, the persistent jokes and foolery; though Watkins, who had a solemn side, was less of an offender than most in her eyes. Thomas's friends found his funny-man act endearing. Perhaps her inability to join in the laughter was an ingredient in Caitlin's sense of isolation. Of Dylan's friends in general she wrote that 'being deadly serious myself, I deplored their apparent lack of seriousness on any one subject'.

If she ever heard Dylan and Vernon reading aloud from Professor Barone's manual of English–Italian conversation, which Watkins had found in a second-hand bookshop, she can't have been amused. Among their favourites was the dialogue with a tram conductor:

'Here is your ticket: take care about not lose it; if a controller should arrive he would let pay to you a double ticket.'
  'Conductor, will you let me stop or no? I have sounded twice and the mechanician does not stop!'

'*And it is just*. We have many stations for stopping for which one is not here.'

Professor Barone's section on Proper Names included Bab, Balthasar, Hilairy, Hippolyt, Hug and Hyacinthus; Thomas said it would be a great help in naming their unborn child.

Vernon Watkins had first met Caitlin a year earlier, when she went to Wales after her marriage, describing her as 'a beautiful and very nice girl, with wonderful gold hair like the incarnation of light, and still blue eyes like flowers. When she smokes a cigarette she looks very like Dylan and her remarks are like his, but softer, and in a lower key.' Watkins had memories of this early Caitlin.* At Pennard one evening they were playing Lexicon, a word-game with cards. His parents were playing, too. Caitlin usually lost. On this occasion she was delighted to find she could make a longish word. Dylan looked over her shoulder and, one eye on Mr and Mrs Watkins, murmured that No, no, she really couldn't, she mustn't. Caitlin complained bitterly. 'ING gets eight points,' she said, 'and K is another six.' Eventually she gave in, but suspected it was a plot to stop her scoring.

At Sea View, when Vernon came visiting with a present of plums — earning a salary, he helped keep them afloat with cash and little gifts — Dylan, lying on a sofa, put out his hand and asked for one. This awakened Caitlin's puritanical streak; perhaps she was feeling hot and pregnant. She snatched the bag from Vernon and snapped, 'No, he has to get up and fetch a plum if he wants one.'

He began wheedling. 'Ca-at. Can I have a plum? Just one.' She didn't stir. 'Ca-at, can I have a plum? A very little one.' Turning to go into the kitchen, she bombarded him with fruit. When she had gone, he picked up a plum that had fallen in his lap and said, 'Right, now we can get on with our poems.'

Watkins, who idealised his friend, wrote a poem that commemorated life at Sea View, 'To a Shell'. It begins:

> At last, beautiful shell,
> Lie there crushed: but the sea
> Cannot obliterate yet
> Faith I remember well:

* Later he told them to his wife Gwen, whom he married in the war. She included them in her book about Thomas and Watkins, *Portrait of a Friend*.

> A house facing the sea.
> Hard and bitterly
> Though waves beat on that wall
> From the swirling quicksands of debt,
> I swear that it cannot fall.

Meanwhile Caitlin had not been faithful to Dylan. Pregnant in late April 1938, nine months or so after they were married, she seems not to have been certain, at first, that the father wasn't someone else. The child, a boy, was born at the end of January 1939. Fortunately it looked like Dylan – 'It had bulging eyes and a turned-up nose. I was so relieved.'

The subject is difficult, not least because in her old age Caitlin dismisses sex as an unfortunate experience that gave her little pleasure. What was once a natural taste for it is brushed aside. When she is unforthcoming about a particular aspect, it may be a reluctance to dwell on the matter, or failing memory, or both.

The first she told me about her former anxieties over the children's paternity was in a letter of 1977, when, my biography of Thomas having been published without any assistance from her (and the libel lawyers having breathed again), we began a friendly correspondence in which she remarked that her children were a constant reminder, with 'their funny looks and his brains', of

> *who* it was who, *miraculously* – because they could so easily have been somebody else's, but God, not me, saw to it that they weren't – fathered them.

It was another fourteen years before I asked her directly if it was true that they could have been 'somebody else's', and got the answer, 'Yes. In fact, easily. That's why I put God in.'

But uncovering more detail about the earliest years was impossible. Her replies were strategic: 'I wasn't an absolute Madonna or perfect. I never said that. There were people it could be pinned on, it's true. Who? I can't remember. I used to flirt around a lot. Quite harmless, but it certainly did end up occasionally going to bed.'

Opportunities would have occurred both in the New Forest and Wales, not least when visitors came down from London. Sex in haste was not to be ruled out; after all, it was no more than Augustus John had taught her to expect. Elaborate preliminaries (Caitlin said, when she was old) were disagreeable. Sex was 'something done in the dark and silently'. The sight of a naked man, she insisted, was unwelcome: 'I found men were very attractive *in* their clothes.' She pointed out that a man needed to take off only 'a tiny bit' of clothing in order to 'get that *thing* out'. By implication the act itself was low and contemptible, a necessary evil.

Later on it was to be Dylan who had the reputation for infidelity. He was the womaniser who left the child-bound Caitlin by a smoky hearth while he gallivanted. Even that is a not entirely accurate picture. At the start of the marriage it was not the picture at all. 'It was Dylan,' she wrote, 'who preached at the start, as no one has preached before, the importance, the beauty, the imperative duty of constancy, and the vilely repugnant and unforgivable act of infidelity.' She also wrote of the 'common infidelity of the flesh, spectred shadily over our early marriage bed'.

Whatever Thomas's ideas of marital freedom when he was bragging to Emily Holmes Coleman, in the event he shrank from Caitlin's unfaithfulness. He was jealous; friends observed it over the years. Caitlin knew it. 'It was Dylan worried the most at the start,' she wrote. 'I was far too arrogantly smug in myself then, and never doubted Dylan as my odd personal baggage for keeps.' In Cornwall, after their marriage, he was upset when Augustus John turned up in his car, and Caitlin went to sit in the front, leaving him in the back; again when she disappeared during a pub-crawl. In Gower, he and Caitlin once walked out to the Worms Head, together with Vernon and a good-looking friend, Wyn Lewis. The Worm is a half-tide island, approached over rocks that flood quickly. Caitlin and Wyn were returning well in front of the others when they all realised that the causeway was being covered. The first two reached the mainland without much trouble. Vernon and Dylan might have been cut off. According to Vernon, the prospect of being marooned on the island between tides while Caitlin was alone with a fanciable man made Dylan frantic. They had to wade through the rising sea to avoid this disaster.

Poems that Thomas wrote at the time can be read as autobiography. 'I make this in a warring absence', originally 'Poem (for Caitlin)', was written by September or October 1937, having taken two months or a year to write, depending on which of his accounts one believes. In a rare 'explanation' of a poem, written for an academic admirer in 1938, Thomas said it was about jealousy arising between the heroine's absence and return. Overloaded with complex images, it is not a rewarding work, but Thomas's summary in several hundred words removes any doubt about its drift. 'The "I", the hero [. . .] feels that her pride in him and in their proud, sexual world has been discarded.' The concluding lines, 'And though my love pulls the pale, nippled air,/ Prides of tomorrow suckling in her eyes,/Yet this I make in a forgiving presence' were translated by Thomas as, 'Forgiven by her, he ends his narrative in forgiveness: – but he sees and knows that all that has happened will happen again, tomorrow and tomorrow.'

A further and more explicit explanation of the same poem was given to Desmond Hawkins, who sought guidance when he came to review the book which contained it, in 1939. Thomas wrote of conflicting statements about the woman 'in whose absence, and in the fear of whose future unfaithful absences, I jealously made the poem'. The 'explanation' is as convoluted as the poem; both hint at painful truths being uncovered.

Thomas says that by cataloguing what he knows of the woman, both good and bad, he means to decide for himself 'whether I fight, lie down and hope, forgive or kill?' He concludes that 'The question is naturally answered by the questions in the images and the images in the questions'. This presumably means that the poem is its own answer: he is using it to let off steam, not as a guide to future behaviour. He could face up to Caitlin's promiscuity, but only within the safe confines of a poem.

A poem written two or three years later, between March and June 1940, 'Into her lying down head', is riddled with statements about infidelity. Sending a draft to Vernon Watkins, he thought of borrowing the title of Meredith's poem, 'Married Love', or alternatively calling it 'One Married Pair'. He told Watkins that 'for some reason' he had written a note under the poem in his copybook, beginning 'All over the world love is being betrayed as always, and a million years have not calmed the uncalculated ferocity of each betrayal or the terrible loneliness afterwards.' He may have been thinking partly of his own infidelities. But the poem's opening lines are unequivocal:

> Into her lying down head
> His enemies entered bed,
> Under the encumbered eyelid,*
> Through the rippled drum of the hair-buried ear . . .

* In a reference to Thomas's sexual jealousy, Caitlin has said that 'he wrote in a poem somewhere about this thing under the sleeping eyelid – but those were not his words. I must ask someone to look them up.'

We are told about a 'Queen Catherine howling bare'; 'Caitlin' is a Celtic form of 'Catherine'. The narrator has a 'runaway beloved' and his 'faith' has been 'undone'. A priapic figure who sounds as if it could be Augustus John is wheeled in, perhaps prefiguring other lovers:

> A furnace-nostrilled column-membered
> Super-or-near man
> Resembling to her dulled sense
> The thief of adolescence,

who makes his 'bad bed' in her 'good night'. She, arguably Caitlin, has 'announced the theft of the heart/In the taken body at many ages'. He, arguably Dylan, is unable to share 'Her holy unholy hours with the always anonymous beast'. He knows there are lovers, but not their names. In the concluding section,

> One voice in chains declaims
> The female, deadly, and male
> Libidinous betrayal.

The closing lines of the poem, as they appeared in Thomas's *Deaths and Entrances* (1946) and his collected works thereafter, were watered down from the original version that Vernon Watkins saw. An explicit line, 'The filth and secret of death is sweeter with the sun than these inconstancies', disappeared. The original spoke of 'A loveless man' and asked,

> Betrayed will his love betrayed find an eye or a hair to hate?
> Will his lovely hands let run the daughters and sons of the blood?
> Will he rest his pulse in the built breast of impossible, great God?

In other words, he asks (as in the 'Warring Absence' poem) if he can bring himself to hate, or even to use violence. Alternatively, should he turn to religion for help? The final line suggests instead a gloomy acceptance of events:

> Over the world uncoupling the moon rises up to no good.

Thomas was a poet of eager introspection. His method of dealing with Caitlin's unfaithfulness in those early days, when he was still coming to terms with it, was to have it out on paper, in words, within a poem. In later life she said that it would have been better had he confronted her, seeking revenge, instead of 'letting it flow past'. In one recorded case, near the end of his life, he did respond angrily. He intercepted a letter from a lover, and kicked her in the face; probably he was drunk at the time. She had to drape herself in a scarf and wear dark glasses before she could go out, but seems not to have complained.

Violence was not his usual response. Having detected an infidelity in 1940 (some months after he wrote 'Into her lying down head'), he refused to sleep with her for a while. When he thought there might be infidelity, he was inclined to pretend it wasn't happening; which is a not uncommon formula between husbands and wives. 'He wiped it out,' Caitlin said, 'or pretended not to know. He did make a few protests, but rather feeble ones. Once he threw a fork at me. Can you imagine anything feebler than a fork?'

Caitlin's response to his unfaithfulness was different. For years she thought there was nothing to be jealous of; it is possible that she was right. She now says that she suspects him of spending a night with a woman when her first child was born, in 1939. Even so, at the time she saw it as no threat to her. When she did begin to take his infidelity seriously, later in the marriage, she was enraged. She 'wanted to kill him', and began to attack him physically.

For Caitlin, the traditional 'dual standard' whereby a man's lapses were overlooked, but a woman's had implications, was reversed. 'If he did it, it was a crime of the first order. I just absolutely went mad with fury, jealousy and everything, would not accept it under any conditions. There was nothing emancipated about it at all. I thought, *I* can do it because it doesn't mean anything. My attitude to going to bed with a man was rather like a man's attitude to going to bed with a whore.'*

She makes no apology; she was what she was. Her liaisons didn't matter because she regarded herself as 'the dancer with the marvellous body', whereas he was the intellectual. 'Even then I recognised that he had more brain than I did. So if I was sitting in the wilds doing nothing, I thought it was a waste of me and my body and all that. I'd got to have

* Quotations in this and the following paragraph are from conversations in 1978, when Caitlin was sixty-four, and more forthcoming on the subject than she became.

my life. And I always wanted to be top of the tree – I had this "great-courtesan" and God knows what illusions.'

She patronised him, seeing him as the man of words who needn't bother his head with her little flings. Her feelings for him, if she is to be believed in what she says now, were never passionate. 'We were very close. But I always thought we were like two children.' Part of his power over her lay in his poetry, or rather in the fact that he was undeniably a poet of stature who made his way in the world by means of his craft. She thought it important for him not to compromise, but to live a 'pure' life as a poet. She told George Tremlett that 'people like Dylan [. . .] need special care to enable them to do their own special work': a dubious claim, and one that Thomas never made on his own behalf, but believed in by Caitlin. Ten years after his death she wrote (in her book *Not Quite Posthumous Letter to My Daughter*) that 'I don't believe for a second' that 'Dylan is not the greatest of poets'. 'Poetry' helps to explain her power over him as well as his over her: she was willing to take him as seriously as a professional poet as he did himself.

At the root of this may be Francis Macnamara, the lost hero of Caitlin's life, the dazzling would-be poet who deserted them all when she was an infant, and had to be replaced in her life. The way her rage at her father has survived over the years suggests how important a figure he was, and how much he made her suffer.

The good news was that Caitlin needed a poet. The bad news was that to be betrayed by the poet she thought she could now control, as she could never control the cruel Francis, would conjure up that betrayal of earlier times. The role of successor waited for Dylan Thomas like a man trap.

7

Trial by Marriage

The Thomases' first child was born on 30 January at Poole Hospital, not far from Mrs Macnamara's home at New Inn House, and named Llewelyn Edouard, with a nod to its Welsh and French ancestry; 'Llewelyn' was spelt in the correct way, without the second 'll' of the anglicised style. According to Caitlin, the birth was unusually dreadful. She was in labour for twenty-four (in another version, forty-eight) hours; the staff said they had never heard such screaming. Her mother, she complained, told her neither about sex nor childbirth, using similar words to describe both experiences to her and Brigit, 'After the initial pain it is quite pleasant.'

Her account in 1991 of the birth made a connection between her suffering then, and the occasion when, as a child, she feigned illness in order to have her appendix removed, but lost her nerve at the last minute and was forced to undergo surgery by an enraged doctor. The nurses in 1939, she said, had been told by the same doctor not to go to her, but to let her suffer; there was even a card above the bed with the instructions. Caitlin purported to believe this. 'It was my punishment,' she said. What she certainly believed in was retribution. Like her appendix operation, the birth of Llewelyn Edouard became a moral tale. With the child himself, she says, she was besotted.

It was the beginning of April 1939 before the Thomases were back at Laugharne in Sea View. They had left behind debts, and couldn't return until they were met; so Dylan told his agent, David Higham, who was being urged to extract the thirty-pound advance for his forthcoming collection of poems and stories, *The Map of Love*. They returned still owing money. County court summonses from tradesmen waited in the wings. Caitlin breezed into shops, putting things down. She wrote once of her assumption, which she admitted was illogical, that 'I should be served rather than serving others [. . .] I am still unable to conceive that I am not entitled to go into a shop and buy whatever I want.' Across well rubbed counters in Laugharne passed food, drink, cigarettes and the tobacco she used for rolling her own, all on tick.

Their life of chronic poverty got under way, with Llewelyn now to be catered for. They were equally hopeless with money, the difference between them being that Thomas was the one who worried. He had what he thought a brilliant idea, his 'five bob fund', which required only ten subscribers who would send him a trifling five shillings each per week. His admirers failed him. The start of the Second World War in September made the prospects for a poor writer still gloomier, although he finished the splendid stories for *Portrait of the Artist as a Young Dog* on time soon after, and busied himself avoiding military service.

Caitlin's reliable friend Rupert Shephard reappeared early in 1940 with his wife, Lorna Wilmott, when they arrived in Laugharne for a holiday. Nicolette had suggested they go there. They stayed at Brown's Hotel and spent most of their time with the Thomases. They were introduced to Richard Hughes and his cellar, and the ferryman took them across the estuary to the home of Ernest Rhys,* by then in his eighties, who told Dylan stories of Walt Whitman and Swinburne. Shephard painted Dylan and Caitlin on different occasions in the living room. She lies on a divan, reading. He sits in an old basket chair with a notebook, the baby's bath hanging on the wall behind him, a towel on the back of the chair.

Lorna Wilmott kept a sharp eye on life at Sea View, and wrote about it in a journal. The family, she said, 'gave us a lot of pleasure and more pain'. She described the scene:

Caitlin, wrapped in complacent simpleness, sits balancing the offspring – an amazing godlike child bursting with happiness and golden curls – on his pot with one hand and shaking the frying potatoes on the fire with the other . . . [She] is as wild and unscrupulous as he – we clashed rather. I felt an outraged hen whose chick has been unfairly attacked when she was – I think maliciously – unkind about R. to me – they are curiously naive and

---

* Rhys (1859–1946), a London Welshman, was a poet and editor who is best remembered as the first editor of Dent's Everyman Library.

make a virtue of it, rather delighting in making their destructive comments to solemn people more inhibited by manners . . . [When drunk] one happy night I answered Caitlin vituperation for vituperation. Rupert sat silent and unhappy tearing up cigarette boxes and even I felt a bit embarrassed when I woke next morning, but she strangely liked me much better for it.

The Thomases were like a little tribe, roaming in search of pastures and sustenance. They still appeared at the doors of her parents or his when it suited them. In the summer of 1940, as France fell and German armies assembled across the Channel, the tribe was in Gloucestershire, along with other hungry artists, at the home of John Davenport, an eighteen-stone critic and man of letters: a wit and mimic, inclined to be a bully, and a good match for Thomas. He had money, fast running out, with which he rented the Malting House in the town of Marshfield, a Georgian residence in honey-coloured stone with a squash court and garden at the back.

For months Davenport held court there. The writers William Empson and Antonia White were guests. So was the composer Lennox Berkeley and the musician William Glock. Beyond the adults – busy arguing, drinking, writing reviews and poems, playing two grand pianos in the music room – was an underworld of children and small animals. Someone found Llewelyn in the gas stove. Antonia White heard screams and splashing from upstairs, where Caitlin had decided Dylan must have a bath, and was attacking him with a sponge. Davenport supplied Caitlin with a record player, and she would lock herself away and dance, while he and Thomas went off to the pub and composed a ponderous literary satire published long after as *The Death of the King's Canary*.

Glock, later Sir William Glock, Controller of Music at the BBC, was aged thirty-two, an ambitious man, blond and well built, attractive to women. He was having an affair with Davenport's wife Clement. When Glock (who was rehearsing for a Promenade Concert in September) and Davenport played duets on the grand pianos, it was said that Clement turned the pages for Glock but not for her husband. Caitlin, too, was drawn to him, looking rapturous when he played Schubert and Mozart, and Glock was ready to oblige. They had to avoid arousing Clement's suspicions as well as Dylan's. The plan they concocted was to be both away at the same time, Glock presumably in London, where he was chief music critic of the *Observer*, and Caitlin

Yvonne Macnamara with Caitlin, her youngest child, on the beach at Doolin, holidaying in the west of Ireland. Probably 1915.

Francis Macnamara (right), who liked to be seen as a thinker, ignores his infant daughter, Caitlin. See page 15.

More Irish holidays. The painter Augustus John (below) was a family friend; he also seduced Yvonne.

Doolin House, Francis's family retreat. It was burnt down later, during the 'Troubles'.

Just good friends. Nora Summers (right of picture), rich man's wife and occasional painter, with Yvonne Macnamara. They had a sexual affair that lasted many years.

Nora with her husband Gerald about 1917, when he was an army officer. Yvonne's marriage had already broken down. The children are Caitlin (left) and her sister Nicolette.

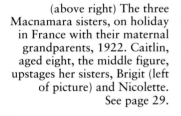

(above right) The three Macnamara sisters, on holiday in France with their maternal grandparents, 1922. Caitlin, aged eight, the middle figure, upstages her sisters, Brigit (left of picture) and Nicolette. See page 29.

(above) Aged twelve, Caitlin is precociously aware of herself. The boy pointing a gun is Vincent Summers, Nora's only child. See page 29.

New Inn House at Blashford, in the New Forest, the former pub where the Macnamara children grew up. Caitlin remembered gloom and dripping elms.

(above) Gabriel Lopez, art
student, on a visit to
Blashford. Not long after, he
gassed himself because Caitlin
didn't love him.

(above left) Rupert Shephard,
painter, was another of the
young men smitten by Caitlin.
Years later, as Nicolette
Macnamara's second hus-
band, he became Caitlin's
brother-in-law.

Nicolette Macnamara marries
Anthony Devas, painter,
1931. Augustus John attends
as father-figure.

Caitlin, aged twenty, with her friend Kitty, daughter of 'Cuckoo' O'Brien, 1934. Behind them is Ennistymon House, once the Macnamaras' principal house in Co. Clare.

(right) Vera Gribben, the dancing teacher who briefly inspired Caitlin to follow the Isadora Duncan school. (below) Caitlin prepares to perform on the foreshore, somewhere in Ireland.

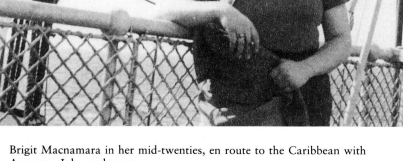

Brigit Macnamara in her mid-twenties, en route to the Caribbean with Augustus John and party.

(above) In a green shade. The unmarried Caitlin and Vincent Summers in the 1930s, perhaps at the Summers' house near Bournemouth, Green Worlds.

(above) Posing for Nora Summers, who liked nude studies.

(right) In Cornwall, with unidentified friend.

in west Wales, calling on Dylan's parents and proceeding to Laugharne on some spurious errand. The lovers would then meet in Cardiff, which is forty miles from Swansea in the direction of Gloucestershire, and spend a night at a hotel. It was probably late August or early September. According to Caitlin, this was the first time she had planned an affair, as opposed to little lapses. For all her talk of casual affairs, she liked to feel that she was 'in love', satisfying the romantic itch.

It was necessary to look her best for Mr Glock. Clothes were always a priority. She knew that her figure and colouring called for vivid accoutrements. Once, when Dylan received a cheque from a magazine, she hurried to spend it on a gold swimming costume. The woman telling the story agreed that it was an extravagant thing to do, but who could object when she looked so marvellous in it? As Caitlin got older, and sensuality more or less deserted her, she retained an appetite for the look and feel of clothes, recalling the most beautiful garment she ever bought – for five pounds, from a theatrical costumier – a creamy dress with purple grapes 'bursting out between two white as marble breasts'. She liked tight-fitting clothes, avoided trousers and dwelt on the feel of silk stockings under a skirt.

On William Glock's behalf she gathered up possessions from Sea View and sold them at knock-down prices in a pub. In the War, thousands of people were on the move, leading odd lives. Caitlin said they would not be returning to Laugharne. Furniture donated by a Macnamara aunt went for a few pounds. There were Welsh blankets and crockery from Carmarthen market, where she loved to shop. With the proceeds she bought dresses and underclothes in Cardiff, and arrived resplendent for her assignation.

After all that, she complained, Glock was not on form. Over-awed or merely nervous, he was unable to perform. He agrees this version of events, adding that 'Caitlin was not indifferent'. She says that 'we just lay there, gazing at the ceiling and the shadows. I got nearly frantic.' Her mother had told her that it was the man's job to warm a woman up, and she felt unable to make the first move. Bold and uninhibited at one level, she could be awkward and shy when it came to revealing herself.

In her own account, she was invariably drunk when she slept with her husband, and love-making was never a 'beautiful experience', with him or with anyone else. The positions of love were grotesque; she couldn't relax; men didn't touch her in the right way. 'I probably made myself as hard as a rock, closed up tight like an oyster. I didn't want to give myself to anyone.'

After their unsatisfactory night in Cardiff, Caitlin and Glock parted as soon as they could, he to spend a day or two elsewhere so they would not arrive back at the same time, she to return as quickly as possible to the house-party. Glock says they didn't give up but tried again at Marshfield shortly afterwards; this time they were successful. God's wrath continued to work, however. Granny Thomas wrote to her son, perhaps innocently (but not in Caitlin's view), spelling out her daughter-in-law's movements, which showed up the missing night. The lapse having been brought to his attention, Thomas had to do more than write a poem, and they had a row; this was the occasion when he suspended sexual relations.

But there seems to have been a poem as well. Echoes of the episode can be heard, or imagined, in Thomas's 'On a Wedding Anniversary'. The poem was meant to mark a third anniversary, which in their case was 11 July 1940. However, Thomas's slow methods of composition meant that a poem could be unfinished well after the date implied. That may have happened in the present case, leaving it to be completed in late summer or beyond, after the Glock affair. The poem used wartime images of air-raids to describe the sky 'torn across' a 'ragged anniversary'. A gloomy, uncertain piece,* it could have sprung from the mood that Thomas described to Davenport early in 1941, apologising for having rushed away from Marshfield a month or so earlier – 'I was very muddled and unhappy, and didn't feel a bit like having any contact at all – until the muddles were straightened in my head.'

After the long summer at Marshfield, Caitlin found herself back with her parents-in-law outside Swansea, in their 'awful little match-box house'. Granny Thomas fussed and chattered. Her husband ignored her, did crossword puzzles with Dylan and made his secret sorties to the pub. Following Caitlin's wicked escapade, extra duty with dustpan and brush was no doubt expected as an act of contrition. There is a glimpse of her in the same Thomas letter to Davenport in

---

* The poem described here is the version published in the magazine *Poetry (London)* in January 1941. Thomas later made it shorter and sharper for *Deaths and Entrances*, the form in which it is generally known.

January 1941, wearing a man's hat and spending the day mopping up after the pipes burst. She felt she had come down in the world; perhaps she had.

In wartime conditions, with paper rationed and publishing inhibited, it was impossible even to scrape a living from the kind of writing that Thomas did. He was still angling for a country cottage, thinking of settling Caitlin in one, should he be sent to work in a munitions plant. After a series of heavy raids on Swansea early in 1941 – nearly three hundred people were killed, and the town centre destroyed – Thomas's parents decided to stay with relatives in rural Carmarthenshire. Uprooted again, the tribe returned to Laugharne, where the Richard Hugheses took them in at the Castle. Hughes himself was in the Navy, stationed at Bath. The Thomases were there a few months, stealing wine from his cellar – they hoped that soldiers stationed near by would be blamed – and tins of food from the kitchen.

At last Thomas found congenial work, writing film scripts for Strand, a company that was making propaganda films for the Ministry of Information. This meant moving to London. Caitlin decided at once that she must go with her husband. It was hardly practical to take an infant with them; or, if it was, Caitlin preferred not to try. Dylan's salary would be ten pounds a week, riches compared with anything they had known. Llewelyn had to be left behind in Blashford, where her mother and unmarried sister Brigit would look after him.

Later on, Caitlin said that she suffered agonies of guilt over this decision – 'I remember poor Llewelyn gazing out of the window to see us go.' He returned to his parents now and then, but it was years before they had him back for good. Caitlin's reasons were simple and imperative. She was young; she wanted a good time. 'Something made me – something hard inside. I wanted to be in the in-place where the action was. I wasn't prepared to sit back and be the virtuous woman, you know? I just left the baby and followed Dylan. That was probably a very wrong thing to do, and a virtuous good woman I don't suppose would have done it. But I wanted to live and see everything and do everything and *be* somebody. It was following not so much Dylan as my own ego that wanted to live and do things.'

The move took place in August. Dylan was in London. Caitlin took Llewelyn by bus and train. Unable to be a practical traveller, any more than she was a practical cook or a practical housewife, Caitlin turned the 150-mile journey from Carmarthenshire to Hampshire into a comedy. It was another dozen years before people began to preserve Caitlin's letters in any quantity. But her letter to Frances Hughes from Blashford on 5 August 1941 has survived:

> After the worst journey in the world, you may not believe it, but Llewelyn travelled from Cardiff to Bristol alone and I followed four hours later to find him black from head to foot in the arms of a woman porter. What happened to him on the train God only knows as I was left struggling with a suitcase and masses of people on the platform ... while the train departed with Llewelyn inside.
>
> I had a harrowing time phoning through to various stations & failing to locate him, till at last I got to Bristol where I heard shouts of 'Anybody lost a two year old baby?'
>
> He appeared quite unconcerned although he'd had no lunch & I was dying for a drink. I also found my parcel of rations etc which by then had melted into a solid pulp – and we were pushed into the Salisbury train among a lot of hilarious sailors who stuffed chocolate into Llewelyn & stole a pound from me.
>
> When we got to Salisbury the porter, to be in harmony, immediately threw the famous suitcase under the train where all L's clothes were strewn on the line – I abandoned everything & rushed for a taxi but the blasted military took them all so we missed our bus and didn't get here till *ten*, so you'll admit it might have been more peaceful.
>
> I've already remembered things we have forgotten – the old ration books (in the dressing table drawers) & margarine coupons – would you be so good as to give what there are to Sid Davis as we owe him 26 & will send the rest when we get them.
>
> I hope you don't think we took your hospitality for granted as we are apt to be rather too 'at home' in other people's houses – but it is our way of appreciating our good fortune and your exceeding good will in tolerating us [. . .]
>
> I hope not to lose Laugharne for ever, and advise you not to move. Will let you know developments.

So Caitlin returned to the in-place where the action was. She was not in London all the time. There were rural interludes. But for the next three years their lives revolved around the capital, their private disorder subsumed in the greater disorder of a city at war. They lived where they could. Nicolette and her husband Anthony, the painter, put them up, in emergencies, and Thomas repaid them by urinating on the floor. It was assumed that he felt the need to protest at his bourgeois in-laws. With Caitlin, gestures were unnecessary: she simply ignored polite society and its rules. Generous, when she felt like it, in giving away a dress or a scarf if someone admired it, she was equally casual about others' possessions. Nicolette was furious when Caitlin used her expensive perfume, or gobbled the Devas children's ration of two oranges when no one was looking. Caitlin told her not to be so mean.

Yet her certainties had to live alongside the continual uncertainties of marriage to Thomas. The first surviving letter that she wrote to her sister Brigit, in 1942, suggests a gathering uneasiness. If it emphasises her husband's shortcomings and says nothing of her own, it is also a reminder of the passive streak in her nature when faced with someone who had clearer ideas of his needs than she ever had of hers. Dylan, she wrote, was

> a positive model bourgeois husband one day and the next suddenly disappears, and I may not hear of him till perhaps several nights later he strolls in a little battered & contrite but not one word of explanation – then once again the home-lover is in residence. It is all very baffling & causes me great consternation as to what manner I should assume – or what action I should take.
>
> Since I am nailed here by all the laws of womanhood through the centuries – I have no choice but to endure – or go to Blashford if I had the fare!

Hammersmith, said Caitlin, was too polite and tasteful for her liking, and in any case they had to leave their address (it was a studio, borrowed from the author A.P. Herbert) within a month.

> I can't help fretting all the time for something more active & more intense than this slow convalescing of sensation. I have fixed my eye on Scotland as a [?horny] hole worth exploring to put a crust on Llewelyn's innocent skin. By what machinery we shall get there is not for me to say. These are but dreams and conjectures but when a kettle overboils it's got to spill somewhere . . . There is a woman called Naomi Mitchison with a forty-acre farm & only two people to work it up there – I am putting all my hopes in Kitty Cuckoo, we might emigrate together.*

* The writer Naomi Mitchison was living on the family farm at Carradale, Campbeltown, and various painters and writers stayed there in the War. Caitlin found somewhere nearer home to escape to on visits, the village of Talsarn in west Wales. Kitty Cuckoo was Kitty O'Brien, her Irish friend, living in London.

In public, drink helped conceal her awkwardness. Her dancing at pubs and parties was a sight to see, violent and sometimes beguiling, until she crashed into a table or a fellow drinker. The violence ran nearer the surface now. Jack Lindsay, a writer who knew them both, decided she was angry with Dylan because her own career as a dancer had been sacrificed, and she wanted to feel that he was leading the intellectually pure life of a poet, as she imagined it. Instead he was writing film scripts and playing the fool. She told Lindsay that Dylan was 'corrupt through and through. It's not for me to save him from himself. If he can't do it himself, let him rot.' This was the betrayal of vocation. Lindsay noted that while Thomas gave as good as he got in their everyday tiffs, he couldn't withstand her 'really high-explosive blasts. He never stood up to her, once she got going.'

The tone of the half-dozen letters and fragments that are left of Thomas's wartime correspondence with Caitlin, when she was not in London, is nervous and placatory. He wants her to want him, he swears he is telling the truth about the money he hasn't got, he is a bloody fool, he hates the film business, he loathes the Gargoyle Club (haunt of arty drinkers), he is alone and miserable in their leaking studio. The squalor, at least when Caitlin was absent, was not exaggerated. The studio, as permanent a home as they had in London, was one room in Chelsea, more of a shack in a dilapidated row of shacks. A woman next door kept cats, and the reek penetrated the boards between. But squalor was not enough; there must be no suspicion that he might be enjoying himself:

> There is *nothing* to do without you; so terribly terribly sad to come back to our empty barn, lie all night in our big bed, listening to the rain & our mice and the creaks & leaks and the [air raid] warnings; so sad I could die if I hadn't got to see you again & live with you always & always . . .

Thomas was not always alone in the big bed. Pamela Glendower, a drinking friend of them both, was in it in May 1943 when Caitlin was a mile away in St Mary Abbot's Hospital, having her second child. Glendower was afraid that Caitlin would find out and attack her, but she went undiscovered. Excusing Thomas, and herself, she says that all he wanted was company and a shield against vampire nightmares: a need he played on with more than one woman, though the fears themselves may have been real enough. Other girl friends can be glimpsed, a woman at Strand Films, someone else with a deformed leg. An actress, Ruth Wynn Owen, fell in love with Thomas but denied she slept with him; he wrote her glum love letters, supporting the theory, often aired by his friends, that only Caitlin mattered. Caitlin herself is unlikely to have been blameless in London. M., a good-looking Welsh friend of Dylan's, was in and out of the leaking studio; years later Dylan caught them in bed together in Laugharne.

The child, a girl, was said to have been conceived beside the River Aeron in Cardiganshire. She was christened 'Aeronwy' but was often called 'Aeron'. Caitlin stayed in the Talsarn district more than once, with Thomas travelling down when he could. The house was being used by a family from Swansea, whose daughter, Vera, had been a childhood friend of Dylan's, and who had taken to Caitlin when she first met her, before the War. Vera's husband was away at the War. She would never hear a word against Caitlin, entranced by her casual bohemianism, so far removed from the South Wales she and Dylan were brought up in – 'I had more fun with Dylan, and with Catty too, than with anybody else, before or since. He was such a selfish little bastard, it was surprising to find him married to someone it was so easy to get on with.' When remittances from the salaried Dylan failed to arrive in Talsarn, she saw Caitlin scribbling one of her ruthless notes, 'calling him a lily-livered so-and-so'. Thomas wrote back abjectly to say that he wasn't, at the same time failing to enclose any money. But Vera had no doubt that Caitlin was 'capable of making short shrift of Dylan'.

Aged twenty-nine when Aeron was born, Caitlin in wartime was at her peak: fecund, spirited, still a honey-pot for men, who were more numerous and less attached than in peacetime. Evening drew the Thomases out with all the other drinkers and escapers, in and out of uniform. Aeron remained with them in London, and had to be left behind in the studio. It alarms Caitlin, thinking back: 'Quite calmly we used to leave this child in her cradle and go out to the pub in the sacred pub hours. We never dreamt of not clocking in. We just left her there howling under the bombs.' This may be overstated; in 1943 the worst of the raids were over, and the flying bombs and rockets had not begun. But Caitlin has long decided that penitence becomes her.

Gwen Watkins – who married Vernon near the end of the War – remembers seeing her in Chelsea pubs with a man or two. Dylan might be across the saloon, holding forth to his cronies – John Davenport,

Tommy Earp the art critic, Tambimuttu the Indian poet and editor, Constantine FitzGibbon (in American military uniform) who would write a biography of Thomas. 'In the War,' says Watkins, 'men were on the look-out for pretty women. She took everyone's attention. You felt you really wanted to stroke her cheeks – she had a complexion like apple-blossom, luminous. She wasn't tall. She looked up at a man. She had a dimple in one cheek, and by moving her mouth she could make it appear.' Thomas, watching her flirt with a young officer, would lose the thread of his story.

According to Theodora FitzGibbon, Constantine's wife, most of Caitlin's finery came from 'a little woman who collected clothes made from beautiful velvets, Indian silk, damasks, nankeen, georgette, chiffon, ninon; a stream of beautiful names for forgotten materials'. The wartime 'Utility' standard for new garments made women hungry for attractive dresses, wherever they came from. Thirty years after the War Mrs FitzGibbon still had one of the items Caitlin gave her, a 'long, tattered raw silk cream scarf, which I used to wear as a blouse, draped sari-fashion'.

Nicolette Devas devoted a page in her family biography to an evening dress that Caitlin bought at Hammersmith Broadway for five pounds. It was 'a gaudy, music-hall dress with a cheap lace fichu and a body of bright pink shiny taffeta'. Caitlin added red ribbons at the neck. Against the odds she looked marvellous, reminding Anthony Devas of a princess by Velasquez. When Nicolette tried it on, 'the mirror reflected a tawdry Christmas-tree doll of a woman: I lacked Caitlin's supreme confidence, her certainty that she was beautiful, and her grand, bravura manner.' Caitlin appeared in it at the Pheasantry Club, in the King's Road, dancing wildly and getting a shout of 'Olé!' from Augustus John. Later she took to wearing her little pink number in pubs. At the Tate Gallery fifty years later she can still be seen in it, painted by Devas.

Caitlin remained restless and unfulfilled. She wrote covert poems. *Story of a Woman* may have been written during a wartime interlude, perhaps in Chelsea. Sometimes she even tried to understand what it was that women did about the house that gave them creative satisfaction. She envied and despised them at the same time, 'those lucky wooden ones' to whom 'the kitchen stove is a lyrical poem, inspiring them to fresh heights of endeavour'. It was only a caricature of the happy housewife that she saw; try as she would, she lacked the imagination to consider what other people's lives were like. The Thomases once stayed a night in Swansea with the Watkinses. In the morning Gwen attended to her small daughter Rhiannon, flicked a duster, washed the breakfast things. Caitlin, following her about, said, 'Do you do this often?'

Neither Thomas was easy to live with. Both had a predisposition towards chaos. When (near the end of the War) Caitlin was on her way to Hampshire to visit Llewelyn, Dylan saw her off at Waterloo Station, but managed to put the luggage, with her handbag and tickets, on the wrong train, which left without her. This was another version of her losing Llewelyn at Cardiff, or of Thomas's failure to appear and be best man on the day Vernon Watkins married Gwen. Thomas, at least, could turn mishaps into anecdotes with which to regale more admirers in more pubs. Caitlin had nothing but the aggravation of their joint impracticality.

Her temper was uncertain. Scenes in public came easily to her, a way of drawing attention. Gwen was at a Watkins–Thomas outing, again near the end of the War, when the four of them ate at a Chinese restaurant in Soho. Caitlin called the waiter over and said, 'This is disgusting stuff!' Lunchers stopped eating as a row broke out between her and Dylan, with Caitlin shouting that she had a good mind to throw the food at the waiter, and Dylan replying that if she wasn't careful he'd throw it at her. Later in the afternoon they went to a cinema to see a Marx Brothers film, always a favourite with Thomas. After a quarter of an hour she was saying loudly, 'Oh God, this is awful, I can't stick this rubbish.' People shushed her. She took no notice.

Gwen Watkins, no admirer of Caitlin (or of Dylan, for that matter), thought that for all her egregious behaviour, she was, in the end, the more wronged of the two, soon to be 'permanently embittered by her life'. And, 'although she made me uneasy and often indignant because of her behaviour in public, I was firmly on her side and against Dylan's treatment of her. Her life seemed to me intolerable. I thought mine was hard enough. I suppose the poet's wife has never had a bed of roses to lie on.'

Still, a poet was what Caitlin wanted and what she had got. To a degree she realised this, and was able, after his death, to contrast 'the small mortal Dylan', full of vanities and temptations, with 'that other monstrous immortal oddity' who forged 'roaring thunderbolts' in his workshop. In his lifetime, though, these fine words seemed less appropriate.

During the final year of the War, Thomas began what turned out to be his last spell of intense creativity. Like hundreds of thousands of others, he and Caitlin kept clear of London as much as possible because of the pilotless bombs that began in June 1944, followed by rockets from September. Some of the time they lived in Carmarthenshire, at a pair of family cottages, Blaen Cwm ('The End of the Valley'), where Dylan's parents had lived since they left Swansea, D.J. cursing their neighbours, who were his wife's relatives, under his breath. Llewelyn and Aeron were with them; the rooms were small; when the council sewage lorry was due to empty the outside lavatories, all that the cottages had, D.J. vanished for the day, more disgusted with life than ever.

For a while the Thomases were at New Quay, on the Cardiganshire coast in the far west of Wales, renting a bungalow on the cliffs. Near by lived Vera, the friend who was fond of Caitlin. While they were there, Vera's officer-husband came back from assisting the Greek guerrillas, bringing his sub-machine gun with him. One night, after a row, he sprayed the Thomases' bungalow with bullets, 'to put the wind up those buggers' (he was a war hero, so a court set him free). Under these unpromising conditions, which as usual included a chronic lack of money, and the need to keep writing film scripts, Thomas produced eight or nine poems at Blaen Cwm and New Quay, some of which would join the small group by which he is best known: 'A Refusal to Mourn the Death, by Fire, of a Child in London', 'A Winter's Tale', 'Poem in October'. The most famous of all, 'Fern Hill', was written in the aftermath of the machine-gunning.

After the barren War years, Thomas had reconnected himself to the 'vegetable background' (in Caitlin's phrase) of rural Wales, a country of crooked romance that lived more in his mind than anywhere else, and would later be caricatured in *Under Milk Wood*. Caitlin realised its importance to him; no doubt he realised it himself; but it didn't offer a feasible solution for the future, since they both hankered after too many fleshpots of one sort or another to find peace in those rainy, run-down parts.

In the short term they had to continue the search for survival. The documentary film work dried up after the War, though Thomas began a new career as a radio writer and broadcaster, which might have been the basis of a modest prosperity, if anything so mundane had occurred to either of them. From 1945 they had less to do with organising their lives than did a patron who arrived on the scene, Margaret Taylor, wife of the long-suffering historian A.J.P. Taylor. Mrs Taylor, forty years old, who had a taste for young writers, enjoyed subsidising Dylan Thomas, and it was she who found homes for them during the remainder of his life. Caitlin looked on with amusement, not seeing her as a threat; she became angry, though, if she thought that Dylan was abasing himself before a patron, as he was happy to do when he thought more pounds might flow from the abasement.

The Taylors first met him before the War, when Norman Cameron, who had been at Oxford with Alan Taylor, recommended the young Dylan as a poet of promise. Taylor didn't like his poems and thought him a disagreeable sponger, but Mrs Taylor kept her eye on him. In 1945 she invited them, or perhaps they invited themselves, to Oxford, where her husband was a lecturer at Magdalen College, and they lived for a while in a summerhouse by the Taylors' home. This was too small for Llewelyn and Aeron, who were usually in the house, with the Taylor children. All the Thomases were unwelcome to Taylor.

In private Dylan sang for his supper. He encouraged Mrs Taylor in the poetry she was writing, sending her long painstaking critiques that he is unlikely to have shown Caitlin. His flattering concern that their benefactor should continue to write poetry would have aroused her scorn, or worse. According to Caitlin, Mrs Taylor – 'a noble woman who drove us crazy', alternatively 'maudlin Magdalen Maggie' – once wrote to Dylan, 'Going to bed with you would be like going to bed with a god'. He may or may not have succumbed; unquestionably Mrs Taylor was deeply entangled, let her marriage disintegrate on his behalf, and mourned him when he died. But to amuse his friends, and make sure Caitlin was appeased, he heaped scorn on her. Elisabeth Lutyens, the composer, heard him say, 'I'll have to see if I can squeeze Maggie's left breast and get some money.'

In the previous few years, Caitlin had coped with life in a filthy studio in Chelsea, various flats in London, most of them belonging to other people, a primitive cottage, a flimsy bungalow and a damp summerhouse by a river. There had been much talk of their going to live in America, but nothing came of it. Any opportunity to escape was to be seized. In August 1946 Thomas was commissioned by the magazine *Picture Post* to write an article about 'Puck Fair', the ancient festival in Killorglin, Co. Kerry, where a billy-goat caught in the mountains is crowned 'King Puck' for three days of haggling, drinking and pagan performance. He and Caitlin went with two friends, Bill and Helen McAlpine, who had money. The women shopped in Dublin for tweeds and flannels, the men drank themselves silly with Guinness, and when they got to Co. Kerry they ate the kind of food – steaks, shellfish, cream – that was still in short supply in post-War Britain. The article was never written.

Caitlin's father had died in Dublin not long before (among his reported last words were 'Tried in the scales and found wanting' and 'Put the goat out'), and this was her first visit to Ireland since she left it with Rupert Shephard ten years earlier. But she was not in nostalgic mood; she rarely was. A detour to Ennistymon and the Falls Hotel was ruled out – years later she wrote, 'I am ashamed to say the real reason was, though I invented various others, that I thought Dylan was not tall or good-looking enough to do my old reputation justice.' He was 'not a dazzling enough catch to parade before my way-back handsome boys'.*

The following year, 1947, the chance of serious foreign travel came their way, to Caitlin's delight; Dylan was less enthusiastic. Edith Sitwell, who regarded Thomas as a wayward protégé, was still trying to cure him of his desire to live in America. A committee that she headed at the Society of Authors awarded travelling scholarships, and in March it was persuaded to give £150, its entire grant for 1947, to Thomas, with a recommendation that he go to Italy. Britain seemed a good place to get away from that spring. An arctic winter had combined with shortages and industrial troubles to produce weeks of power cuts. Posters looked down on unkempt cities, where bomb-sites were untouched since the War, telling the nation that only exports would save us. 'We're up against it!' was a government slogan of the day. 'We work or want.'

They left in April: Dylan, Caitlin, Llewelyn, Aeron, Caitlin's sister Brigit and Brigit's child Tobias. Brigit had taken the surname Marnier by deed poll in 1944. She remained the odd woman out among the sisters; and the most reliable. Travelling by train, they lost their luggage on the Swiss-Italian frontier, regained it in Milan, stayed at

---

* Today the Falls Hotel boasts 'Dylan's Bar' (there is no evidence that he ever went near the place), and there has been talk of Dylan Thomas weekends.

Rapallo, which was too expensive, and in the middle of May found a villa in the hills outside Florence.

'The children beastly, the wine ample,' Thomas wrote to Margaret Taylor; he reminded her about the house in Oxfordshire that she was trying to find them, adding 'thank you thank you for the desk'. She sent him English magazines and books as if he was an invalid, which in a way he was, suffering an enforced convalescence from too much dissipation and too few poems – after his fertile year at the end of the War, another silence had fallen. He did write a poem in Italy, 'In Country Sleep', but he feared it was being done to order, and it has a hollow ring that suggests he was right. It may be about the need for faith, a commentary on his own uncertainties.

In any case, Italy was too hot and alien for Thomas's deep-dyed provincialism (which was his strength) to enjoy. He wrote to the critic Tommy Earp to say he was sick of beautiful hills, of chianti and of Florence itself, 'a gruelling museum'. For Caitlin, the opposite was true. She loved the villa, the swimming pool, the meals prepared by a cook. She bloomed in the sun. When they were out, men 'stripped me naked with their goggling eyes, travelling round from breasts to bottom'. (Gwen Watkins once remarked that Caitlin would 'strip at the drop of a hat', adding that 'so would I have done, if I'd had her figure'.)

The more she enjoyed Italy, the more Dylan hated it. This was the summer she gloated over, talking in Sicily in 1991. He was the one who languished, out of his element. She said he deliberately fell into the swimming pool, fully dressed, in order to attract attention. The letter he wrote her, after she left him at a café table in Florence,* was abject. He loves her for ever and ever but he has lost her. He writes of touching her 'holy body' with his 'rotten hands'. He is 'the sore on your arm, which I made, your unhappiness and your pain'.

Caitlin can't recall what they were quarrelling about, unless it was unfaithfulness. She concedes that, to her knowledge, he wasn't unfaithful to her in Florence. Perhaps it was some infidelity in Britain, brought up to clobber him with, a diversion away from her own behaviour. She has both admitted to infidelity during the holiday and denied it. If she did have a lapse, it is most likely to have been after Florence, when they went to Elba in late July and ended their holiday

* See page 6.

with a couple of weeks in the little town of Rio Marina. A translator in Florence had recommended it to the Thomases as being (Dylan wrote to the McAlpines) a place of fishermen and iron-ore miners, with good bathing. It sounds more to her taste than his, to be endured as part of the business of appeasing Caitlin. The nearest he came to bathing was when he lay in the shallows in the heat, a straw hat shielding his face, reading the latest *New Statesman* from England.

Caitlin was in and out of the water all day, and in the town she was not always with her husband or sister. There was certainly a budding romance, whether consummated or not, with the proprietor of their hotel, her 'beautiful Giovanni', whom she found attractive. She regarded Giovanni as a piece of unfinished business, and filed him away for future reference, before the tribe went north again, back to grey skies and the life of compromise.

Mrs Taylor had kept her promise and found them somewhere to live, the Manor House in the village of South Leigh, ten miles west of Oxford. It sounded grander than it was, little more than a cottage, with no electricity, no means of heating water except over a coal fire, and no inside lavatory. Their patron put furniture in it and arrived frequently by bicycle to keep an eye on them. When Alan Taylor published his autobiography in 1983, he said it was his money that bought the house. It was a gesture to his wife, on condition she stopped financing the hated Thomas. 'My foolish action,' he wrote, 'of course brought me no reward. Margaret was soon giving Dylan more money than ever.' The house, which cost a little over two thousand pounds, was not given to the Thomases. They were supposed to pay rent to the Taylors, but it is unlikely they ever paid much.

To support the family, Thomas had his patron and his broadcasting work; for a while he wrote feature-film scripts, and although this didn't last, it raised his income sharply. In the tax year 1947–8 he received more than £2,400, handsome earnings for a freelance writer then; his accountant, a new acquisition, successfully claimed that six hundred pounds of this was 'business expenses'. But there were few visible signs of prosperity at South Leigh; the money trickled away as usual.

Caitlin had to work hard in their primitive house. The former Cordelia Saleeby, who was at the Slade in the 1920s, and knew Caitlin as Nicolette's younger sister, was living in the village with an actor, Harry Locke. Cordelia Locke was another of the women, a sizeable band, who instinctively sympathised with Caitlin and saw her as beauty entangled with the beast. Heavy kettles had to be boiled, coke brought in for the stove; Caitlin slaved away 'like a peasant', a sack tied round her waist, while Dylan (if he was there at all, and not up in London doing a broadcast) rolled a cigarette or read a book, waiting for her to slosh hot water over him in a hip-bath in front of the fire. Cordelia saw her as lovely, battered, dishevelled. Later she wrote of nostalgia for their kitchen on a winter's night, children's clothes airing by the fire, an oil lamp casting a circle on the table, pictures torn from magazines pinned to the wall, Christmas decorations gathering dust long after Twelfth Night, and Caitlin, 'proud and haunted, blowing her nose with tremendous vigour into a spotted handkerchief'.

Stews were still their staple diet. 'Her idea of cooking was to buy a calf's head with eyes gleaming and its ears sticking out of the pot, and jam the lid on.' With the children she was 'a rough loving mother, like a dog with her puppies'. The evening before Llewelyn, aged nine or ten, went off to boarding school, his hair cut short and his jacket too big for him, she and Cordelia spent the evening sewing name-tapes on his new clothes. Caitlin was 'beside herself with grief'. But the English middle-class custom of sending sons away as soon as possible, almost unheard of in Dylan's South Wales, was convenient to both the Thomases.

Their quarrels had grown worse. In the spring of 1948 Dylan and his sister Nancy were at Blaen Cwm, where their parents were having a crisis: Florence Thomas had broken her leg, and D.J., an invalid himself, needed to be looked after. A letter from Dylan alternates between describing the dismal scene on a Sunday ('snowbound, dead, dull, damned') and apologising for behaving so badly ('senselessly, foully, brutally') to the woman he loves forever, to whom he will never again be a senseless beast if only she has him back, because 'Christ, aren't we each other's?'

Both the Thomases needed violence and colour in their relationship with one another. The few surviving letters from Dylan to other women that in any way count as 'love letters' sound half-hearted, like those he wrote during the War to Ruth Wynn Owen, of whom he was fond. Caitlin's letters to him are all lost, many of them supposedly burnt at his mother's instigation after his death, but one assumes that they, too, were explicit about feelings. They were probably more direct, as well, since there is a deviousness about many of his letters to

Caitlin, as he tries to placate her and wheedle his way back into her affections. The overwriting makes them sound dishonest.

Philip Larkin, writing about the Dylan-Caitlin letters to Kingsley Amis in 1985, said that 'what struck me most about them was that he might never have met her before [. . .] no friendliness, nothing to suggest that they had a life they shared and enjoyed [. . .] All snivelling and grovelling and adoring and so very impersonal'. There is enough truth in this to be uncomfortable. At their worst, the letters are so concerned to stop her being angry with him that they lapse into a catalogue of appeasement. They are meant to keep her sweet. If they sound unhealthy, it is because Thomas's dependence on his short-tempered wife (for whose short temper he was partly responsible) cloyed the relationship.

Their readiness to pick at private wounds fascinated their friends. Cordelia Locke found them 'destructive', yet able for that reason to make others confront their own problems. 'If you got to know them you were emotionally clobbered. They broke up marriages. A woman in the village left her husband . . . they had this effect on people. One also drew an extraordinary amount of strength from them. I was a bit low, one marriage breaking up, so perhaps I was susceptible. But they had this electrifying effect. If you asked Virginia Woolf's question, *Who would you most like to see walking up your drive now?*, the answer was them.

In spring 1948 his parents came to South Leigh to be looked after until Florence was walking again. Their dog, a mongrel called Mably that they could no longer look after, came with them. Between the children – this was before Llewelyn went away to school – the old people and the tireless attentions of Margaret Taylor, little writing got done. Dylan, left there briefly (with a woman to look after his parents) while Caitlin took the children to visit her mother, wrote one of his doleful letters, saying what hell it was, with Margaret Taylor lecturing them about art, Alan Taylor arriving on his bicycle and making scenes on the road, his father discussing saucepans and operations. 'Come back, my love. There are lots of huge lettuces, & I love you.'

Caitlin was the strength of the family. Her mood had hardened as she grew less inclined to put up with an erratic husband. A letter to Brigit dated 19 May suggests a Caitlin who had left the vague young woman far behind. Her voice had acquired an edge:

Well you may ask what am I doing – what am I not doing, constant unremitting work of the lowest order for five people who are utterly dependent on me for their livelihood (and that thought alone scares the life out of me) two very young, two very old and sick,* and Useless Eustace Dylan† – it's no joke I tell you – and would move heaven and earth to have you here.

But honestly what have I done to deserve this further trial – and on top of everything they [her parents-in-law] have the gall to disapprove of our way of life, our friends, in fact any form of life at all that does not put death first. Your bitterly loving Caitlin.

Thomas shut his eyes to domestic friction. If the children were difficult he wanted them kept out of his way at meal times or when they were travelling as a family. Burst pipes and smoking fires were not his department. Women, surely had always coped with such things. He earned the money, however erratically. Not surprisingly, Caitlin saw herself as the real provider, in the sense that she supplied the conditions for him to work in, and in the deeper sense that she was the mature half of the partnership, he the feckless child with the gift, in the end dependent upon her. Shortly before Christmas 1948, Dylan was knocked off his bicycle by a lorry and went to hospital with a broken arm. Cordelia was near the scene of the accident, and went to Caitlin to break the news. Caitlin was reading a Penguin thriller, listening to Radio Luxembourg. Dylan's broken arms were nothing new. She was not impressed. 'Showing off as usual,' she said, 'always has to be the centre of the stage. Dylan, Dylan, Dylan, and what have I got? Another bloody baby to feed and change and prop up.'

She was pregnant with her third child, and the South Leigh experiment was coming to an end. Thomas liked life in villages, but he had done only hack work in South Leigh, and began to convince himself that if he could return to Wales, and especially to Laugharne, his creative powers would be renewed. Margaret Taylor, who had chosen South Leigh because she wanted him near at hand, had no option but to agree. According to Cordelia Locke, Mrs Taylor had visions of returning with them, and setting up a threesome. If so they were quickly squashed. As for Caitlin, she felt an affection for

---

* They were not quite as ancient as Caitlin made them sound. D.J. was seventy-two: Florence was sixty-six.
† 'Useless Eustace', a character in a *Daily Mirror* strip embodying male slothfulness.

Laugharne, despite the curses she rained on it later, and she let herself be persuaded that it would be good for Dylan's work. The writing of poetry remained part of their contract.

Mrs Taylor and the Thomases reconnoitred Laugharne, looking at a house called Gosport, then seeing if a lease of the Castle, where Richard Hughes no longer lived, was available. It was not. Finally the Boat House, a property below a cliff and almost at sea level, came on the market. Mrs Taylor paid three thousand pounds for it, two-thirds of her capital, and spent a further £136 on repairs to the roof and verandah. Again the Thomases were supposed to pay rent for it.

Before they moved, Dylan went abroad again, this time unaccompanied, to Prague, where guests from many countries had been invited by the Czech Government to see a writers' union inaugurated. A letter home spoke of bad food, biting cold, nice people and his 'terrible loneliness'. 'Dylan, the bugger is in Prague, God stiffen him,' Caitlin wrote to John Davenport. She suspected he had been with a woman. The fact that he brought her back some blouses (she said) put the matter beyond doubt.

In April 1949 they moved to Laugharne, where their third child was due to be born in July. Almost at once Thomas began work on a poem, the first since his half-hearted effort in Tuscany two years earlier. 'Over Sir John's hill', written within a few months, was a coming to terms with his own mortality. Its tone, brooding over the Laugharne seascape, was elegaic, ostensibly mourning the birds who are preyed on by the hawk above the hill. It invoked the natural world of helpless creatures, including Man —

> We grieve as the blithe birds, never again, leave shingle and elm,
> The heron and I . . .

If Laugharne was to be a fresh start, the poem was a good omen. Caitlin had an interest: 'Sir John's hill', with its evidence of a poet back at work, meant he had not been entirely corrupted. Its theme was one she understood. She knew his fear of death, and later on wrote that 'it was I stood between him and death. I was his chosen death in life', whatever that meant. Thomas came from a long line of Welsh preachers and chapel-goers, and in the poem he was conjuring up a pantheistic God; although there is always a suspicion that when he used religion, he was doing it to create convenient special effects. It was Caitlin who had the primitive sense of a real God, waiting behind the clouds with real thunderbolts of retribution.

In the meantime, and looking on the bright side, she had a local woman to scrub and Hoover, the sea to bathe in, and credit at J. Eric Jones, Grocer, Stationer, Wine & Spirit Merchant. On the stove the perpetual stew still bubbled.

8

Boat House Blues

The Boat House stands at the head of a corridor of sands. At low water a modest river, the Taf, passes under its windows, making channels to the open sea several miles away to the south-east, where two further rivers join to form an estuary into Carmarthen Bay, marked by shoals that were known as 'Trawlers' Dread' in the days of sail. At high water the sea covers the sands and mud-flats to within a few yards of the house. On the horizon is the western tip of the Gower Peninsula and the serpentine Worms Head, reminders of Swansea.

Dylan Thomas was surrounded by reminders of his past. His parents came to live in Laugharne at the same time, to a house in the main street called Pelican that he rented for them. His mother's cousins and nephews were still to be found on farms inland. Fernhill, where Thomas stayed as a child with the aunt whose death was the reason for his poem 'After the funeral', is not far off. Laugharne itself he had known since childhood. He was in Dylan Country. Whether it was ever Caitlin Country is less certain.

They lived better than they had, in an airier house, its six small rooms and a kitchen arranged on three storeys. When approached down the angled path from above, it appeared to have only two storeys, but on the far side the land fell away to a back garden, below the kitchen level. This was the 'harbour', surrounded by a wall with an opening through which the sea came on spring tides. The boat yard had been there, in the days when it was the ferryman's house. In summer weather Caitlin used the harbour as a sun-trap. Cliff Walk, then an overgrown lane running out from the town,*

* It has been surfaced for visitors and renamed 'Dylan's Walk'.

overlooked the Boat House, and passers-by were always curious. It was said that she sunbathed in the harbour without clothes on. A rumour went round that she was still diving into the sea when she was eight and three- quarter months' pregnant. She ignored prying eyes, treating village conventions with a friendly contempt. Laugharne to her was in the same category as fishing villages in the west of Ireland, a melancholy place of delusions and apathy, not to be taken seriously. There are people in Laugharne today who suggest that since it was a place that both bred and attracted eccentrics, the Thomases were nothing special. Still, they were a better class of eccentric.

The baby was born on 24 July, after a hurried journey to Carmarthen, ten miles away, in a taxi driven by one of the Williams family who ran most of the services in Laugharne. Caitlin lay in the back, suffering without inhibition; it was the natural thing to do. She had been worried about the pregnancy, which was accompanied by varicose veins, telling Brigit that it was more than she could cope with in her 'decrepitude', surrounded as she was by 'overpowering worries'. Aged thirty-five, Caitlin already felt herself wearing out. But the child, as usual, delighted her, with Dylan's soft features and the blond curls that ran in the family. He was given an Irish name, Colm, and a Welsh one, Garan, which means 'heron'.

The Thomases were soon familiar figures about the place, no longer the young unknowns they had been before the War. It was easier to run up bills now that Dylan Thomas was a voice they heard on the radio. He was the one that people took to. They knew about writers, characters who pretended to be working when really they were boozing. She was stronger stuff. 'They loved him,' Margaret Taylor said, 'but they never loved her.' It was not that she ran up bills, but that she ran them up defiantly, as if she was entitled to. Further, Caitlin looked too attractive, even in her mid thirties, and her way with men was too forthright, for the village (which usually means the women of a village) to be at ease. Her presence was felt when she walked about in her bright plumage. Even repairs to her clothes caught the eye – a black jumper darned with yellow wool, thick blue stockings darned with red. A woman asked her once about the stockings. 'If I do them in navy blue, nobody notices,' said Caitlin. 'If I use red wool, everybody knows I can do it.'

She was not inclined to go into people's houses, though she could be friendly enough, if she was in the mood. At Brown's Hotel, one of the pubs favoured by the Thomases, and the nearest to the Boat House, she could be seen alone at the bar in the morning, drinking a glass of beer and rolling a cigarette on her thigh with one hand, a feat much admired. Dylan might be in the same room, sitting with three or four cronies by the window. If someone came up to her, she would chat; otherwise she was silent and withdrawn.

Dylan took a more active interest in the place, from a safe middle-class distance, turning the gossip into anecdotes to amuse visitors with. The reality was a village with a history of poverty, violence and feuds. The Williams family, who had done their share of feuding, ran buses, taxis and the electricity generator that powered the place; when Tudor Williams went to bed, he stopped the generator and the lights went out. Fights and even a death were said to have marked the skirmishes of the 1920s and 1930s between the Williams family and rival bus operators. The police station had twenty-six rooms and one constable, whose job was to enforce order, especially when there were drunken fights, without bothering the courts. Laugharne was treated like an enclave with its own rules, which included a punching from the law when the constable was a boxer (as he was at one time), and implied a certain licence for rough behaviour as long as the police-man's authority wasn't challenged when he chose to exercise it. When the portreeve, the mayoral figure who heads Laugharne's corporation, gave his annual breakfast on a Sunday, for men only, followed by morning service, the constable made himself scarce when they left the church to begin a day's drinking in the pubs, illegal on a Welsh Sunday until more recent times.

Thomas liked the place because it was wayward and undemanding. To Caitlin's irritation he often spent his mornings in the kitchen of Brown's Hotel, where Ivy Williams, wife of Ebie, another of the clan, let friends come in and gossip while she cooked and scattered ash from her cigarettes. The company chose horses for the day's racing or gambled small sums on a game with a spinning device, like a primitive roulette. Usually Thomas found time to visit his father, now chronically ill with heart and other problems, to help with the crossword. Afternoon was the time for working, in what had been a bicycle shed on the cliff path above the Boat House. The estuary views included Sir John's hill, half a mile away. He might be there from two o'clock in the afternoon till 6.00 or 7.00 in the evening. Taking Aeron for a walk, with Colm in the pram, Caitlin would hear him muttering as they passed, and know that writing was in progress. Silence meant he was reading a thriller or had fallen asleep.

Caitlin came to idealise that year, 1949: 'the last period of happiness or near-happiness that we had together', she told George Tremlett. Thomas's letters show him as harassed as ever by money, borrowing where he could, taking fees from the BBC for scripts that were never written and so making enemies among its officials. He made his usual visits to London, broadcasting and borrowing. 'I'm in a hell of a hole. I see no way of getting out of it,' he wrote to Princess Caetani, a New Englander who had married an Italian prince and was now, in her seventieth year, an active patron of the arts. Her Roman magazine *Botteghe Oscure* paid handsome fees for manuscripts, which Thomas customarily asked for in advance, concocting ornate begging letters.

After 'Sir John's hill' he entered another barren period. Debts were part of the problem. A careful housekeeper might have made them solvent, but Thomas never gave any sign of wanting to be married to such a paragon, though he did complain at times about Caitlin's spending. The real question is why he allowed his life as a writer, about which he had once been stubbornly professional, to get into such disarray. Beneath the anxieties about money were deeper anxieties about himself and his future as a poet. He was embracing chaos as a means of escape. He described a death-dream, where he found his own skeleton in a cave.

An apparent solution, consisting of well paid travels in America, turned out to be only the problem, coming at him from a different angle. Within a month of returning to Laugharne, Thomas had been invited to give a public reading in New York City by John Malcolm Brinnin, the newly appointed director of the Poetry Center at the Young Men's and Young Women's Hebrew Association. The visit was planned for early in 1950, and supplementary readings in many places across the country were eventually arranged by Brinnin. At first there was talk of Caitlin going with her husband. He told the McAlpines in November that he hoped she would. Two weeks later he was telling his American publisher that what she needed was a rest cure in the sun, and that he thought of sending her to Elba, which she liked. Elba was on his mind; no doubt Caitlin was prompting him. Early in 1950 he was telling the Italian princess – perhaps in the hope of a free holiday – that they both loved the place.

If Caitlin dreamt of a romantic adventure with Giovanni, the hotel proprietor, nothing came of it at the time. She looked nearer home, and began to have brief encounters with men in Laugharne. Later she would sanitise these by suggesting that they followed Thomas's 1950 visit to America, and were in retaliation for his misdeeds there. But on one occasion she admitted they began earlier – that 'when Dylan was on his long trips to London, I automatically went with whoever of the local boys was available, that I was attracted to. And then of course when I realised *he* was doing this kind of thing [in America], I would do it in a spirit of revenge.'

Leaving Caitlin in Laugharne (where, she had said earlier, she refused to remain while he was in America), Thomas flew to New York on 20 February 1950, and began three months of engagements, reading poetry chiefly to audiences of students and their professors, and achieving a limited fame, on university campuses, in the process.

Brinnin became a friend and admirer, although his self-imposed role of lecture agent made him uncomfortable, as Thomas, blundering about America, missed engagements and gave offence. But the poet charmed more people than he offended, and his readings, of his own work and others', became definitive for thousands of that generation. Legends of drunken misbehaviour were created overnight, encouraged and sometimes invented by Thomas. Self-mockery was a useful disguise.

Letters to Caitlin, emphasising his loneliness, rose to fresh heights of appeasement. He omitted the lionising and groaned about what a 'pilgrimage of the damned' it was, a nightmare filled with strangers, mitigated only when, in the spring, he reached the West Coast. There he was able to offer her glimpses of San Franciscan food and weather, in advance of the life they could lead there together, when he decided which job at which Californian university he would accept. Skilfully covering his tracks, he told Caitlin what she wanted to hear, ridiculing his progress (a 'fat, redfaced comet'), swearing that she was all he needed: 'I want to touch your breasts and cunt, and I want every night to lie, in love & peace, close, close, close, close, close to you, closer than the marrow of your soul.'

She, in turn, wrote him the letters he needed on his travels. Brinnin saw him with the first, received in Westport, Connecticut, on 27 February, and so written soon after departure. Thomas, he recorded, had been waiting for this every day, 'yet now that it had arrived he seemed reluctant to open it'. When portions of the letter were read out to him, Brinnin thought they had 'the quality of folk-poetry'. Thomas added that Caitlin was 'the only one for me'.

Later he received a 'lovely letter', followed by 'your beautiful letter, my true love, & your very good, but heartbreaking, poem'. Caitlin's poems, she once said, were written only when she was 'driven beyond endurance with myself and my circumstances'. In Laugharne, with Dylan loose in America, she gnawed at her fingers and wished she was somewhere else. The children were demanding and she resented them. Being Caitlin, she didn't pretend otherwise. A letter to John Davenport and his wife (23 March 1950) said she hesitated to ask them to Laugharne because of the children ('battalions of young, and so called innocent, life killers'); added that they were company of a kind she could easily dispense with, since 'nothing in the world makes one feel so far away from the fruits, whatever they are, of civilisation'; and went on:

> Poor Dylan doesn't sound very happy in America, and is horrified by the glut of gusty, noisy, money and power obsession steaming and screeching over the terrified head of a cowering poet!
>
> I daresay he is enjoying himself, in his own particular way, with his own particular friends, but he doesn't tell me that, being a Welshman, and knowing my domestic storms. They are as cunning as buggery and as obvious as the day. The Welsh, I mean.

If Thomas had returned weighed down with dollars, as seemed possible at one point, a lot would have been forgiven. Brinnin thought three thousand dollars a feasible profit. In the end the tour brought in a gross income of more than $7,500, or £2,800. Small amounts were posted to Caitlin, and Brinnin cleverly sent her a handbag via Dylan, wrapped up in gift paper, which, unknown to him, contained eight hundred dollars. The rest had gone, some of it on extra air and rail tickets when Thomas failed to keep to his itinerary, much of it on taxis and entertaining his friends. His business expenses, no doubt generously expressed, were accepted by the British tax authorities as being about a thousand pounds. This left a comfortable sum, well over ten thousand pounds in today's money, to be swallowed up by the black hole of the Thomas finances.

No money meant no trips to the sun. The San Francisco plan, if it ever existed, had failed. Thomas went home in June tired and empty-handed. Worse still, he left a love affair smouldering in New York. In his *Dylan Thomas in America* Brinnin identified three East Coast women who slept with Thomas: a poet, unnamed, a professional model who liked poetry, 'Doris', and a magazine executive, 'Sarah'. 'Sarah's' real name was Pearl. The difference between Pearl and the other women who made themselves available in America (and who may have included literary groupies here and there) was that he took her more seriously and may even have thought himself in love with her.

Caitlin says she found him 'sucked dry, tongue-tied, with nothing at all revealing to say'. When she asked about his performances on stage, he derided them. He was not in good spirits. From Washington, DC in May he had written a love letter, calling her his 'sacred sweetheart' and his 'dear golden Caitlin', which contained an ominous sentence about her 'waking up alone in our beautiful bedroom – please Christ, my love, it *is* always alone'. Perhaps his own infidelities made hers more oppressive. Similarly, having made a large sum of money disappear, he was upset to find she had been playing a smaller version of the same game in Laugharne. Despite having been left with ten pounds a week sent via the bank, he told Margaret Taylor, the 'extravagant woman' had managed to chalk up a bill for £150 with the obliging grocer and wine merchant.

There was gossip about her and men. Jane Dark and her husband Howard, a travelling draper, who lived in the town, were with the Thomases at a dance in Pendine, along the coast. It was soon after the American trip; Dylan talked about Charlie Chaplin, whom he had met in California. Caitlin was dancing with an army officer. Her dress was white. Mrs Dark was alarmed to see streaks of menstrual blood appear at the back of it, one of those misfortunes that people remember; another defiant hint of her physical nature. Perhaps it was the same night, when they were back at the Boat House having supper, that Mrs Dark asked Caitlin what kind of men she liked, and was told promptly, 'Tall and athletic.' Dylan looked at Howard Dark, a small man with a moustache, and said, 'Describes us exactly, doesn't it?' Then or later – probably later – Dark was one of Caitlin's lovers.

On the writing front, poems remained elusive. Thomas finally completed 'In the white giant's thigh', begun the previous year, another poem of vast regrets, this time for the dead-and-gone women of a romantic countryside. The difficulties with poems troubled

Caitlin. In July she was writing to people in America she hadn't met, thanking Gene Derwood, the wife of the poet and anthologist Oscar Williams, for a gift, telling her that Dylan was 'depressed at the thought of eternal wage earning, and the poems as impossible to pin down as ever – That is the bugger of the family and don't I know it!' To Brinnin, who was thanked for the bag with its hidden dollars, she wrote ironically that while Dylan wanted only to write his 'non-paying poems' in peace, his family kept demanding 'food clothing tobacco drink' and wouldn't let him: 'the old story of the corruption of the artist through the tyranny of the family [. . .] I couldn't deplore it more from every point of view, my own included.'

Was she blaming herself or Dylan? Perhaps both. A remark in the Brinnin letter, about Dylan having been over-indulged during his visit, hinted that Americans were on the list, too. Caitlin would soon be saying that they had a lot to answer for, beginning with certain women. Already, when Dylan had returned, she was on the look-out; as she said afterwards, 'I sniffed around him as suspiciously as a wild animal in the jungle welcoming its returning mate.' That summer she sniffed out evidence in the shape of Pearl's letters. Thomas had come back from London with one or more in his pocket, having picked them up from his club, the Savage, the address he used for clandestine mail. They were in his coat, draped over the back of a chair, and she found them when she was looking for spare pound notes, which she did as a matter of course. 'I read them with avidity,' she said, 'and was torn to grated shreds for her and for me.'

One can think of reasons why Thomas might have deliberately let her find out, but it was very likely carelessness. He laughed it off, saying she was a barmy American woman, a pain in the neck, another hysterical fan with nothing better to do than fling herself at innocent poets. Caitlin said she believed him. Perhaps she did, given her conviction of long-standing that 'no sophisticated smart efficient woman would have anything to do with Dylan, because as they say, he was like an unmade bed'. But he was also a poet, a romantic figure to some; as he had been to her when they first met. Now he was edging towards fame as well.

Gwen and Vernon Watkins had the Thomases down to Pennard one Saturday in June. Fred Janes the painter and Dan Jones the composer were there as well, with their wives. It was the last time so many of the 'Swansea gang' were together. Gwen found herself alone in the garden with Dylan, when the others had gone to bathe, and he, as usual, excused himself from going near the water. He talked boastfully about America and Americans ('terrifying, fascinating, boring') before they got on to Dickens, that earlier literary visitor to America. Sitting in the sun, they exchanged favourite quotations. 'I had never felt at ease with Dylan,' she wrote, 'but now, for about three-quarters of an hour, I did.' Then the others came back, and Caitlin bickered with him over tea, saying that American whiskey had destroyed his taste buds. To Gwen, Caitlin seemed 'permanently embittered'. It was still early in the summer; Pearl's letters were yet to come.

Nor did Caitlin's discovery and Thomas's denials end the matter. In September Pearl came to Europe, and spent several days with Thomas in London. They went to pubs where he was well known, and even attended a wedding. Brinnin was over at the same time, and the three went on a river boat to Greenwich. When Pearl was absent for a moment, Thomas said, 'What am I going to do? I'm in love with [Pearl] and I'm in love with my wife.' Next day she and Dylan went to stay by the sea at Brighton.

Soon afterwards Pearl had gone to France, Thomas was back in Laugharne, and Caitlin knew all about the arty, well-shaped piece with a fringe and bracelets, because Margaret Taylor had travelled down to tell her.

I gazed suicidally into the tide and was all set money or no money to go on the streets with a baby strapped on my back, when he came back in an unmistakably shaking panic this time and said, 'You don't believe *that* do you?' and I said, 'I do,' and went on packing. But I refused to conventionally go to my mother's, that seemed an even greater humiliation, and I learned bitterly for the first time what it really meant to have no money of my own and to be married to a Welshman.

In addition, she was pregnant again. Her rage against Pearl held up nicely over the years, and long afterwards she was calling her 'a mongoose-gripping cobra'.* She didn't leave Dylan. At one point he thought he had talked her round. He wrote to Helen McAlpine on 14

---

* In 1976, when I wrote to Pearl with some questions, she sent an unhelpful reply that referred to 'ancient infidelities' and the indecency of 'raking through the cold ashes of [Dylan's] life', on the grounds (rather late in the day, one might feel, as far as she was concerned) that it would give 'unnecessary pain' while his wife and children were alive.

September to say he had found Caitlin 'terribly distressed, but [I] managed to tell her that all that that grey fiend had pumped into her ear was lies and poison. And so it was. And Cat believed me . . .' The object of the letter was to persuade Helen to back him up. 'Don't answer this,' he wrote, 'I trust you with everything: which is Cat's happiness.'

But Cat's happiness was a wasting asset. She was not equipped to cope with serious betrayal by the person she regarded as her property, her child, her poet. Caitlin, in her own eyes, was morally as well as physically the stronger. Her husband had a 'baby weakness' that went with an 'unnatural perception of the intellect'. He was supposed to depend on her, so how could she now tolerate the independence implicit in his wicked infidelity?

Dylan was, in her phrase, 'the one deadly, organic entanglement of a lifetime'. Because, as she insisted, her own carnal indulgences were of no importance, she viewed their relationship as a truce between her flesh and his spirit. The real bond between them was his 'gift', his talent – or his genius, a word she likes to toy with. It infuriated her to find that others were now attracted by the lustre of an artist that she had divined long ago, when the artist was still an obscure scribbler with a few poems to his name. 'I took him when he was nobody': the justification, to her, is absolute.

Her presumption was inseparable from her nature. It was she, the object of men's desire, who had favoured Dylan, the little man in stale clothes. If, in addition, she unconsciously chose him to replace her lost father, the poet who never was, he was thereafter indispensable. Infidelity as such was probably never the issue. She objected only when it threatened the inner coils of their relationship. It was true that their lives were already wearing thin. The poetry was waning, and Caitlin knew that 'the tyranny of the family' had something to do with it. They were quarrelling and in debt. But their marriage kept its secret interior, as marriages do. Then came America. After Pearl – who can hardly have been expected to know – nothing was ever the same. Dylan was on the way to being another lost poet for Caitlin.

None of this happened overnight; some of it is conjecture; Caitlin's bristling egotism is hard to channel into logical explanations. But their quarrelling became more violent. When they were drunk, she would drag him on the ground and bang his head against the floor, 'beating the Jesus out of him'; later on she was surprised that he didn't try to stop her more often. In another version, though, 'I would grasp Dylan's "cherubic curls" and pull with all my might, and he would demonstrate his vaunted rat-hold on the throat and come very near to strangling me.' That sounds just as likely. Caitlin has a story about ripping up the manuscript of 'In the white giant's thigh' after a quarrel and throwing the pieces through the window; then rescuing them from the mud-flats before the tide came in. She also claims to have rushed out in her nightdress to save papers that Dylan flung away in a rage. At the University of Texas's Thomas collection they have manuscript pages with grains of sand adhering. They were exhausting games to play.

What were the effects on Thomas of a harsher, unforgiving Caitlin? Her accounts of their quarrels emphasise how they were reconciled afterwards, in bed. But if Thomas in the last three years of his life is to be seen as a man adrift, his powers faltering and his options closing one by one, it is hard not to see Caitlin as one of the reasons. He was, indeed, a dependent man; without the guarantee of her affection, he was in trouble.

The following January, 1951, he was sending her anguished love letters from Iran, where he had gone as a guest of the Anglo-Iranian Oil Company; he was to write a film about how well the company treated the Iranians, who had not yet taken control of their own oil. By now Caitlin had ended the pregnancy, in an 'illicit hellhole', as Thomas described it to Princess Caetani. While he was away she corresponded with the Royal Literary Fund, which, twelve years after he first applied to it, had decided to make a grant, and in the end paid three hundred pounds. She wrote plain, business-like letters – continuing to deal with the Fund after Thomas returned in February – sending details of bills that needed paying, such as school fees. Jones the grocer got fifty pounds, rather less than half what he was owed.

To the Davenports at the end of January she wrote:

[I] have sunk into a kind of introspection that bores me to death, and I don't want to inflict other people with my miserable boredom – what I have been through is nobody's business and so on and so on – so shall we leave it at that. But I am heartily sick of my own devastating company which is singularly fruitless – apart from the blood fruit which sicken me too, and the worst part is there is not another soul spark or livener to make me forget myself for a minute – Only liquor – and liquor alone is not enlivening – It simply increases the moribund – & I've got plenty of that – Ah but hope springs eternal!

My faithful sister, under the skin, writes me – 'Catty, Ducky, what fun, I'm slipping (skipping) down to Laugharne on Thursday . . .' I may be prejudiced, but it's not my idea of fun.*

I had thought I might 'skip' myself up to London to welcome my shark, but doubt if he deserves such a concession, and the queue may be too long – Trouble is I do want an excuse to stir myself out of this Snake Pit.

A letter to her husband left him, he said, in despair. He told her it made him want to die. To John Davenport he wrote ironically, probably when he was back in Laugharne, to say 'how far, far away I feel, here in my *horribly* cosy little nest, surrounded by my detestable books, wearing my odious, warm slippers, observing the gay, reptilian play of my abominable brood, basking in the vituperation of my golden, loathing wife!'

Before his return, Caitlin did indeed skip up to London, describing (to Brigit) how she had to stay with the McAlpines for a week or two because Dylan was delayed. In this version of events, which told Brigit nothing of the Pearl affair, she said that as soon as he arrived, her husband accused her of carrying on with a poet in London (which she vehemently denied), after which

we went on the booze, had a row as usual, and Dylan buggered off in a rage so I never even slept with him – not a very successful reunion . . . and so it went on. But now we are back in the fold and settling down to the old humdrumming of which I am sick and buggered up to the teeth, and the foul rain and the filthy winter turn me sour with disgust. I am determined, whatever happens, to get out of this Poet's nest where the poet never is.

Yet alongside Caitlin's hard-headedness was her appetite for romance of the higher kind. 'Love' was to be looked for in all situations, and although it might and frequently did involve sex, the romantic colouring was important, the having men at her feet. Thus, at the end of the letter to her sister, she describes an interlude in London while she was waiting for Dylan:

* Presumably this is Margaret Taylor, whom both the Thomases laughed at for calling everyone 'Ducky'.

You asked for some moral uplift but I'm sure I stand more in need of it than you – I even had quite a bad fall (in love) in London, doomed from the start to failure, with a stone deaf poet almost insuperable . . . but my beaten flesh hasn't been stirred for so long I was quite overcome and can't get the thing out of my system. What possible chance anyway does a poor mother have for sidestepping. It has made me even more cantankerous.

The poet (not the one suspected by Thomas) was David Wright, who remembers Caitlin as 'very intelligent, absolutely honest, great fun, charismatic and with a cutting wit'. Among their encounters during her week in London, he called at the flat where she was staying, and found she wanted him to take her to a party given by the painters Robert Colquhoun and Robert MacBryde. When he refused, because he was having dinner with a girl friend, she insisted on making him a sandwich. When he ate it, he found it was full of garlic. There was no sexual affair. The nearest they came to it was when 'drink and desire' led Wright to suggest lunch at a pub near his flat. He went to the rendezvous 'with a heavy heart and bad conscience', since he didn't want to upset the marriage. But 'nor did Caitlin, for she had the good sense not to turn up'. Perhaps it was enough to have been asked.

In Laugharne, domestic problems didn't stop Thomas writing poetry. Three poems were completed in 1951, making it his most productive year since the War. 'Do not go gentle into that good night' was addressed to his dying father, a statement urging defiance. It was written out of disappointment at D.J. Thomas's resignation to death. It may also have reflected the son's awareness that he himself was too passive, letting events wash over him. 'Do not go gentle' was written by the spring, as was 'Lament', at one time 'The Miner's Lament', a bawdy song for a retired libertine, 'the old ram rod, dying of women'. Its jaunty style, sprinkled with naughtiness, was in the consciously comic manner that Thomas was developing for *Under Milk Wood*, which would bring him more fame than anything else he wrote. 'Wick-dipping moon' and 'a black sheep with a crumpled horn' (in the poem) are from the same stable as 'Come and sweep my chimbley/She sighed to me with a blush' (in the play).

Thomas was a lifelong composer of comic verse and scatological limericks for his friends, but these private entertainments were kept apart from the poetry. 'Lament' breached the wall, the only published poem to do so. Although *Under Milk Wood* may have pointed the way to a future of racy literary comedies, there is no evidence that Thomas saw the genre as a substitute for the real thing; he liked the play but knew it for what it was.

Finally there was 'Poem on his birthday,' which may have been begun in 1949, but was not completed till the summer of 1951. A sombre poem, its narrator is not so much observing mortality as trying to fend it off. It has hints of the nuclear-holocaust fears that were then a new phenomenon. The underlying note is despair, propped up by a last-minute show of optimism. It also marked the end of Thomas's career as a poet. Only the sterile verse 'Prologue' to his *Collected Poems* the following year was to follow.

His career as writer and broadcaster seemed busy enough in 1951, as contemporaries remember and his letters attest. He was becoming collectable, and it would be easier for biographers to chart his progress later on. About forty-five of his letters from that year are extant. No one took much notice of Caitlin. Apart from the Royal Literary Fund correspondence, which is unrevealing, only three of her letters from 1951 have come to light, those to the Davenports and to Brigit, already quoted; the other to Oscar Williams, promising to write him 'a poem that is a poem', if only she knew what that was – 'although I've asked Dylan many times what is a Poem, he is quite incapable of telling me'. Most of the time she is in the shadows, nursing her grievances.

In July she makes a brief, hectic appearance, as reported by Brinnin, who visited Laugharne with his friend Bill Read and stayed at the Boat House. He had expected a country girl but found 'a Celtic blonde beauty', her manner 'a puzzling combination [. . .] of the primitive and the *svelte*', which is flatteringly similar to her own self-assessment of 'peasant and noblewoman'. A tour of Pembrokeshire by taxi, a Williams at the wheel, was marred by Caitlin, who sat in the back with Brinnin and cross-examined him in whispers about Pearl. A 'magnificent lobster dinner' at a restaurant, promised by Thomas, ended up as one lobster between them all, eaten while Dylan and Caitlin were having a quarrel. At the Boat House there was friction about a second trip to America that was being planned for 1952. 'America is out!' Caitlin declared at one point, although the idea had been that she would go as well.

Next morning, a Saturday, calm was restored. This lasted until the evening, when they happened to be talking about sex murderers over dinner at the Boat House, and Caitlin began to ridicule whatever

Dylan said. He flipped a matchbox at her, she flung it in his face, and the next minute she

> reached for his hair and pulled him out of his seat and on to the floor [. . .] Chairs got knocked over, dishes were pushed from the table as, blow for blow, the combatants wrestled toward the kitchen. Gaping, we sat benumbed over our cooling food.

The fight ended with Dylan running upstairs, and Caitlin rounding on the embarrassed Americans with, '*Thank* you for helping a lady in distress.' As penance they had to sit and listen ('not without genuine sympathy') while she harangued them about her husband's in-adequacies, and how America, for which she blamed Brinnin, had gone to his head. She ranted at 'those foul women who chase after him while I'm left here to rot in this bloody bog with three screaming children'. It was two, in fact, Llewelyn being aged twelve and usually away at boarding school; but Caitlin never let details get in the way of her rage. Once again, by morning it was as though nothing had happened.

Troubles accumulated, turned into a comic script by Thomas in letters to people he hardly knew ('my children grow large and rude; I renounce my Art to make money and then make no money [. . .] I quarrel with Caitlin and make it up in floods of salt self pity'), using the monologue as an escape route that made her all the more resentful because it was just a writer being clever; it solved nothing. An unpayable tax bill came in for the year 1948–9, when Thomas had earned £1,600. Gout and back problems overtook him. Caitlin had an attack of mumps.

In the autumn they had a spectacular row, perhaps about M., the friend who used to stay at their 'leaking barn' in Chelsea. Caitlin told a later lover that M. at first refused to sleep with her, but she got him into bed in the end. Dylan caught them at the Boat House. Elisabeth Lutyens went to stay there shortly after, and found Caitlin alone, Dylan having walked out. He had telephoned from Swansea, reversing the charges, to announce hollowly, 'This is the last time you will hear my voice.' Caitlin interpreted that as a suicide threat. He was more adamant than usual about not returning, and Daniel Jones, in whose house he was sulking, had to be used as a mediator. Eventually the two women went together to bring him back, making the journey by bus and train. The reunion was disorderly; Lutyens remembered Dylan kneeling and begging her forgiveness, Caitlin remembered punching him and wanting to kill him. They had to return by taxi because the last train had gone. Lutyens was the only one with money, so she had to pay for the thirty-mile journey. Frequent stops were necessary because Dylan had drunk so much beer. Every time they drew up, so that he could go into a field, he made a pretence of running away in the dark and had to be brought back.

Later, seeing the way they lived, Lutyens took Caitlin's side, dismayed that Thomas expected his wife to 'forgo all independence or life of her own, staying at home as wife and mother', and even resented her going about with their visitor. Lutyens wrote of his 'mischievous cruelty', as when Caitlin ripped up the manuscript of a poem, which he declared was the only one, at which she went down on her hands and knees to reassemble it, while he grinned behind her back and told Lutyens he had dozens of copies.

The women who sympathised with Caitlin rarely mention, perhaps were ignorant of, her sexual proclivities (Lutyens knew that Caitlin found M. 'sympathetic', but didn't believe that she had been to bed with him). If Caitlin was driven to the brink by Dylan's behaviour, he was driven to a different kind of brink by hers.

There is a hint of 'suicide threats' by Thomas. Given his morbid interest in blood, terror and vampires, death by his own hand – one can imagine him enjoying the phrase – may have been no more than another of the fantasies he liked to frighten himself with. His anecdotes about everything were full of exaggerated nonsense, which is what made them entertaining. But after his death Caitlin mentioned suicide in her unpublished *Fool* manuscript:

> He made a few very fainthearted attempts at scratching, with trembling razor blade precaution, the delicate blue veins on his princess wrists, intending, he carefully pointed out, to bleed to death in a gradually weakening trance in a deliciously eternally hot-adding bath. One day he told me he had drunk a bottle of Jeyes Fluid but I suspect that was a plain Taffy lie as no bad effects resulted. Another night he put his head in the gas oven, turned on the gas but [. . .] felt too lazy to persevere with the Grand Opera drama and preferred to come into bed instead.

None of this sounds like a brush with death; none of it sounds very encouraging, either.

Their general disorder was compounded in the autumn of 1951 by a temporary move back to London. Margaret Taylor, whose own mental stability is sometimes in doubt, had decided that Thomas could organise his affairs, and perhaps escape a further trip to America, only if he was able to do a spell of steady work in the capital. It was unclear what this work was going to be, apart from a scheme to write radio comedy for a series that never materialised. But Mrs Taylor bought another of her houses, this time in Camden Town, near railway yards although near to Regent's Park as well, furnished some rooms there and cajoled them into occupying it. Caitlin was disenchanted with Wales, Dylan always took the line of least resistance; so once again Mrs Taylor had her poet under surveillance.

With them Caitlin took their cleaning woman and general help, Dolly Long, a piece of Laugharne that transplanted badly to London soil. Dolly was unmarried but had a child by a soldier in the War. She was a small, stubborn woman, referred to once by Caitlin as 'my personal she-devil', who used to light bonfires too close to the Boat House and lock the children in cupboards. To Caitlin, with vague notions from her Irish side of a peasant sub-world, Dolly was 'one of the unkillable poor'. Once, needing her urgently when Dolly had sent round to say she was ill, Caitlin is said to have appeared at her council house on the new Orchard Park estate above the village, dragged her out of bed, and told her to 'get round to the effing Boat House'. In her dotage at an old people's home Dolly was heard to mutter, 'That bloody Mrs Dylan wants me to clean the place again. Well, I'm not going.' On the other hand, after 'Mr Dylan's' death she kept an old suit of his, which she sent off at intervals to be dry-cleaned; and preserved a worn photograph of Caitlin, smiling wickedly, that she would show to visitors, with its inscription, 'To our one and only Dolly from always sweet Caitlin Thomas. Happy New Year.'

Caitlin, Dylan, Aeronwy, Colm, Dolly and Dolly's little boy arrived in Camden Town one evening. According to Caitlin, Dylan began by nagging and trying to establish order, then mumbled 'See you later' and vanished to the pub. Although it was late and everyone was tired, Caitlin felt compelled to go through the 'nightly ritual of the baby's bath', not because she was fastidious (she said) but because, having mastered one system, she could imagine no other. So 'I set up my papier-mâché bath on two chairs, my Johnson soaps and baby powders', while Dolly crouched in a corner looking frightened.

Another time at Camden Town, when drunk and faced with Dolly's refusal to make supper, she smashed a toy guitar over her head, necessitating stitches; after which, said Caitlin, she was 'as lively as a cricket', until the next time. It was no wonder that when threatened with a talking-to from the master of the house, Dolly replied, 'Mr Dylan won't do nothing, he's nice, not like you.' Dylan used to dig out a bag of sweets (he always kept a good stock of hard-boileds and wine gums) as a present.

Margaret Taylor was a constant visitor, wanting to know what Thomas was writing (very little), trying to have confidential chats with Caitlin about their big naughty boy who had to be curbed for his own good. She had been known to arrive in the morning while they were still in bed with hangovers, and start discussing the previous night's party or pub crawl; Dylan, meanwhile, pulling the blanket over his head, waiting for 'an opportunity to wriggle into his trousers concertina'd on the floor and shut himself into the lavatory for a nice long escaping read'. Children were screaming 'Mummy! Mummy!' all over the house as Mrs Taylor, with a 'Now, duckies, to practicalities!', moved on to her plans for another evening's fun. Once, said Caitlin, she and Dylan were standing in a bar, laughing about old Maggs behind her back, when they realised she was there, listening to them, 'the tears streaming down her mortified face'. It was a sad relationship, cruelly exploiting a benefactor who seemed to thrive on cruel exploitation, and Camden was one of its sourest episodes.

They were still there in the New Year, as final arrangements were made for another American tour, which, despite everything, had been planned with Brinnin. This time Caitlin was to acompany him. The previous autumn, about the time they went to Camden, she knew that she was expecting another child. Strangely, Caitlin had seemed better able to avoid unwanted pregnancies in the past than she was in the present – as though she was now making an effort, conscious or unconscious, to stabilise herself (or Dylan) with another child. But if any such motive was involved, it was overriden by a desire not to be left behind. The pregnancy was terminated. In her words, 'I was ruthless if I wanted to do something. I wanted the baby, too, but I wanted America more.'

For all her talk – and his – about the dangers of America, it remained a promised land. This time there was less emphasis, if there was any at all, on bringing home dollars. A letter to Brinnin asked if he could find them free accommodation in New York, since 'the money I earn we want for The Sights, not for board'. When they sailed in the *Queen Mary* on 15 January Dylan knew what Caitlin was after, an archetypal good time. But her chances were not good.

9

Breaking Point

Caitlin in America raised no expectations except that of being the poet's wife. A bluestocking would have been recognised with delight and asked about literary London, a timorous consort would have been looked after with small drinks and invited to go shopping with faculty wives. Caitlin was neither. She was a smouldering Celt with a cruel tongue who liked her whisky and felt hard done by. There was no part for her in the script.

When she arrived at Pier 90 in New York, dressed for the cold in furs, she was seeing America for the first time. Apart from a glance at skyscrapers, gadgets and hamburgers, she took little notice. A journal she was supposed to be keeping, on which Thomas would base a book commissioned by a London publisher, was soon forgotten, as was the book. Brinnin, their host, a better observer of the passing scene, noted her ill-humour as they relaxed for ten days before Thomas started work. He heard her ask a professor, 'Are they all stuffed shirts like you?'; noticed how she went out of her way to spoil her husband's anecdotes; was beside the poet as he stepped on to the stage for his first reading, and heard Caitlin breathe, 'Just remember, they're all dirt.'

As for Thomas, his caricature in America served him well, the drunken poet from Europe who flouted convention and behaved badly, but not so badly as to make himself disliked. Few of his engagements were not kept; his lecherous posturing at parties ended in stupor; next morning his amiable comicality saw him through, together with the echoes of his brassy, melodic reading. American deference towards European writers as a class was not yet in decline, and Thomas's idiosyncracies were better tolerated than they would have been in Britain: not that he behaved as grossly there.

The delight with which campus America received him only added to the savagery of Caitlin's mood. America in general and Pearl in particular had begun the process of robbing her, Caitlin Thomas, of her personal property. The place was not to be trusted or respected. The journal, had she kept it, would have been filled with the ugly images she used later. 'What I hated most was those young girls and students, pissing their pants in the audience and screaming at him as though he was a pop singer.' His acclaim was unbearable, since it reminded her how he had betrayed her by ceasing to be her poet; indeed, by ceasing to be a poet at all.

She made no attempt to contain her feelings: why pretend, when it was she who was suffering? Her posthumous accusations were wild and often exaggerated. 'How raw, how green' was Dylan before America, 'how touchingly pure and innocent'. He had been 'launched naked as a fresh-skinned rabbit' into a 'mercilessly man-eating culture', which brought him fame that was 'not worth the exchange of his soul'. The idea that Thomas carried the seeds of his own destruction, as she carried hers, didn't appeal to Caitlin. America was to blame, just as later, in old age, the wheel would come full circle, and she would blame Dylan himself for it all. Never herself, never for an instant.

The real case – and there was a case – for trying to save Thomas from the consequences of himself was not one that she was equipped to make, or that Thomas's circle of admirers would have been interested in hearing. All she had to offer was anger. Brinnin – who was much reviled in Britain afterwards for having written it all down, as if a decent fellow would have pretended it wasn't happening – was with the Thomases at a party in Cambridge, Mass., given by the *Advocate*, Harvard's literary magazine. He saw her survey the room 'as if it were crawling with vermin' and heard her ask, 'Is there no man in America worthy of me?' (When Thomas remonstrated with her she left, and when he returned to their apartment much later he found himself locked out of the bedroom, with a note saying, 'Stay out, you scum').

Howard Moss, a *New Yorker* editor, attended a party at the Manhattan apartment of Maya Deren, who made avant-garde films, where Caitlin, 'rather pathetic', put on her dervish-dancing act, smashing glasses and making herself bleed before she crashed on to the sofa where Moss had been sitting a moment before. That evening, he said, it was Dylan who did the looking-after.

Behind her violence were real concerns. Her husband's small besuited figure on an American stage angered her because she thought his attempts at sartorial smartness made him merely ridiculous. Even in Britain she disliked seeing him try, as in his own odd way he did try, when all he did (she insisted) was look like a clown. Should he wear his clerical grey or his dark blue (both cast-offs, one from his preacher uncle, the Revd David Rees, one from a Californian admirer)? What about his threadbare tweeds or 'the shiny brown slinks with the stains down the front'? Should it be a hat or a cap? 'Since the poor bugger only possessed this miserable collection of down-and-out remnants, only fit for a jumble sale, and the ridiculous pathos of the situation killed me, I would lose patience and say, "Put the bloody lot on, you couldn't look worse".'

Caitlin had a sense of dignity, despite her own performances in public when she drank recklessly and exposed herself to ridicule. She was, in her phrase, an 'Irish fighting drunk', and her behaviour, however deplorable, was to her a sign of spirit. It was the passive, grinning, cadging, fawning Dylan that she deplored. As she said, she had no objection to asking outright for money. What she disliked was wheedling and flattery.

Thus an attempt by Thomas to squeeze a thousand dollars from a woman in Cambridge was thwarted by Caitlin's rudeness. Mrs Macnamara, *in loco parentis* for Llewelyn while they were away, had written that his boarding school was threatening to send the boy home unless outstanding fees were paid. Thomas asked the first woman of means he met if she could help, and a lunch was arranged to discuss the matter. Caitlin, who was shopping with Brinnin's mother, insisted on going to the restaurant to glare at them. Her story and Brinnin's differ as to whether Caitlin had already insulted the benefactress, or whether she did this later, but the result was the same. Dylan told her that the cheque book was being dangled 'an inch away from my pocket, and you come along and fuck the whole thing up'. Brinnin's suggestion that they cable money from the American earnings had already been rejected by Thomas, in hopes of the benefactress. The bill went unpaid.

In America, said Caitlin, 'I drank like a madwoman'. Among her emotions, some more worthy than others, was wounded vanity. She wanted to be noticed, like him. 'You never got all that arse-licking in England. He adored it and I don't blame him. I was very envious and resentful because I wasn't getting it.' David Markson, then a graduate student at Columbia, asked if he could bring two friends to the White Horse Tavern – the bar in Greenwich Village that Dylan patronised – to meet him. Caitlin was there, sitting in silence. They listened enraptured to Thomas's monologue. Eventually Caitlin leaned forward, holding an unlit cigarette, and said, 'Will one of your satellites give me a match?' Red-faced, they all obliged, but soon after that she walked out. Thomas talked on for a while, then asked if someone would go to the bar across the street, where she probably was, and buy her a drink. Markson found her there, 'just being angry. I knew enough to apologise. She came back.'

Her most consistent apologist in America was Rose Slivka, who had met Thomas on his first visit, through her husband Dave, a sculptor. 'The world was killing her,' said Slivka, years later. 'She was the artist's wife, and that can be a terrible place to be.' Caitlin, she thought, 'had some sort of vision, and the vision turned to fury'. Few in America were as charitable. Caitlin herself was capable of self-criticism, when it suited her. Mike Watkins, of the Ann Watkins agency in New York that represented Thomas, took Caitlin to lunch one day when Dylan was out of town for a reading. She drank big Martinis, wine and brandy, enjoying herself. He was due back at the office, but had to accompany her in a taxi to Brooks Brothers, where she wanted to buy herself a pink shirt. This was Caitlin being happy. At one point Watkins asked her about Dylan and the problem of his drinking. 'Oh,' she said, 'that isn't the problem. I am the problem.'

The working part of the trip consisted of forty or fifty engagements, of which rather more than half were in New York, New England and elsewhere in the East. Caitlin attended few of the readings. This phase ended at Pennsylvania State University on 17 March. Charles W. Mann, another graduate student, was in the party invited to meet the Thomases after the reading. Dylan was 'jolly and articulate'. Caitlin, next to whom Mann sat on a couch, 'looked frazzled, care-worn and unhappy'. They left to catch a night train to Chicago, on their way to Flagstaff, Arizona, where the painters Max Ernst and Dorothea Tanning were to put them up for a week's holiday. Due to missed connections, unbudgeted-for hotels and the usual leaking pockets, the four hundred dollars Brinnin gave them for extra expenses – their tickets were already paid for – had gone when they reached Arizona. They languished in the sun, penniless. A joint postcard to John Davenport, showing a cowboy rounding up horses, said (in her writing), 'Wild horses wouldn't keep me here! Cat,' followed (in his) by 'Neigh! Dylan.'

Work began again in April when they reached California. There they stayed with Ruth Witt-Diamant, who ran a poetry centre in San Francisco, and who was Thomas's host on his previous visit. Laundry had arrived from New York, forwarded on Caitlin's instructions, a mere forty dollars' worth. Their baggage was formidable; according to Caitlin, in the end they had forty suitcases, most of them borrowed. Among Thomas's West Coast engagements were two readings in Vancouver, where he went on his own. Caitlin is supposed to have discovered that he slept with a woman there, darkening their travels still further. She probably found an amenable man or two, since they were apart on various occasions; his friends said that she did.

Returning circuitously to the East in mid-April, they stopped off at Salt Lake City for a reading at the University of Utah, where Thomas allowed himself to be manoeuvred into discussing poetry with the professor of English, Brewster Ghiselin, and his students, and remarked (in the course of some sensible replies) that 'I'm only a fat little fool ranting on a cliff.' Olive Ghiselin, the professor's wife, remembered Caitlin as 'beautiful but edgy, unresigned to being the background wife'. She also remembered a dinner party at which Caitlin said that she hated dogs, yet they insisted on sniffing around her. 'Of course,' said Thomas. 'They know a bitch when they see one.'

The rows and reconciliations continued. Caitlin has said that in America, their quarrels 'took on the ugly complexion of mania'. A telegram from Mrs Macnamara, 'FEES NOT ARRIVED THEREFORE LLEWELYN DISMISSED FROM SCHOOL', caused a storm when they were back in New York, Thomas having sworn that he had sent the money from San Francisco in time to appease the headmaster. Friends saw him weeping at the White Horse because of the school-fees affair, but the tears may have been for Caitlin's benefit as much as anything. Marianne Mantell, one of the young women who founded Caedmon Records and made their name with Thomas's recordings, heard him groan that Caitlin meant to leave him because of the girl in Vancouver, although he had slept with her only because he was cold. This sounds the authentic Dylan. It is possible that the love-in-Vancouver story was a fiction, invented to explain Caitlin's anger, rather than have to admit to his friends that what had upset her was his performance over the school fees.

As they sailed away, Caitlin wrote a thank-you letter to Brinnin to say he would be doing a 'fatal disservice' to Dylan if he allowed him to 'go through that pantomime again'. 'As for me,' she added, ambiguously, 'such as I am, and however much you think I'd be better under the sod, I shall not be there. Nor anywhere near, ever again, the sacred "Muse".' By 'under the sod' she might mean 'dead', though in the context it sounds as if 'the sod' is Dylan and she is talking about their love life.

But she hadn't given up. It is unwise to look for consistency in her moods. Their fluctuations had a long history, in milder form extending back to her girlhood, and the marriage had built itself around them. Reinstalled at the Boat House in June, she wrote almost dreamily to David Lougee in New York, an earnest young poet and Dylan-fan, asexual as far as she was concerned, describing Laugharne with the tide running in on a sunny day, as she lay in 'our very own, long forsaken, enchanted harbour'. She mused on the rain (which she admitted would soon be making her want to cut her throat), on her 'Queen of Sheba nonsense life in America' and its contrast with 'abysses of domesticity', on the chances of living cheaply in the Spanish sun; she was even nostalgic for New York bars and restaurants, now that she was no longer there, 'the White Horse, the seductive stores, the dazzling lights and all things bright and beautiful'. The letter had a gleam of hope; or was she manufacturing hope for the benefit of a nice young poet? There was still a chance, she wrote, of turning Dylan away from the lure of 'acting', as she called his poetry-reading, and back to his vocation:

We hope to bury ourselves for the next three months from all human contacts, and not even think about the awful business of money, and making a living. Obviously quite insoluble in our case, as Poetry and money are the bitterest enemies [. . .] I am making a last fight for writing, in whatever form, as against acting, and the pernicious star system, which undermine the resistance and veracity of the most upright (ie T.S. Eliot) protagonists. And, let us face it, Dylan is not the most upright or strong.

The plan to ignore the world and write poetry, if it ever amounted to a plan, was ignored. The Inland Revenue was taking an interest in the American earnings. The publisher who was expecting a book about America had to be pacified. Thomas was in London, seeing people about projects that would never come off because they bored or frightened him, then watching a few days' cricket at Lord's, where he claimed to have caught the sun and contracted pleurisy.

Back in Laugharne, 'sitting in my pink skin in a garage' – his shed on the cliff – he worked at a verse prologue to his *Collected Poems*, which were due out at the end of 1952. His publishers, Dent, wanted to keep his name before the public. New poems intended for the collection were never written, among them another 'Poem to Caitlin', a 'Poem to Colm' and a continuation of 'In the white giant's thigh'. In 'Prologue', more optimism is being generated. The poet, 'at poor peace', sees his verse as a metaphorical ark in which he and Creation can escape the flood or the darkness. It eventually consisted of 102 lines, with a rhyme scheme that couples the first and last lines, the second and last-but-one, and so on until 'farms' and 'arms' meet in adjacent lines at the centre. Thomas spent much of the summer pitting himself against these technicalities. It was probably 'Prologue' to which he referred in a letter to Caitlin where he spoke of 'those endless rotten verses of mine, which I almost agree with you about'.

The letter was written from, and to, the Boat House. Caitlin had found one of her husband's essays in sponging, addressed to a wealthy patron, Marged Howard-Stepney, and had taken offence, as usual, at seeing him debase himself.

A Welsh woman of the same age as Caitlin, Marged was interested in the arts and had philanthropic inclinations that were the despair of her advisers. She was unmarried and alcoholic; when she stayed at the Boat House, Dolly Long found bottles of gin in her bed. She was more reserved than Margaret Taylor but no less devoted to the idea of helping a genius. Caitlin, true to her beliefs, saw nothing wrong in enjoying whatever Howard-Stepney crumbs were available. Her abortion at the end of 1951 was paid for by Marged. It was the cringing tone of Thomas's appeal that she objected to.

The offending item was very likely the one that survived in Thomas's papers, beginning 'Dear Marged, You told me, once upon a time, to call on you when I was beaten down, and you would try to pick me up', then turning into a poem:

Once upon a time you told me,
I remember in my bones,
That when the bad world had rolled me
Over on the scolding stones,
Shameless, lost, as the day I came
I should with my beggar's cup
Howl down the wind and call your name
And you, you would raise me up.

There were two more stanzas of this, and presumably it sent Caitlin into one of her rages. The only way he could get her to listen was by internal communication from the shed, to say that what he had addressed to 'that Marged gin woman' was 'horrible, it was dirty, and cadging and lying', and so on. He was in misery, and he knew that she was, too, for his 'callous attempt at a mock-literature of the slimiest kind'.

Thomas also spoke in the letter to Caitlin of his 'loathing and hatred for myself', but one can only guess whether this was contrition or more Caitlin-appeasement. In an abject letter to Princess Caetani in Rome, excusing himself for not having finished the play she was promised, he wrote, 'I don't deserve one warm word but only bashing on the head and then forgetting cold as ice.'

This may have been less self-criticism than an echo of events at home, with their physical attacks and chilly silences. According to Margaret Taylor, Caitlin once refused to speak to him for a month. According to Caitlin, Caitlin hit him over the head with a long torch when they were at Marged's house, all drunk after he had been reading poems to an invited audience there. Poet and patron were 'sloppily absorbed in one another'. The torch was the first weapon that came to hand, on a mantelpiece. Marged said she was endangering the brains of a genius; Thomas seemed unaware that he had been hit.

Donald Hall, then a postgraduate student, stayed at the Boat House in October 1952 with his wife. He had arranged to drive Thomas to Oxford to read at the university's poetry society, Thomas having failed to turn up on a previous occasion. The two sat talking about poetry after the women had gone to bed. Thomas disparaged his own work; he sounded as though he meant it, adding that he didn't intend to do much writing of poetry in future. They were still talking when Caitlin (who had complained that she needed Dylan to keep her warm in bed) shouted, 'For *Christ's* sake, come up here.'

In the morning, Hall watched Caitlin as she prepared Aeron and Colm for school, meanwhile stirring the porridge. Dylan, from upstairs, was calling to her about a tie he couldn't find. Patient at first, she finally shrieked, 'Find it yourself.' The booming voice answered, 'Fuck you, then, you cruel bitch.' Wife and children took no notice.

The winter of 1952–3 was difficult. Thomas's father died in December. A few weeks later 'the Marged gin woman', who was supposed to have been buying the Boat House from Margaret Taylor, and refinancing poet and family, was found dead in her London house. Talk of another American trip made Caitlin despair. Thomas told a correspondent he was 'in a tangle of doubts & debts'. David Higham, his agent, a kindly man whom the Thomases called 'lavatory brush' because of his bristly hair, sensed 'a crisis in your general affairs' and wrote offering to talk things over.

Another view is possible. *Collected Poems*, dedicated to Caitlin, was widely praised. Philip Toynbee in the *Observer* called him 'the greatest living poet'. Whether or not Thomas believed this, the book won the Foyle's Poetry Prize of £250 and was soon selling well. A collection of stories was planned; he was to edit a book of Welsh legends; even the Caedmon records were beginning to earn royalties. In the first few months of 1953 his total earnings exceeded a thousand pounds; the fact that Higham was taking half the money to pay off debts and taxes meant only that his affairs were in competent hands. The legend of how debts had him by the throat at the end of his life was created by Thomas himself.

But this cheerful logic is irrelevant. If Thomas felt trapped and desperate, as the evidence suggests, then nothing else mattered; his reasons were sufficient. John Davenport, who knew him better than most, believed that he spent his last eighteen months in 'a great state of terror' about his personality and his ability to go on being a poet.

At the root of his condition lay uncertainty about his powers, which was always present but engulfed him as youth faded and he failed to come to terms with maturity. I said all this at greater length when I wrote Thomas's biography. What I did not say, because I knew less about his marriage — and would not have been free to say it if I had known — was that his crisis of confidence had another element, the crumbling of Caitlin's affection. In later years she has made so many statements about her and Dylan that they are of little use in deciding what was in her heart during the last bitter phase of their marriage. But if her strength and security had been important to him throughout their life together, and there can be no doubt that it was, then the anger she displayed increasingly after 1951 can't have left him unmoved.

By 1953 there was another factor, her growing promiscuity. Early that year she had a further abortion, again paid for by Marged, who died soon after. Caitlin was uncertain if Dylan was the father. Whether or not he knew this, he must have been aware of her recklessness. She was sleeping with sons and husbands in a small community. Ivy Williams of Brown's knew all the gossip, not least because one of the men was connected with the family. In the end she told Thomas what was going on. According to one of Caitlin's versions (Tremlett, 1986), she assured Dylan it was lies and he believed her, saying, 'I knew it was quite absurd. I knew you would never do that.' No doubt it is less harrowing to think of him shrugging it off. But eight years earlier (Ferris, unpublished) she put it differently, saying that he 'deliberately blinded himself. He didn't want to know it. He did once or twice bring up the subject with me. But he just kind of wiped it out.'

Thomas was a perceptive man. His remark in the 1950 letter from America about her waking alone – 'please Christ, my love, it *is* always alone' – is a sufficient clue. By 1953 he knew, even if he chose not to know. The contempt for him that was implicit in her couplings with local riff-raff, brought home for an hour or two when his back was turned, must have been painful and desolating. There is not much direct evidence of how he responded, apart from the kick when he intercepted a letter; perhaps a *letter* added insult to injury, a literary slight as well. But he had lost his freedom of manoeuvre long before. Caitlin was the strong partner; dependence was in his nature. Her behaviour was part of the price he paid.

Caitlin wrote in *Leftover Life to Kill* (1957), 'He said he loved me; that I was the only woman for him; and, whatever the evidence to the contrary, I believed him, and still do.' His hangdog, over-anxious letters suggest that he could put up with anything except losing her. If he felt she had turned against him – and her willingness to heap humiliation on him made it look like that – he would be in despair. The fact that he was partly or even largely to blame for provoking her with his shiftless ways in the first place didn't stop him suffering. She was able to survive without him; he may have been unable to survive without her. This was the other element in his psychological downfall, which in turn made him reckless with his life, and would lead to his death. Nor was Caitlin in any doubt about his dependence. 'What I am missing with Dylan,' she wrote three months after his death, 'is his clinging to me, and not mine to him.'

By the spring, plans for a third American trip were well advanced. Caitlin had already written to Oscar Williams, in February, to say that

> since [Dylan] has, as good as, given up writing, for the actor's ranting boom, and lisping mimicry, anything he sells is either a rehashed bubble and squeak of adolescence, or a never to be fulfilled promise in the future. Which obviously, when the future comes, and it always does in the end, makes things very difficult.

In March Thomas was telling Brinnin that Caitlin had accused him of going for '"flattery, idleness and infidelity". This hurt me terribly. The right words were: appreciation, dramatic work, and friends.' When he had left for America, in April, Caitlin wrote to thank Brinnin for his efforts to bring her over as well. She went on, rather unfairly:

> I only wanted to tell you, who hate the crude and horrible truth, that if anything bad happens, to me or Dylan, that you are responsible. It is a dangerous thing, tampering in other people's lives, particularly when one is put on a pinnacle, and the other is left to hell, to rot. Not the basis, as they say in America, of a good relationship.

Poetry had let her down. 'I think you are a good person, too, in a limited sphere,' she wrote, 'but it is a mistake to think that *Poetry* is the beginning and end of the world.'

The trip was to be shorter than either of the previous two, lasting six weeks. Besides the usual poetry readings there would be performances of Thomas's play, which had now acquired its final title of *Under Milk Wood*. The BBC, who commissioned the work, had not yet seen it. Thomas was still writing scenes for it when he arrived in America, and Brinnin loaned him the services of his assistant at the Poetry Center, Elizabeth Reitell. Reitell was in her early thirties, a wartime lieutenant in the Women's Army Corps, later an artist. Her first response to Thomas was to find him 'an affected ass'. Her second was to fall in love with him. She was his literary minder, and he succumbed without difficulty. When she was organising a New York cast for the first performance with actors – Thomas had previously given a one-man show in Boston – she decided that 'Dylan would agree to anything as long as he didn't have to do anything about it.' He found it easy to agree to Liz Reitell, or to anyone who offered comforts. Before the affair with Reitell got under way, Pearl sought him out in Boston, and (he told Brinnin) they spent a night together.

None of this stopped letters of a familiar kind arriving in Laugharne, begging Caitlin to wait for him, spelling out his torment. Has she forgotten him? Does she hate him? Towards the end of April he sends her a hundred dollars; early in May, a further two hundred and fifty. Trying to convince Caitlin that there will be money for a holiday, he tells her to look up Majorca in his father's encyclopedia. Near the end of May, despite receiving a 'beautiful letter' from her, he continues to groan. Perhaps they will both die, perhaps she will stop loving him. Majorca is still being promised. The dream has acquired a house and two servants.

Under Milk Wood was well received. There was a plan to write the libretto for an opera by Stravinsky, to be commissioned by Boston University. Thomas should have been prospering. He returned to Britain at the beginning of June 1953, the day of Queen Elizabeth's Coronation, and lapsed into the Laugharne routines. This time it was Liz, not Pearl, who was warned to send her letters care of the Savage Club. He wrote on 16 June to say he had missed her, more of a good-friend's letter than a love letter.

It was to be a quarrelsome summer. Thomas revised *Under Milk Wood*, scratched away at a poem about his father's death, 'Elegy', and did some broadcasts. He wrote to the American poet Theodore Roethke, who planned to visit Ireland, to say that 'Caitlin, who comes from County Clare, and I want to go to Ireland, too'; it was about the nearest the Thomases came to foreign travel. A letter to Daniel Jones, arranging to meet in Swansea, said, 'Isn't life awful? Last week I hit Caitlin with a plate of beetroot, and I'm still bleeding. I can't finish a poem or begin a story'; it included a joke about drinking disinfectant.

Vernon Watkins visited Laugharne with a friend. Thomas read poems, beginning with one by Caitlin; Gwen Watkins suggests he was being conciliatory. If so it had no effect. As Thomas read 'Over Sir John's hill' and reached the line, 'Fishing in the tear of the Towy', pronouncing 'tear' to rhyme with 'bare', Caitlin repeated the word as 'tier'. They screamed the word at one another, back and forth, 'until Dylan, his face congested, shouted, "For Christ's sake, the bloody word is *there*, I wrote it!"' Aeron ran away; Colm began to scream; their parents sulked, wrapped up in their own unhappiness.

Brinnin reappeared with the American photographer Rollie McKenna, of whom Caitlin was fond. As usual, American projects were discussed. 'I had one strong and simple reaction,' wrote Brinnin: 'he should stay in Laugharne and get on with his work.' But he knew that Thomas was seeking excuses to get away. They talked about lecture tours and Stravinsky and living in California, with Dylan trying to entice Caitlin into the conversation, and Caitlin remaining withdrawn. No decisions were taken.

The agony was prolonged a little longer. Drafts of a letter to Princess Caetani, one of the sheets dated 26 August 1953, are touched with delirium. No such letter is in the Caetani archive. It was worked at but never sent, a tortuous spinning-out of words by a man who is disconnecting himself from reality. All the drafts begin, 'What can I say?', and consist of variants on a single image. He has tied himself up in a sack, blindfolded, weighed it with 'guilt and pig-iron', and thrown himself into the sea, which is full of despairing down-and-outs, 'so that time and time again I must wrestle out and unravel in a panic, like a seaslugged windy Houdini'.

His games with words at the expense of deeds had been taken to the point where action was impossible. If it was what he feared, it was also what he desired. Feverish and incapable, he locked himself up inside the letter. Phrases are crossed out and rewritten, laboured over as though he is writing a poem. But it is just a begging letter, which never even gets to the point of begging:

> up to their sockets in snails
> up to their ~~sockets~~ skulls ~~in quartz~~
> up to their skulls in crabs
> don't I smell fishy as I ooze webfooted
> ~~stink of down-at-eel ink fish~~
> cuff my hands to jingle my darbies
> like a ~~teeny~~ puny wheezy Houdini
> covered with seaweed like a halfpenny Houdini
> ~~such a pea green free for all of the glassy dead~~

What visitors saw (perhaps all that Caitlin saw, too) was the uneasy surface of these depths. One of the last to visit the Boat House was David Gardner, a young cameraman with the BBC, who had filmed

Thomas's only solo appearance on television earlier in the summer, reading a story about a charabanc outing in the series *Speaking Personally*. Because the BBC had no television studio in Wales, Thomas had to be sent where they could utilise a roving outside-broadcast unit from Bristol, which was visiting North Wales to televise a circus and a religious service. He was fitted in at St Asaph, a small town with a cathedral, using the Dean's library. Gardner was the cameraman.

Gardner had read Thomas's poetry; a journalist had told him that the poet was 'married to a by-blow of Augustus John'. After the broadcast they sat drinking at the local hotel till three in the morning. Thomas suggested he call at Laugharne one day, and a month later Gardner did so, arriving outside Brown's in his two-seater motor just as Dylan walked around the corner with his drinking friend Howard Dark. Gardner stayed the night at the Boat House, and took to what he decided was 'the very pleasant, dignified Caitlin, very courteous and kind', at one point incurring jealous glances from Dylan. What stayed in his mind as unsettling was a conversation about poetry on television, in which Thomas said that only bad poetry would be suitable, and began to recite:

> I must go down to the fucking sea again,
> To the fucking sea and the fucking sky,
> And all I ask is a tall fucking ship
> And a fucking star to steer her by.

It was still a forbidden word, though not at the Boat House. There was something manic about Thomas's use of it.

The new trip to America, which had been inevitable from the start, was arranged for October. Boston University was no longer likely to be subsidising the Stravinsky opera. The idea was that poet and composer would meet in California and begin work without financial backing, but Thomas's letter on the subject was hedged with uncertainties. At first, Caitlin was to be with him in America; then she was to stay behind.

In Laugharne, he had his hair cut by Mrs Dark, and was fitted up with a nice pair of trousers by Mr Dark, supplied at cost price. When he was leaving with Caitlin – who was to accompany him as far as London – he is said to have turned back three times to say goodbye to his mother.

In London he delivered *Under Milk Wood* to the BBC, at last, and the producer, who was Douglas Cleverdon, had it typed. A day or two later Thomas lost the manuscript in Soho, and told Cleverdon that he could keep it if he found it; a casual remark that would one day put money in lawyers' pockets. While in London the Thomases stayed with the Lockes, Cordelia and Harry, who now lived in King Street, Hammersmith. Cordelia saw that Caitlin was dreading Dylan's trip; she was also opposing it, and 'refused to pack a sock for him'. Her attitude was cold and unforgiving. After he left, on 19 October, giving a dramatic thumbs-down sign through the window of the airport bus, Caitlin is said to have 'thrown herself into Harry's arms' – the Lockes were with her in a taxi – and sobbed, 'I'm a widow-woman.'

In New York Thomas wrote no letters, or at least none survives. For two weeks he went about his business of performing in *Milk Wood*, reading poems, drinking heavily and pursuing his affair with Liz Reitell, on whom responsibility for looking after him fell almost entirely. Brinnin was only briefly in New York. By accident or design he stayed in Boston, beyond reach of Dylan's destructive friendship. To Reitell, twice married before she met Thomas (and twice more afterwards), he was, or became, the love of her life. She clung to his endearments, while recognising the strength of his attachment to the woman in Laugharne. No doubt it was a relief for him to have some affection without the customary Caitlin storms thrown in. Caitlin has said proudly that he didn't want a 'doormat wife' and 'needed opposition as much as I did. I am convinced that I am the only person who consistently opposed Dylan.' But there was something between a doormat and Caitlin on the rampage.

According to Reitell, Dylan wanted to stop drinking and was making 'strenuous efforts' to get better. If so, it was an intention at one level that he undermined at another. He knew he was unwell but did nothing about it. On 27 October he seemed particularly upset; it was his thirty-ninth birthday. His behaviour in public was sometimes deranged, and he told Reitell more than once that he was afraid of going mad. Caitlin he referred to as 'my widow'. He spoke of 'escaping' from her. Escape was on his mind; Houdini came into the conversation. Physically he had deteriorated over the previous year. He was asthmatic, prone to blackouts, almost certainly had potency problems, was racked with gout, and suffered continual gastric upsets and hangovers. Reitell's doctor, Milton Feltenstein, treated him, specifically for gout and gastritis, injecting him with cortisone.

On the night of 3–4 November, Tuesday-to-Wednesday, when he had been two weeks in America, he broke down, wept, babbled about Eden, said there was 'an illumination' about Caitlin, and, after a foray on his own into Greenwich Village, returned to Reitell at the Chelsea Hotel, boasting that he had drunk 'eighteen straight whiskies', almost certainly a lie. He slumped to the floor with his head on Reitell's lap, saying, 'I love you but I'm alone.'

This time the rhetoric may have been true. Caitlin, still with the Lockes at Hammersmith, had written in a rage, apparently incensed by receiving a small amount of money with no accompanying letter. Her letter had no salutation.

> There is only one thing worse than not having money and that is to have it flung at you as though you were a sow in a sty.
>
> So thank you very much, and it is not enough to cover remotely what needs paying, and I need more.
>
> I don't care what you say after this, nothing will ever make me go near you again.
>
> I knew you were abysmally weak, drunken, unfaithful, and a congenital liar, but it has taken me longer to realise that on top of each one of these unpardonable vices, you are a plain, stingy, meany as well.
>
> And that, along with the 3 score and ten repetitions of the same monotonously low behaviour, has just somehow done the tilt.
>
> After this dose of concentrated humiliating ignominy, I am, once and for all, finished.
>
> So please consider yourself free as shit. Caitlin.

In other circumstances the letter might have turned out to be less final than she sounded. 'Plain, stingy, meany' is a line from a quarrel, not a renunciation. The letter, too, instead of ending dramatically with 'free as shit,' started up again, working through her grievances. On the other hand, its artlessness was its power. It was Caitlin at the end of her tether.

> And when I say I shall kill myself, or go on the streets, I am not joking, I mean it. I think you underestimate a certain desperateness in my character. I shall try to stay alive as long as I can for the children, that are yours too and you care so much about, but when it gets to the point of being as unbearable as [?Donnadieu] found it, and no simple point to make it worth living, which it did and is, then, in spite of the children, I am bound, one way or another, to snuff myself out.

I have never before been quite so miserable, and that is true, or left in quite such depressing circumstances, and will never understand your motive for deliberately making me suffer, when you have quite genuinely to my mind, but then I am an awful fool and this proves it, seemed to love me. In an attic, unwanted, with no money, while you snigger and snicker, and swank and betray me, it beggars description. And your behaviour by not sending that one word which would cost less than a farthing of your precious time – is unforgivable, eternally and for ever *unforgivable*.

Will you please send me more money as soon as you can, as I can't bear being summonsed in all directions, and they are your bills as well as mine. Also to keep me intact till Christmas, as I think I must see that through, whether I want to or not. After I don't know. But this time you need not bother about putting the words in, not that you did before, it doesn't matter any more. I would suggest, that since you are so happy in America it would be wisest to stay there. There is, without exception, no wife in the whole of creation treated like I am, and at last it's over, for better or for worse. And no more slop talk, let's at least cut that out – you may be good at it, but it stinks to high heaven, turn it on one of your new adulators, it always goes down. Whatever you do or say, however foul, always goes down, fuck you.

It's never before happened to me that people stop in the street to ask what is the matter, why am I so downhearted, and would I like 3 pennies for my fare home. If only they knew I hadn't got a bloody home, and it's the last place in the world I want to go. And I want this to be quite clear that when something, which will if I am driven any more, happens to me, it is *not* unintentional and *you* are unreservedly the cause of it.

By having a lump of iron slop, instead of a man's heart in your flabby breast, and if there was any justice, which there isn't, no good would come of it.

The proof is – me with the bleeding heart am bleeding to death, you with a big bag of hypocrisy are crowing on your dunghill.

The letter carried no hint of an admission that her actions may have contributed to his, just as his contributed to hers. But attack, for Caitlin, was always the best form of defence. In the event, Thomas never saw the letter. The envelope was franked in Hammersmith on the evening of Monday 2 November, addressed care of Brinnin in Boston. On the night of the 'eighteen straight whiskies' it may not have left the United Kingdom.

The following day, Wednesday, Thomas recovered momentarily, only to drift into sickness and alcoholic delirium, attended by Reitell. That evening Dr Feltenstein injected him with half a grain of morphine, a dangerous dose for someone in such a debilitated condition. His breathing was affected, and he went into an irreversible coma. His despair had put him in the way of encouraging death; he had found the only possible way out of the trap.

Caitlin's letter, meanwhile, was somewhere *en route*. Anything she said or did now mattered nothing to him: only to her.

10

A Life of Her Own

Caitlin heard the news on Thursday evening. She was in the audience at the Memorial Hall in Laugharne for a live radio programme in a Welsh Home Service series called *Vintage Town*, which included a contribution that Thomas recorded before going to America. About half his talk was used, an amiable minute or two about 'this waylaying, old, lost Laugharne'. During the broadcast a telegram was handed to Caitlin, to say that Dylan had been 'hospitalised'. Her first reaction, she says, was to put the news out of her mind. She 'seems to remember' going on to a dance after the broadcast. The pattern of how she would behave was being set even before Thomas died.

One of her problems was that she wouldn't dissimulate. When she felt grief, she showed it. When she felt angry, or needed a drink – or, from now on, physical comforting – she behaved accordingly. Tact or propriety didn't come into it. What the world would see of Caitlin the widow, as she became the someone-different who can wait a lifetime to emerge, and for most people never does, was a wild and reckless woman. She spends her old age deploring it. There were always other Caitlins behind the scenes, wiser and self-critical. But most people had to take her at her face value.

On the Friday, she went to London and stayed overnight with the Lockes in Hammersmith. After a send-off lunch on Saturday, probably organised by Margaret Taylor and paid for by the McAlpines, she boarded the plane for what was then a twelve-hour flight to New York, and settled down to drink duty-free whisky. A telegram to Oscar Williams, the kindly poet, said she was arriving at Idlewild at 8.00 am on Sunday, and would someone please bring money to pay her excess fare; she took plenty of clothes.

The weather in New York was cold, with sleet. The Slivkas, Rose and Dave, were at the airport with a station wagon they had borrowed from Rollie McKenna. Cheeks pink, hair radiant, Caitlin seemed in high spirits, brushing aside Dylan's condition as if, now that she was there, her presence could awaken him. The whisky was still at work. Escorted by police motor-cycles that the British Consul had organised, they swept into the city, and deposited Caitlin at the Slivkas' house in Greenwich Village, for her to take a bath and change before going to the hospital.

Thomas had been admitted to St Vincent's, also in the Village, twelve blocks from the hotel where he collapsed. It was reputable and not too expensive, built as the first charity hospital in New York a century earlier and now run by the Roman Catholic church. Friends and hangers-on gathered there over the weekend; too many for comfort. Among the inner circle was Brinnin, half in love with Dylan and apprehensive about Caitlin; David Lougee, the young poet, star-struck with them both, who said that 'Dylan worshipped her. I would have, too'; and Ruthven Todd, a London poet who had known the Thomases since the Thirties and now lived in New York.

Caitlin, wearing a black dress, arrived with Rose Slivka and at once began causing trouble. 'Is the bloody man dead yet?', or a question along those lines, set the tone. A small crowd in a corridor was keeping watch on Thomas through a glass panel. Lines were connected for feeding and monitoring, and he was inside an oxygen tent. Left alone with him in the room, she was aware of the audience on the other side of the glass, and, as she was apt to do, wondered how she ought to behave. Her abiding sense of ignorance plagued her. Just as no one had told her what to do in bed with a man, or in the throes of childbirth, so, apparently, there were no instructions for how to behave with a dying husband. She was very drunk. An attempt to roll a cigarette was not successful. It occurred to her that Dylan might need warming up, so she tried to get her body on top of his. On both counts, the risk of breaking the tent and of blowing it up with a match, she had to be restrained and taken out. Rose Slivka says she even tried to pull the lines from his body because they were in her way.

'He died for me before he left,' she wrote, squeezing maximum drama from the situation, for which one can hardly blame her. 'That other staged death of the flesh was but a corroborative complement to the poet lost in himself.' The image of the man in the tent assumed gross proportions. She remodelled him – certainly when she tried to make literature out of it later, but perhaps at the time, in her frenzy, as she rushed about the corridors at St Vincent's – seeing him as a child she was losing, her 'cherished beloved child that was so much a part of me that more than any other child that was torn out of me with roaring protests, he was torn out of me that dying instant'.

On a more prosaic level, there were exciting death-bed scenes to witness. So far only Brinnin and Reitell had been allowed to sit with Thomas. Reitell was still in the hospital when Caitlin arrived. She was keeping out of the way, although Caitlin had never heard of her. Perhaps they were introduced in suitably tactful terms. All Brinnin says in his account is that Reitell was 'sitting alone at the far end of the corridor'. But Caitlin later chided him, in a not unfriendly letter, for having 'the effrontery to introduce me to those drabs of wet nurses who so considerately jump into bed with Dylan, just for his sake'.

If Caitlin had known about Reitell as the mistress in whose arms her husband had collapsed, she might have sought her out and delivered the 'smashing punch on the nose' that she talked about in later life. As it was, she tried to strangle the trembling Brinnin, who represented America and its poisonous lures, while Rose, who was not herself, screamed, 'Go for the jugular, baby!' Being athletic, Caitlin did some swinging from curtain rails, for no apparent reason, and also broke a figure of the Virgin and a crucifix, not a wise thing to do on Catholic premises. In her old age she explained that this was not random sacrilege but anger that God had repaid her devotion by depriving her of Dylan.

After biting an attendant on the hand and clawing at a nun, she was put in a straitjacket. Rose, screaming and crying on her behalf, was put in one as well, but quickly talked her way out of it. When Caitlin was strapped up, she began flirting with an Italian doctor. But instead of persuading him that she was harmless, like Rose, she became malevolent, according to Lougee, asking him how he would like to be castrated, then threatening to harm his children. Eventually, with cash provided by Feltenstein, whose conscience may have been troubling him, a private ambulance took her away, still tied up, with the Slivkas and Ruthven Todd in attendance, to a private clinic on Long Island. There, out of restraints, she remained for two or three days, weeping and wandering about the wards in an institutional shift with tapes at the back. She says that she begged a psychiatrist to let her go because 'I have got to see Dylan', and he replied, 'I suppose you know your husband is dead?'* He had been dead since midday on Monday 9 November.

Brinnin and Reitell had maintained their vigil at the bedside. 'We sometimes took his hands in ours,' wrote Brinnin, 'sometimes spoke softly to him in the last hope that some small word of love and comfort might penetrate the limbo in which he lay.' It was Brinnin who gave the cold feet a squeeze a moment after death; Reitell who whispered to the corpse and kissed it on the forehead. This was too formal and well bred a scene for Caitlin. It may be that unconsciously she arranged things so that she would not be there; this would explain Todd's story, that she went into the clinic voluntarily. To sit dutiful and wifelike at the bedside, concealing her thoughts behind the simple mask of grief, might have been beyond her capability. The sorrowing was real enough. She was haunted by the hospital scenes, by 'the familiar hands that always broke my heart, lying as they had lain in sleep' – hands were full of meaning for her, her father's, square and ugly, her own, that she inherited from him and constantly gnawed, and Dylan's delicate pair, like fish-fins, she said. But she was still furious with him. It was his folly that had brought him back to America. It was his uselessness that had made her write the letter from Hammersmith. Behind the grief was her conviction that their marriage had been over. Now that he was dead, she was free.

The Slivkas looked after her when she left the clinic, and she and Rose spent the best part of a week in one another's company, staying in adjacent beds half the day, talking about everything except Dylan, taking hours to dress and bathe, stumbling about in a dream interrupted only by alcohol and shopping expeditions. Rose had an unaffected sympathy for Caitlin that kept them in step, letting her slow down to her friend's recuperative pace. One of their trips was to Lord & Taylor's, intending to buy another black dress. Instead they bought one in shocking pink velvet. 'Don't ever tell anybody,' said Caitlin. She asked Rose if she thought it likely that the townsfolk of Laugharne would ever think she looked like a proper widow. 'If only you had a

---

* This is Caitlin's version. Ruthven Todd, who was at the clinic, said that she signed herself in as a voluntary patient, which means she could have left whenever she chose. No single participant's account of a day like that is going to be trustworthy. The ambulance invoice for twenty-five dollars can be believed: so can the bill from River Crest Sanitarium, $137.00.

little less shape,' said Rose, smiling, 'everyone would think you looked *much* properer.'

Rose liked Caitlin's nature, 'funny, cruel and real', and continued to take an understanding view of her as the artist's wife, relegated to second-best. She was with her when a deputation of the American Welsh arrived in their best suits, bearing a cheque that Caitlin thought miserly; at a memorial service where Caitlin sat at the front and Reitell was somewhere at the back; at the pier where she boarded the *United States* on 17 November for the voyage home. But Rose was friendly with Elizabeth Reitell. Her private view was that Dylan (who once asked Mrs Slivka to sleep with him) lived a messy life, and that Reitell was 'a secretary, a soldier, an adorer', who, when Thomas was adrift in New York, 'at least kept things straight'.

None of this was divulged to Caitlin. But word of it must have got through, because some time afterwards a letter came from Laugharne, asking if it was true that she was friendly with that Reitell woman. Rose replied that she didn't want to have to defend herself. She never heard from Caitlin again.

The funeral, at Laugharne, was arranged for 24 November, two weeks and one day after Thomas died. Only one of the children – Colm, the youngest, aged four – was at home, being looked after by Dolly Long. Aeron, aged ten, was at a Hertfordshire boarding school studying ballet and drama; her Aunt Nicolette went there to break the news. Llewelyn, aged fourteen, at Magdalen College school, which he hated, had been told by his headmaster. From his mother he heard nothing, nor did he expect to.

Llewelyn had developed a stoicism: 'I never missed my parents. I never knew them.' He found her 'not a bad mother in the usual sense, but inclined to be cruel, feckless, thoughtless'. Any kindness she showed, like the presents she gave, required the recipient to be there in person, 'as if she needed her children to show their reaction'. His long stay as a child with his grandmother in the New Forest was not, he says, a source of resentment; his mother's often-expressed guilt about it was unnecessary. What he resented was the school, the bloody boarding school. Beyond that are other perceptions. 'I was never golden,' he says. 'Colm was golden. He still is, a bit.'*

* Colm's views about this, or anything, are not available: he disliked the idea of a book about his mother, and declined any part in it.

On the day of the funeral, Caitlin (who had caused scenes going back on the ship) did nothing especially outrageous. She spent two hours getting ready. Because the Boat House was so inaccessible, the coffin had been left at Pelican, old Mrs Thomas's house in the main street; now and again Caitlin slipped up to the top floor, where she had secreted a bottle of whisky. Afterwards she wrote scornfully of the crowd that came, the 'raffish Londoners' and 'Swansea boys in their best provincial suits', but at the time she was quiet, pale and composed. Among the six bearers and four reserves were two of Caitlin's local lovers, actual or impending; one was Howard Dark, the travelling draper, whose good Welsh trousers had been passed over in favour of a foreign suit, supplied to clothe the embalmed body, and which, as the Laugharne joke went, Dylan wouldn't have been seen dead in. The hands were gloved; it was noted, as though proof of American insensitivity, that Dylan never wore gloves.

When the coffin passed down the aisle of St Michael's Church, Caitlin leaned over Daniel Jones, who was next to her, and touched the lid. David Gardner, the cameraman, who had come over from Bristol as a mourner, not for the BBC, thought it 'a nice gesture, I think rehearsed'. During the interment she thought of jumping into the grave, on the grounds that it would have looked 'pretty sensational'. But Dr Jones had her arm locked in his, even if she had been serious.

A piece of crucial business was enacted or set in motion during the day, when Jones spoke to Stuart Thomas, a Swansea solicitor and friend who had also known Thomas, about setting up a trust that would administer the income from Thomas's work, which was expected to be small, for the benefit of Caitlin and the children. They brought in a third person who was at the funeral, Thomas's agent, David Higham. At the time it seemed no more than a necessary formality. The existing estate consisted solely of bad debts. Caitlin's views were sought and she agreed. Whether she was ever sober on the day of the funeral is another matter, but in any case the trust deed wasn't drawn up and signed by her for many weeks.

In time Caitlin would seek to prove that she was unfit to sign anything for the remainder of the year. An affidavit from Cordelia Locke said that at the funeral, Caitlin (looking 'very lovely in a black dress') appeared to be 'controlled in a terrible sort of way'. Caitlin's sister Nicolette did rather better, attesting that on the night following the funeral, Caitlin decided to kill herself by jumping over the cliff.

Nicolette tried to humour her by saying they would jump together, and they proceeded towards the edge. At the last minute Nicolette pointed out that if she jumped she would ruin her coat; at which they turned back.

The pubs were busy, and Caitlin was watched for signs of misbehaviour. Always at her worst when she knew people expected it, she gave a disappointing display, under the circumstances. At Brown's she knocked pints of beer off a tray and wetted Fred Janes, who was carrying it. She flung aside a box of chocolates that a well-wisher was offering, and managed to insult several people. Vernon Watkins – who had difficulty persuading the bank to give him a day off – watched the goings-on with dismay. Once, Caitlin leaned her head on his shoulder; he kissed her forehead.

According to Laugharne folklore, the evening ended with Caitlin doing high kicks in her black dress under the street lamps; old Mrs Thomas, who had much to cope with – husband and only son, as well as only daughter, had now all died within a year – whispered to friends about her daughter-in-law's shameless exhibition. Caitlin spent the night sedately enough, according to her own account, sharing a room at the Castle, which opened its doors to guests, with Nicolette.

Conventional mourning didn't appeal to Caitlin. At Brown's, following the funeral, she had recognised David Gardner, greeting him as 'the little boy' who had previously come to stay. Anxious to help the penniless widow, he offered her money, which she refused. Her problem was loneliness, she said. Next week she intended going to London; why didn't they go up together?

He had to meet her in Swansea, where she was visiting Stuart Thomas, the third prospective trustee. Thomas, a saturnine but witty solicitor who gave good parties with his wife Eve, assisted his father in a small family business; later on he ran it himself. It was 1 December. Gardner says that Caitlin insisted on drinking whisky at ten in the morning. She signed some papers and they took the train to London, where they made for the Locke residence in Hammersmith. Caitlin had been drinking steadily ('Call that a sole?' she said to the dining-car attendant on the train), and in the evening, when they were all at a pub in King Street, she attacked a stranger.

Gardner, a young man of Welsh origins, not sure where he stood, withdrew from the proceedings and fell asleep in the third-floor room that Cordelia Locke had offered him. During the night Caitlin went into his room, and swung herself out of the window while clinging to the velvet curtains. The curtains broke and she fell, fracturing her collar bone. Because the house was at the end of a parade of shops, a flat roof projected at second-storey level, so the fall was not more than about eight feet. Gardner, who was to be a close friend for the next couple of years, concluded that she was hanging on to the curtains and daring God to punish her, in the knowledge that she didn't have far to fall.

Again she found herself incarcerated. The hospital that treated her injury had her seen by a psychiatrist, whose case notes described her as 'the youngest of four daughters of an Irish poet – a friend of Yeats, Augustus John etc'. His information came from Nicolette, who liked to be colourful – 'Patient has always been impulsive and difficult. She is apt to be suddenly violent [. . .] She was a brilliant dancer and writer.' The psychiatrist observed that she was now a chronic alcoholic, drinking half a bottle of whisky and 'much beer' every day, and briskly diagnosed her as a paranoid psychopath. Years later (when Caitlin was pursuing her claim of having been incompetent to sign the trust deed) the same doctor said it was 'suicidal melancholia', but the daring-God theory sounds more likely. She was to make various suicide attempts over the years, always half-hearted:

Nicolette had her taken to a private clinic outside London, at Virginia Water, where she stayed several days, writing sane letters about her future. David Gardner was told he had been 'simply wonderful', and to remember that she was 'downright bad':

> It is true my sorrow is genuine, horribly horribly genuine, that is why I am trying so desperately, and unsuccessfully, to kill it. But that is not going to stop me being the biggest bitch on earth if I feel like it.

She told David Lougee that she jumped out of the window 'trying to break my broken heart. No success as usual, and they can't even prove me mad, so got to let me out'.

America was the place she had her eye on – ironically, considering all she had said about the country. Colm and her mother-in-law could go with her. Ruth Witt-Diamant, who had organised the San Francisco readings, wrote to say they could stay at her house; in the meantime she ordered butter, bacon, sweets and whisky to be sent to Caitlin from Fortnum's in London to help them over Christmas.

Laugharne, as a place to live, was out of the question. Margaret Taylor, who had problems of her own, Alan Taylor having finally left her, was anxious to sell the Boat House to Caitlin at the knock-down price of thirteen hundred pounds. But Caitlin didn't have thirteen hundred pennies, and in any case, as she told Brinnin, Laugharne was 'a permanently festering wound' that she had to escape from. 'All I can think about is Dylan, and where he is lying, while I am lying alone, and what is happening to his head, and hands, and body'; though the phrase about 'lying alone' was not strictly true. When she left the Virginia Water clinic, on or near her fortieth birthday, she sent Gardner (who had returned to his base in Bristol) a telegram to say, 'Can't you come, Don Juan?' He soon joined her in Hammersmith, and they became lovers. At Christmas, when she was back in Laugharne, he came to stay at Brown's. Daniel Jones and his wife were at the Boat House, but Gardner moved in for a day or two when they had left. After that he was a frequent visitor; he says Caitlin insisted they shouldn't use the double bed upstairs where she had slept with Dylan.

On Boxing Day she wrote to Lougee ('Darling D') to say that she was 'full of brandy, wine, beer, whisky, gin; all the poisons in creation, so take no notice of what I say. I shall not start getting good till after Christmas. The trouble is starting: anything.'

Marriage had subdued but never erased her certainty of her own potential. Perhaps it was simply the response of a woman who was inwardly unsure, needing to keep up her spirits with endless demonstrations of herself in public. Life was a drama with her at the centre. When, aged twenty, Caitlin Macnamara went back to Ireland, which meant the deep waters of her earliest memories, it was 'like a story that had happened before, where [I] could foretell the sequence of events, and recognise [my] favourite passages'. Visiting Paris before she met Dylan, she was 'the heroine of an enchanting farce'. Such illusions helped her, as they help many, though few carry them to such lengths. The trait doesn't 'explain' Caitlin but at least it suggests a way of looking at her. Thus some of her frustration with being Mrs Dylan Thomas arose from his failure to be a satisfactory part of her story (in which he was her poet, her private treasure), while at the same time she was dragged into playing a walk-on part in his.

Now that he was dead, she could be herself again, the leading player. Caitlin had a powerful streak of self-indulgence, inherited from her father; at the same time she was aware of another kind of life, rigorous and creative. This harsher Caitlin may have developed her belief in punishment and 'just desserts' to try and counter the inherited failings that she found in herself, among them Francis's coarse promiscuity in sex. She certainly despised her father for having dissipated his talents in chattering and drinking. It was this puritanical Caitlin who regretted her husband's weaknesses in the same department, while respecting his endeavour, for most of his life, to keep the writing of poetry as a thing apart. Her own talent for dancing, if ever she had one, had long since vanished in drunken ecstasies. Were she to achieve artistic individuality, it would have to be as a writer. She tucked away the idea for future reference.

Her original intention was to leave Laugharne early in 1954. Thoughts of Mediterranean skies and the man who owned the hotel on Elba cheered her up through January. Leslie Daiken – vaguely remembered as someone connected with the media, a wit and drinking pal, probably platonic – sent her a set of teach-yourself-Italian records. Before she could leave, arrangements had to be made for Colm, aged four. He was having nightmares and panic-attacks. Caitlin tried to persuade her mother-in-law to look after him, with Dolly Long to do the work; unfortunately, as she wrote to Daiken, 'his Granny is being tough about keeping him while I am away, in fact, I don't think she will, the bitch'.

Florence Thomas irritated Caitlin at the best of times, with her chattering and her ideas of decorum. Now, the old woman's sharp eye was on everything she did. Florence's greatest pleasure was to talk about Dylan and the past. Caitlin once threatened to kill her if she didn't stop, then was filled with remorse to hear her say, 'You and the children are all I have left in the world.' Later, Caitlin wrote about her with sympathy, a woman 'attuned to catastrophe' who accepted her son's death – 'not as I did, cracking with revenge, breaking with murder, but with what . . . might have been almost a sigh of relief as though tidying away in a bottom drawer the outgrown useless baby's bootees, scalloped socks, the fleecy white shrouding shawls'. In 1954 they were the wrong natures to be left together, with their memories of two different Dylans.

Poverty and how to avoid it took up a lot of Caitlin's time. With so much sympathy being expressed for the poet's family, she naturally hoped that hard cash would follow, and she pursued any hint of it.

Funds in Britain and America were collecting thousands of pounds. Nothing, though, had been handed over – in some cases it wouldn't be, for years – and the fund-raisers' first priority was the children. Unwise remarks by Caitlin to newspapers made benefactors hesitate. In an interview with the *Sunday Express* she spoke of looking forward to a holiday on Elba, followed by residence in her native Ireland, since Wales held no attractions; her photograph was captioned 'I've a cheque book now'. Welsh mayors and subscribers were displeased. In New York they heard rumours of unwidowlike behaviour. 'Why are those bastard Americans so down on me, making all these ridiculous difficulties,' she wrote to David Higham, raging at 'that sanctimonious *them*'.

The Trust to handle Thomas's work, which had now been set up, was sending her eight pounds a week to keep herself and Colm, while it sorted out the debts. Hopeful creditors – milkmen, radio producers, poets, Brown's Hotel – waved bills and ancient dishonoured cheques. Eight pounds was a fleabite to Caitlin, though it was a living wage at the time. A few drinks and meals and pairs of shoes, and it had gone. Like Dylan, she believed in taxis and first-class tickets. 'I am incapable of travelling cheap,' she told her friend Daiken (12 February), 'and would rather be rich on a dunghill than starving to death in a castle.' The Trust had no time for this. It made anxious noises about the future, some of them no doubt to impress Caitlin with how serious things were. Its first estimate of annual royalty earnings was an average of five hundred pounds, lasting for only six or seven years. Instead, the income rose quickly and went on rising for decades, until the estate was earning that amount in a week, even allowing for the effects of inflation.

It took a while for Dylan Thomas to become established as a popular figure. As late as 1962 his former friend, Constantine FitzGibbon, was declining the trustees' invitation to write the official Life on the grounds that all Dylan ever did was scribble poems and be amusing. But Thomas was already a candidate for the public's gallery of mad artists; even the names 'Dylan' and 'Caitlin' would soon be popular for children of literary parents. His books and recordings became valuable commercial properties.

The Trust was officially in business from 28 December 1953. The settlement, which was irrevocable, allowed the trustees to accumulate capital and pay income, half to Caitlin, the other half divided among the children, to be held in trust for them till they were twenty-five. Daniel Jones the composer gave literary advice on texts. David Higham the agent handled the works themselves and collected the income. Stuart Thomas was in day-to-day charge of the Trust from his office in Swansea.

The town, then in the process of being rebuilt after the bombing, embodied the lower-middle-class provincialism in which Dylan Thomas was always at home, and which Caitlin despised. A network of businessmen, doctors, solicitors, accountants, council officials and university lecturers lived congenial social lives in the western suburbs. Kingsley Amis, a lecturer at the local university college, was there, about to be famous with his first novel, *Lucky Jim*. His later poems about 'Aberdarcy', a disguise for Swansea, describe the amiable philistinism he rubbed shoulders with. He was in the town until 1961, and became a lifelong friend of Stuart Thomas. Caitlin herself would have counted as a friend of Thomas and his wife Eve at one time, but the friendship was tenuous and lay outside Swansea, in London pubs and restaurants in Rome. In 1954, when no one knew how the Trust would develop, Caitlin was soon accusing the trustees of 'Welsh bourgeois meanness' and making enquiries to see if they could be got rid of (they could not). Jones, due in London for a Dylan Thomas function where Caitlin might be present,* told a friend, 'You'll recognise me quite easily. I shall be in a full suit of armour.'

London, which she visited on brief sorties when she could, was as far as she got for the moment. Elba was deferred. She told Stuart Thomas on 7 February that it was important for her to stay near Colm,

> otherwise he will think I've gone up in the sky too, where he thinks all the other Thomases have gone . . . On the other hand if I am literally driven out, by the hounds of loneliness – I have only just started being completely alone with the child, bar Mably dog, and Dolly, half human half animal, in the day; it all depends how I shall weather it; I shall just pack up, snatch up the boy and go, in spite of all impediments.
>
> But I intend having a try the tough way first.

The letter also enclosed a bill for Colm's shoes; said she couldn't

---

* 'Homage to Dylan Thomas' at the Globe Theatre, 'A Programme of Poetry, Dance & Music'. Edith Sitwell, Louis MacNeice, Richard Burton, Edith Evans and Emlyn Williams were among those taking part. Caitlin was present, not enjoying herself.

afford a rag for her back; complained that one of the trustees, Dan Jones, had been round the shops in Laugharne on behalf of the Trust, forbidding them to give her credit ('What am I, a half wit, you all make a big mistake'); and took mysterious objection to Stuart Thomas's letter that returned her husband's personal 'effects' from America ('do you find it absolutely necessary to use such vulgar terms to me, when sending along tuppence worth of trash; wouldn't "things" be more suitable; and you could save the effects for your posh customers').

Caitlin herself is convinced that she made a prompt exit from Laugharne, that 'within a few weeks, I had gone', and others have taken her word for it. A notice at the Boat House tells visitors that Caitlin and the children left 'shortly after Dylan's death'. But it was more painful than that. 'Please help me,' she wrote to Daiken; 'I am as helpless as a Siamese twin, when it comes to parting with this body of Laugharne.' She found some solace in hanging on – behaving badly, defying ostracism, choking on her complicated memories. 'They wanted a saint and a scapegoat,' she wrote later, 'so in primitive clay they fashioned them out of us [. . .] and the whiter they painted him, the blacker, by contrast, they painted me.'

Having invited censure, she did all she could to deserve it. Whatever she was – hurt, grieving, furious, poor – the world had to know about it. 'I long for the violence and drama of a strait-jacket,' she wrote to Nicolette (4 January). Vivid stories circulated, some of them true. In Swansea she created havoc in a pub and even worse in Daniel Jones's house, wrecking a room, making sexual advances to a visitor, attacking Jones's wife. At Laugharne, books and broken furniture from the Boat House bobbed on the tide. Men slipped in to see Caitlin when they hoped no one was looking.

Granny Thomas, who presently moved out of Laugharne altogether, was not equipped to take a compassionate view. She told her friends about the goings-on, with details. So did Caitlin.

Letters she wrote to David Gardner, whom she caricatured as a sweet boy in love with a wicked lady, show her fascinated with her own condition and perfectly aware of what she was doing. On 12 February she wrote from the Boat House:

I always have the impression that you are in holy terror of being swallowed up, devoured, clung to; and finally masticated up into shreds of drowned cabbage [but] I am not a clinger, never have been, and what I am missing with Dylan is his clinging to me, and not mine to him; because I have never done it, and never will [. . .]

If I go on, as I have been this last week, alone; though it is barely a whole week yet; on this fantastically virtuous bender; I shall be so disgustingly upright, nobody will be able to get near me at all. And without the drink, that is serious drink [. . .] I don't talk at all, and I don't want dirty old sex, and men, within miles . . . so perhaps some people will be wishing for the good old bad Caitlin again. That's what comes of doing everything to excess, good and bad. And that is why I did not yet trust myself with a visit to London; being on the *merest* brink of redemption [. . .]

But at the end of the month I intend stepping out with some other classy girl friend, Ivy Williams [of Brown's Hotel] to London, and the high spots. *Not* 'Under Milk Wood' for me thank you [the BBC re-broadcast the play in February]. So *please* dear David, try to be there, money or no money, it would help us both.

After the visit, she was writing to Gardner to say that 'I have never had a good person before', that she needed him, that 'You are the only person can make me come, every now and then, at great trouble, with infinite patienza.' At the same time she was warning him to keep away from her. Other letters ticked off her shortcomings, 'the super bitch' who was 'the scourge of Laugharne' and 'going steadily downhill' while 'scandal accumulates daily'. During another London visit in May, when Gardner wasn't there all the time, she was arrested for being drunk and disorderly and kept in a police cell. It began, she told him, with her 'being on the loose, alone, and unhappy. So much for your chaste girl friend; let us banish the last illusion'.

Caitlin needed confessors. She wrote to Daiken on 18 June:

I have not had a man since[—], which is over a week ago; and that little spot of animal madness; though I assure you an animal would be a lot more sensitive; cost me the last shreds of my tattered reputation [. . .] I hardly dare go to the Browns [. . .] except out of bravado, as all the genteel cows look through me, and the saucepan boys pinch my bottom on the sly, as though I were the lowest whore, that should be felt, but not seen in company. Me, a whore, I wish I was, I would be a lot better off; but that is a skilled job that I am quite incapable of performing.

Nicolette was sent a letter on the same day. It began by swearing 'not to say a word more about my fascinatingly morbid, to me, condition; with which I have bored the pants off everybody, even my own', but soon came back to the ever-interesting topic:

I live in a kind of Coventry; and my social life consists of sitting, when I can have it, in a gloom-dripping, half-empty, frigidly-hushed pub of smug, self-righteous, genteely-bristling-with-indignation faces; carefully averted from monstrous me. The whole bloody bunch of morons make me sick, to tell you the truth, and I couldn't care less, but it does make living among them a lonely and silent affair. [—] is the worst, like a rabid bitch on heat, since I played around with that oaf [—] the one who fancied you [. . .] So really, my dear, I must pull myself together, and get out, while the going's good, and before I am given the boot.

I am concentrating on September, for Elba and Eldorado; much the same peasant community as this, by the way, only Italian. And trying to get the rusty wheels of the [presumably American] fund, sitting pretty on a discarded scrap heap, into action; and make it produce some steam, which it refuses to do so far. It will be a hell of a tough job.

Caitlin was involved with a number of men in Laugharne, but it would be difficult to make a list, and there would be no point. In old age, when she could be persuaded to talk about her casual lovers at all, she liked to see them as primitives (or 'village oafs'), quarrymen and miners with good strong bodies who got on with the job. She did have a weakness for the type, but she wasn't fussy. She had another weakness, for men of short stature, perhaps because they weren't perceived as a threat. Tall, physically dominant men had menaced her in the past: her father, Augustus John, the disappointing Caspar. People had to be incorporated into her life, and Dylan Thomas, the poet she selected, was (in her words, later on) a shrimp. David Gardner, deeply involved and in love with her in 1954, was small-statured. So were at least two of the Laugharne contingent, one of them the Howard Dark who was present when Caitlin said that she liked 'athletic men', and Dylan replied sarcastically, 'Describes us exactly.'

Dark, with his van of clothes, was a sociable tradesman who went duck-shooting and liked women; his wife divorced him (for cruelty) after Caitlin's time. His manner was crafty and insidious; Dylan called him 'the gnat'. But he wasn't a 'village oaf', and Caitlin seems to have enjoyed his company and regarded him as a friend as well as a lover. Writing to him from abroad, she complained when he didn't write back. An undated note, probably written from Laugharne, reads, 'Darling, Darling, Darling, Darkie, Dark. Terribly with you. Cait.'

Wickedness appealed to Caitlin. When she was in the mood she exaggerated both the extent of her depravity in the village, and the effect she had on the inhabitants. If they could, she wrote in *Fool*, 'they would sling me up by the heels to a cross bar in the middle of the Grist square, tar and feather me and burn me alive'. She sounds angrier than she needed to be, heaping scorn on 'those low-trash poor, complete with three-piece polished unsittable suites', owning small motor-cars and 'gargantuan giant Hoovers'.

She derided the men for going off on the bus at seven in the morning to do labouring work at the 'Experimental' along the coast at Pendine – a high-security establishment where explosives were tested, with bangs and columns of smoke; the Cold War brought prosperity. She derided them again for going home at five 'to contemplate their fat wives bending over the kitchen range'. Did she hate the townspeople because they hated her, or because they annoyed her for constituting a closed community with a will as iron as hers, on which she could make no more impression than she and her Macnamara forebears had ever been able to do in Co. Clare? Something made her vituperative. What she quaintly called 'birth-control rubber millinery' had 'not yet reached this backward area – they prefer to fish it out after with a knitting needle or an extra long strong bodkin, or wait for normal delivery and surreptitiously stuff it up the "chimbley".' It is an odd outburst, given Caitlin's own track record in this area.

For most of 1954 she went to and fro between Wales and London, but found herself still tethered to the Boat House,

ceaselessly making beds [. . .] throwing things out, old clothes, papers, especially papers; it seemed I should never rid myself of the curse of print, handwriting, letters with people at the end of them [. . .] And the familiarity of his presence breathed on me in every room and most of all in our room, in our bed that we had grooved together in a joint hollow in the middle. I fell for the whole bag of cowardly evasive tricks, drinking myself to death, useless men, mock suicides. Not one of them worked, possibly because I did not, deep down, expect them to.

The Trust bought the Boat House from Margaret Taylor in June, so there was no longer any fear of losing it. Caitlin manoeuvred with the trustees, occasionally purring, usually showing claws. 'Not yours,' she signed a letter to Stuart Thomas. Details were beneath her; she was purposely vague about the kind of things people in offices were interested in. Asked by the solicitor for the date of her birth, she said it was 1914; asked about her marriage, she wrote, 'Can't remember, but, judging by Llewelyn, about 16 years back'; she was only a year out. Often she felt deserted, or posed as a woman deserted – impossible to be sure which – when urging the Trust to send more money,

> if not for my sake (as all the dear friends so kindly say), for Dylan's. It would certainly be a major miracle if somebody did something for my sweet sake alone. But that would be too much to ask. Dylan would be the only person to do that; and God help you all if he was here now.

On another occasion she told Stuart Thomas that she was ashamed of having been in 'such an incapable state, not even able to stand up', when they last met. But she was 'not, as might appear, entirely irresponsible, and soon I shall get much better. I am just waiting for the sun.' As it happened, it was one of the wettest summers for years. She bought a dinghy for the children and named it 'Cuckoo', and they all rowed in the estuary.

Aeron remembers picnics. Still at the Hertfordshire school, she had seen little of her mother since her father's death. Nicolette, she says, suggested that the Devases adopt her, an idea that infuriated Caitlin. Llewelyn doesn't even remember picnics – 'In the Aeron world there may have been. In the real world we lit a fire and came back.' But he was older and better equipped to assert himself than his sister, who was only ten when Dylan Thomas died, and who for years languished in Caitlin's embrace. The phrase isn't hers. Both she and Llewelyn are circumspect in what they say about their mother. Neither is at ease when asked about her. Some of Aeron's memories are unhappy, but they become unimportant (she says) when she meets her mother and they revive their intimacy. Llewelyn is more detached and sometimes sardonic. Detachment was a skill he soon acquired. Dolly Long's family still have his book of pressed plants – 'Unknown, Cliff Walk, July 27 1954. Great Bindweed, Bell-house, Laugharne, August 11 1954.'

By August Caitlin had decided to take the plunge and go to Elba. The Trust could afford to buy the tickets, and Colm would go with her. She told Brinnin she was 'filled with a mixture of terror at going, and despair at the hopelessness of trying to start something new'. Ostensibly the 'something new' included writing. Letters during the year referred to it half-heartedly. 'I have been told to write,' she said. 'but what about? [. . .] I have a lot of things to say, but don't know which way to say them.' She had written something about the village halfwit, Booda, a deaf mute who was suspected, a year or two earlier, of going to a laundrywoman's cottage and killing her for the money under the mattress. He was charged with murder but acquitted and now was back in Laugharne, where he lived in the abandoned Ferry House near the Boat House, and sometimes appeared outside, looking in at Caitlin through the windows. He was once seen coming from the direction of the Boat House, laying a finger under his nose, pointing at the town clock and lolling his head to signify sleep; this was taken to mean that the man with the moustache, Howard Dark, was still in bed with his mistress.

Margaret Taylor was another of the subjects, and Caitlin resurrected a 'poisonous panegyric' she had written about her in Dylan's time.

> Do you realise [she wrote to Daiken] she is completely devoid of principle, conscience, or respect for the truth; and most people have a little bit hanging on somewhere: hence her ritual phrase – 'Now Catty, deary, you must learn to be *Elastic*.' Well she has anyhow, and it seems to suit her. I can't help it if I am crumbling cast iron.

Nicolette was sent both pieces to see what she thought of the 'awful Maggs diatribe' and 'that other bit of Booda punk', but Caitlin lost interest. Other people were less important; her gaze was riveted to herself and her life with Dylan.

Stuart Thomas made the travel arrangements, via Calais and train to Genoa, the port for Elba. Sufficient money to live on had to be finessed out of the austere financial system of the Fifties. Under the Exchange Control Act of 1947, only miserly amounts could legally be taken abroad and spent on pleasure. Forms had to be filled in on behalf of Caitlin, seeking fourteen pounds a week for three months to maintain mother and son. This was allowed only because she was going on business, 'to write a book on Elba'.

She went there early in October, arriving, well primed with chianti, at the small, noisy mining town of Rio Marina, where the family had stayed seven years earlier. The same hotel gave her the same room. Soon it became a 'bloody island'. It was her decision to be on it, yet at the same time it was as if she were at the mercy of events, as so often before, the vague-natured woman who first appealed to Dylan Thomas. Once again she was cast up on a shore.

11

Love Stories

It was Caitlin's fate to make things even more difficult for herself than she made them for others. A mining town on an island, in a country with unreconstructed views about how women should behave, was a chancy venture. Winter was coming; she had a small child with a troubled history at her side. Had she wanted orthodox rest and recreation, a hundred places in southern Europe that catered for the English would have been glad to take her sterling.

Her reason for choosing Rio Marina (population 2,500) was alarmingly straightforward. Giovanni was at the hotel, the man she met in 1947, and probably took as a lover. Caitlin described him with her usual bluntness in *Leftover Life to Kill*, the baroque, pain-racked book she began to write on Elba and finished, with difficulty, nearly two years later. She wrote:

> There was a man, when Dylan and I were here, who I thought possessed the ideal qualities: solidity, latent strength, tough as a rock, yet soft spoken, instinctively sensitive, and unembarrassed with learning; in short, the perfect leaning post. And a beauty of his own. I had saved up this man, The Church, for years, as something unique, an invaluable refuge, next to whom I could live happily for the rest of my years.

The pseudonym Caitlin used was transparent, Giovanni's surname being 'Chiesa', the Italian for 'church'. As well as owning the hotel, the Elba, he was something important in the municipal offices. He was married and by 1954 had a grown-up family. When Caitlin reappeared she found him 'as kind and good as ever'; but he had put on weight and lost some of his hair. The seven-year illusion died, and she was soon looking for additional solace.

Once she was installed at the hotel, sleeping with Colm in the room that she and Dylan had shared, the place became like all the other places, difficult and unrewarding. Elba was a straw she had clutched at. Sex coloured much of her time on the island, either doing it or avoiding it or being censured for it – hasty couplings on the bed when Colm was out of it, or lying under olive trees on wet afternoons, or huddling in stone huts on broken sofas, all against a background of scandalised Elbans whispering 'Prostituta, prostituta!' Affairs, she wrote, gave 'the illusion of something going on'. Some of the time, at least, she thought herself in love, though not with Giovanni. Nor was it beyond Caitlin to be leading her life on Elba with one eye on her book as well. She wanted material to write about; she said so to Brinnin the previous February.

Giovanni slept with her as a matter of course, beginning as he meant to go on, by jerking a fork over his shoulder to indicate the bedroom door. Before long, and to Giovanni's fury, she was entangled with 'Joseph', an attractive eighteen-year-old who worked in the iron-ore mines, and was anxious to improve his English. As she pointed out in the book, Joseph was only three years older than her son Llewelyn. He called Giovanni 'Mussolini', and his behaviour was almost as demanding as his rival's. With his 'wonderful whirlpools of dankly greasy, black grass hair' and 'the breadth and hardness of his thighs in their tight trousers', he was like 'a callous child' in his manner of seduction, 'the first person who had got anywhere near me since Dylan'. The hostility between her two lovers, together with an attempted rape when she was drying herself after a bathe, and fairly innocent friendships with one or two other pretty boys and a dustman she felt sorry for, filled the void, and kept tongues busy.

Old friends were not forgotten. 'I am beyond the beyond', she wrote to Daiken at the end of October, with what sounded like satisfaction. She wrote mischievously to John Brinnin's mother to say that she intended telling her son about 'all the awful things that are happening to me, deep in the heart of: Elba'. Howard Dark in Laugharne was asked (21 October) why he hadn't written. Had something happened? The letter went on:

Or don't you love me any more; I am very sorry, it may be vanity, but I don't believe that. Or are you just playing me up; that seems to me the most likely, knowing you as I do; but do you think it is quite fair, with me so far away, eating my heart out.

She pretended to be staying on Elba indefinitely, thanks to his 'very *un*gallant behaviour', and ended, 'You will be pleased to hear, there are compensations here.'

A month later she was complaining about the 'hopeless letter' he had sent her ('I thought you would write like you talked, which would have been fine and beautiful'), telling him she was 'drowning in wine'. David Gardner, she said, talked of coming out, 'but I am putting the damper on that. I have too many complications already.' Dark received a pat on the back for helping her through 'that awful time', no doubt the months after Thomas's death. 'Are you behaving yourself?' she asked. 'I am by no means perfect yet. Wait for me.'

Caitlin now had at least four men on the go, Dark and Gardner in Britain, her landlord Giovanni and Joseph on Elba (as she wrote once to Gardner, 'I like to see my lovers lined up in static melancholia through the long years, awaiting philosophically the Caitlin call to arms'). Her life abroad was a mixture of monotony and excitement. The privations were worse than Laugharne's. There was no such thing as a hot bath, the winds were freezing, money was short (a running correspondence went on with Stuart Thomas, who kept invoking Bank of England regulations), she had no sanitary towels, she grew too fat for her clothes, Colm had problems, Dylan haunted her. 'So this is what you wanted,' she imagined him saying. The town was unbeautiful, dirty with human excrement, dusty with the red ore that lorries delivered to the harbour. But she liked some of its moods – at dusk, 'up the stone slabbed market street, where the long ghostly sheets dripped from the windows', and the pancake shop revealed itself 'in the warm half light, with the wonderful red blown coals, illuminating the big oven', while shadowy figures stood near by, mouths watering.

Soon after she arrived, when it was still mild enough to bathe, she rented a house above a bay as a daytime alternative to the hotel. If voyeurs were getting 'an eyeful of stray breast or bum' when she bathed, what did it matter? She told Dark it was 'just like the Boathouse, over the sea'. The terrace looked down through olive trees to the water. She wrote in *Leftover* that:

anybody but me would be content with this. The bottle of red wine in front of me, and the long bread, the hard parmesan cheese [. . .] One day, for no special reason that I can remember, I suddenly felt whole again; and God, what a change. I was a new person, somebody I had forgotten a long time ago; I wanted to sing, and jump, and hug everybody, and kiss them. But it only lasted a day, then the wind came again and sent me shivering back where I had come from.

Letters to Stuart Thomas said she owed money to Giovanni and gave indignant lists of necessities: rent for the house, a coal stove, school lunches and an overcoat for Colm, the washing, the cheap wine, the tobacco. But she wasn't coming back before 1955. 'Don't think life is easy here,' she wrote, 'it is not, but I want to stay on, for my own reasons.' As she put it in *Leftover*, 'how would I dare go back, as raw, as sore, as unsewn up, as I had ever been, if not more'.

Perhaps her ultimate motive was self-mortification. Augustus John, when he read *Leftover*, said that 'while apparently in a perpetual state of disgust with the world in general, [she] seems to have chosen instinctively the lowest and dirtiest dram-shop of a mining town in Elba as her refuge from it'. She described one or two semi-spiritual interludes, including a walk to a mountain Calvary to avoid a would-be lover, where she 'sat on a flat stone, eating bare bread and drinking the mountain moss-sweet water, from cupped hands'. Guilt and sensuality went together.

To be seen as a woman undergoing an ordeal was certainly one of her intentions. She said so in letters to Gardner. Whether it was the ordeal she wanted, or a reputation for enduring ordeals, or even an excuse for keeping him away, is less clear. 'Please don't think I came here to *enjoy* myself,' she wrote on 20 October. 'I do things because I've got to do them, with a combination of the pioneering and missionary spirit, though what I expect to get out of it, I have no clear idea. I only know that for me it is the hard way, and always has been.' She went on to say that to let him visit her on Elba would be an 'indulgence' that she couldn't permit herself.

Three months later, in January 1955, the threat of an embarrassing appearance by Gardner had receded, but Caitlin was still talking about ordeals. The letter was headed 'The House of Lust; Nothing could be further from the truth'.

Cheri,

There are two things you are not allowed to say: one is to prate of happiness; the other to basely suggest that a man to me is just another cup of tea! On the contrary a man is not half so reviving: he is primarily unnecessary, utterly unsatisfactory, and ultimately a pain in the puss, in the neck, in the belly: a drag, a scold, a nagger, a queen saucepan fishwife . . . and what is more I have not got one, and that could be the trouble. At least I have only got a half of two, and the proprieties and *raging* decorums are *almost* insurmountable.

How many times have I got to tell you, sweet innocento, that this is not a holiday for me, it is a test by fire and ice, with a lot more ice than fire. And what I have done, and am doing, takes all my courage: and that is something I fancy I have got, if nothing else. Will you never learn that I am not a frivolous person, I only wish I were. And I dream of England nostalgically, with all its imagined warm associations which I know do not exist for me any more, including you.

Ordeals notwithstanding, Joseph was undeniably a compensation. He was another who commended himself by being dependent. 'I knew I loved Joseph; he was much easier to love because he had a distorting need, an overpowering want [. . .] for the world I represented to him.' The young miner clung to his glamorous English teacher who would save him from a lifetime of Elba. 'You are my only hopeless,' he told her.

Giovanni was disgusted with all this. Caitlin's lax ways were disgracing him, and he went to great lengths to make her behave, trying to involve her with the women in his family (she ignored them), threatening her with eviction (her weeping defeated him), even handing her a written denunciation. 'Even at Rio,' he wrote, 'there are women who misbehave, but they do not display themselves publicly, and they know how to preserve appearances, as you do not.' With admirable candour (or shameless exhibitionism) Caitlin chose to include this reproof in *Leftover*, where it occupied four pages. One sentence, which originally followed the one quoted, was deleted from the final manuscript, either by Caitlin or (more likely) an editor who didn't want the author to be seen in too harsh a light. It read, 'Instead you have put yourself in the position of being gossiped about by everyone: do not think they praise you; they compare you to a bitch on heat.'

Most of the time Caitlin was indifferent to what people thought.

'My not caring was my strength,' she wrote in *Leftover*. The way she said it – 'they could not understand that I did not care about the things which were life and death to them: I had had my death' – suggested to her readers that her behaviour was the result of her widowhood rather than what was more likely, the result of being Caitlin Thomas.

Her rages seem to have been less intense, as though her flight into another world where none of the old rules applied was itself the safety valve she had lacked when she was married. But after a carnival she pushed a man down a flight of stairs and had to be put to sleep with a doctor's injection.

By Christmas her remittance-money was approaching the Bank of England limit, when she would have received four hundred pounds, out of which, as pained voices reminded her from the Trust, she was not even managing to pay her hotel bill. Caitlin wasn't listening. In January she popped over to the mainland to buy some face cream, and while she was there invested in a bottle of expensive scent, which did her a power of good 'as I poured it profusely down my clinging, pink woollen vest'. Then there were pretty bras and a bathing costume and stockings and dolls, the latter for local children, including Joseph's sisters, as well as for 'my Aeron daughter, more beautiful and wicked than any of the dolls'. Back in Rio Marina she ordered three bottles of champagne in a row to celebrate imaginary birthdays with friends in a café.

A dollar cheque received by the Trust in January, and sent on to Caitlin direct because (being in dollars) official sanction wasn't needed, proved difficult to cash on the island. In February she was writing to Stuart Thomas to say she was 'financially destitute' and 'things were out of all control'. She wanted to see her other children but couldn't face living in Wales. Daiken got a letter headed 'Buco (Hole)' beginning 'Darling, Darling, Darling, Daiken, Daiken, Daiken, Please, Please, Please'. This restated the old problem, money, and added the new one, Joseph:

Help, help, there must be somebody cares about me, or isn't there? That reminds me, I want to bring a boy back, very young and very exceptional; he wants to work in England among other things.

This was a forlorn hope. There were scenes with both Giovanni and Joseph. Giovanni (she said) offered her money if she would give up

Joseph. In March he precipitated a crisis, writing to the Trust to say that the hotel account had been unpaid since Christmas, and suggesting ominously that in view of 'her well-known name' and the 'surrounding circumstances', the sooner Mrs Thomas was back in England the better. It was, he added, probably unnecessary to point out that if the matter didn't receive immediate attention, he would be forced to inform the British Consul at Florence and the local police.

Stuart Thomas squeezed another two hundred pounds out of the system – the Bank of England kept wanting to know what was happening to the book – and Caitlin was told to make arrangements to leave. So her self-imposed exile came to a clumsy and humiliating end. Yet she managed to absorb it, like other disagreeable experiences, as though she accepted all along that mortification was the point. She didn't try to conceal her misery at leaving Joseph; even Giovanni Chiesa, who had found her too much of an embarrassment, came in for a few regrets.

It was no use thinking of Dylan – that would start 'a longing on another scale', for which there was no relief 'except that I should always see him and re-create him through me'. Caitlin sought the reader's pity as she described the packing up and leaving. 'This is it, this is the finish, a beaten voice said inside me [. . .] And all the king's horses, and all the king's men, couldn't put Caitlin Thomas together again.' In April she was back in Britain. Some time later, Joseph made his way to London and telephoned her at the number she had given him, Cordelia Locke's in Hammersmith. Cordelia told him that Caitlin was not there, and she had no idea of her whereabouts. 'Oh, lady,' said Joseph, 'it cannot be so.'

When David Gardner met her at Victoria Station, she greeted him with, 'Hello you, I'm pregnant,' but he was inclined not to believe her. For a while she stayed in Hammersmith, 'trying to polish off the monstrous book'; the Boat House was uninhabitable after storm damage. In May she and Gardner went to Ireland, a journey, she said, that busybodies urged her to make as part of the therapeutic process. She found

> a sky not keeping its place at all [. . .] invading, and swamping and making magic of the land, till the land was alight with sky, and the sky was blowing with islands of land; and the stone walls and the gorse and the smiling donkeys flew upwards [. . .] So I was going in search of the smell of a twenty-year-old magic: to see was there any left for me, or was there not.

Whatever she found, she didn't write about it afterwards. The smiling donkeys, flying upwards, are in the style of Dylan Thomas, and it may be that the Ireland of her earlier years was now too distant an episode, buried under too many memories of her marriage, to be conjured up on a casual visit, or at all. Gardner says they spent a peaceful week at Ennistymon, encountering at least one of her men friends from the Thirties, and being taken home to meet his wife and eat boiled bacon and cabbage. There were no scenes, but at Dublin on the way back she was drunk and quarrelsome, and Gardner returned alone. In June she was certainly pregnant. Gardner was sure the child was his, and was anxious she should continue with the pregnancy. Whoever was the father, Caitlin applied to David Higham for fifty pounds for 'a necessary operation', and it was done illegally, as were most abortions then, at the Lockes' house.

That summer she was supposed to be finishing the book. It had acquired its title, *Leftover Life to Kill*, by July, and Higham thought that what he had read was 'exceptionally good', although he didn't know if it was publishable. This was to be the book's problem for the next eighteen months: it contained striking passages, and bore an individual stamp, that of an almost manic self-indulgence. But it was still inchoate and shapeless, and some of its word-play had echoes of Dylan Thomas.

A further difficulty arose. In America, John Brinnin had been writing his own account. It was being prepared for publication there, and, if no problems arose with libel, in Britain. *Dylan Thomas in America*, originally subtitled 'An Intimate Journal', dealt fairly with Caitlin, but contained details about her behaviour (drinking, losing her temper, fighting her 'private marital war') of a kind that would have alarmed most British publishers in 1955. It was difficult to find any single passage that was defamatory, but the overall impression was of a difficult woman, determined to get her own way. It may have been a fear of giving offence as much as a fear of being libellous. The book as a whole was condemned by some, when it appeared in Britain, for its 'vulgarity', which apparently meant that Brinnin showed Thomas as an artist with bad habits and unworthy friends. He had not been dead long enough for this to be acceptable. The fact that Brinnin was a devoted admirer was thought to be no excuse. Biography was still regarded as a gentlemanly business. Edith Sitwell, who reviewed the book – she described Brinnin as her 'much-valued friend' and

169

Thomas as her 'dearly-loved friend' – thought that the sordid aspects of the story were 'no business of the public'.

David Higham's agency was handling the British rights. Unwilling to proceed without consulting Caitlin, he showed her a proof copy of *Dylan Thomas in America* and got her agreement not to object, in return for the right to state her objections at the beginning of the book. Since Higham was going to be Caitlin's agent for her own book, she had reason to cooperate. Apart from flashes of temper in the past, because Brinnin reminded her of America and her husband's infidelity, she was well disposed towards him, writing soon after Thomas's death to say that 'I do realise how much you have done, suffered, loved; and I do thank you.' But his book trespassed on what she regarded as her property. It also spelt out details of Thomas's affairs with Pearl and Reitell.

In her preface (which Brinnin said he thought was 'wonderful') Caitlin wrote that

> I am not quarrelling with Brinnin's presentation of Dylan. It is impossible to hit back at a man who does not know that he is hitting you, and who is far too cautious of the laws of libel to say plainly what can only be read between the lines.

The book, she said, was one-sided and restricted to a short period of Thomas's life (this was true). Her task was to 'try to show what went before', and she hoped to produce 'a better truth than Brinnin's'. This showed unnatural humility for Caitlin. For once, she was not sure of herself.

The real effect of Brinnin's book on Caitlin was that it drove her to state a case – not in *Leftover*, which was now a manuscript waiting for an editor, but in a new book altogether. The old one was put aside, and some time in 1955 she began to write *Am I the Perfect Fool?*, a work devoted to Thomas and her relationship with him, which has already been quoted. Writing to David Lougee from the Boat House on 1 January 1956 ('New Year's Bastard Day') she said that Brinnin's 'astonishing tour de force' had 'spoilt the summer for me with the dirty taste in my mouth', adding:

> And he is responsible for me getting into such a mess and muck trying to write an answer back, and show another, different, side of Dylan. All I am

showing is that I can't write; that I am blind and confused, and obsessed by myself: me, me, me, to distraction [. . .] But I have sworn not to move from this funereal Wales till I finish it, so will be here for ever and ever bloody more.

Fool was less a reply to Brinnin, though his name was often invoked, than a desperate attempt, triggered off by his book, to make a record of the marriage. The question in the title meant: am I a fool to think I understood Dylan and our life together? The answer was a qualified 'No'. Like *Leftover*, the book was unpublishable as written; unlike *Leftover*, it was never refurbished and shown to a public. In theory Caitlin on Dylan was an attractive proposition. But her writing was too dense, confused and episodic, and the second book lacked the saving grace of the first, an alternative theme – her escapades on Elba – that gave the marital drama room to breathe.

What *Fool* did have were raw, unstructured insights into the marriage. She wrote about the sexual jealousy that was there from the early days, and admitted that she was sometimes the guilty party – 'And when I had the mumps once, as though that was not undignified enough at my age, Dylan discovered a letter of mine to a certain person, couched in over-intimate, tender terms; and he came straight at me, and gave me such a kick in the face with his shod foot.'* She noted Thomas's suicide attempts. She remembered his saying that he didn't want to live to be a drooling old man with gout, 'waited on by a bitch like you'. She said that if it had not been for the children, 'I would have left Dylan a million times and a million years ago'.

What she described was manifestly the same florid, hyper-active marriage of *Leftover Life to Kill* as published, but the *Fool* version was uglier, and it showed that their troubles had a long history. The *Leftover* story was in the mould of lovers torn apart by death. It followed her to Elba, and presented her wild deeds as the acts of a grieving widow. Her nature and her marriage were trimmed to make them fit this version.

This is not to belittle the grief. Both versions breathe desolation. 'If I waited a million years, I could not forget Dylan: he will not come blundering down the path again [. . .] and bang at the door impatiently and shout, "Cait, come down quick and let me in." There will be nobody to bang at the door for he is in already' (*Leftover*). 'Our

* Caitlin had mumps in August 1951.

deepest love, which I can feel at this instant in the flaying agony of the Boat House, Laugharne, [is] as clean, intact and intolerable as it always was, now that it is too late' (*Fool*).

In 1955 Caitlin thought of having Dylan's body exhumed and reburied in the garden, facing the sea, having decided that the churchyard was not worthy of him. Thomas's grave was in a modern extension to the churchyard, too bleak for her liking. 'If the grave is in the Boat House garden,' she told the trustees, 'I shall be able to tend it myself . . . And when my time comes to join him, I hope to be buried alongside him.' The Home Office said she could have a licence, price two pounds. There was even a plan showing where the grave would be, just the other side of the forecourt in front of the house. But the Church authorities weren't happy.

For much of the year Caitlin remained in Laugharne, amending her manuscripts. Wyn Henderson was there sometimes, doing what she liked best, pottering about in the world of artists. Caitlin was in good company. Between the Wars Henderson managed a London gallery for the American heiress Peggy Guggenheim; she ran a small press with Desmond Harmsworth, the painter (and Lord Northcliffe's nephew). Dylan Thomas, in his Cornwall days, was merely a notch on her gun, another artist who had needed her services.* Her lovers were said to include one or two millionaires, and stories clung to her of an interest in eccentric sex, and indeed eccentricity of all kinds.

To Caitlin, who could organise nothing successfully, Wyn was a worker of miracles, a woman of the world who could find a psychiatrist, type a manuscript or understand a train timetable, meanwhile telling bawdy jokes and organising a party: preferably with someone else's money, because she never had much of her own. On the other hand, she never starved. Gwen Watkins thought her 'a kind of vampire who lived on other people's emotions', which seems harsh. Caitlin had reservations, but so she did about most people. The relationship suited them both, and Wyn was more loyal to it than her friend, praising Caitlin's 'incorruptible honesty and steadfastness'. While staying at the Boat House around 1951, Caitlin had shown her, in Dylan's absence, some of her own poems, including one called 'On

---

* Wyn Henderson (died 1976) said that when he was younger, Dylan Thomas left a poetry notebook with her for safekeeping. It was in cheap blue covers, smaller than octavo, and vanished from her flat after his death. She named the person who had it.

Being Married to a Drunk'. Henderson wrote, 'When I thought of the happy, carefree young Irish colt that had married Dylan in Cornwall from our "Lobster Pot" I felt the utmost compassion as she read these poems aloud, and shrank from the thought of the damage that had been done to her by life.' Now in her late fifties, Mrs Henderson was still thriving.

As usual Caitlin was often in London, leading an unfashionable social life. She didn't choose, or was unable, to cultivate friendships with the well known, though sometimes she bumped into drinking pals of Dylan's. David Gardner met Louis MacNeice and John Davenport when he was with her, and felt he was getting a taste of literary London. Her letter to Leslie Daiken ('Dear Sir Leslielot', 7 November 1955), giving him the address where she would be staying, made fun of her plans:

I shall be arriving shortly, so please give my secretary a ring, or drop in your card. My visiting days are Wednesdays and Fridays, from six to seven o'clock sharp. Kind remembrances. Your affectionate friend (Mrs) Caitlin Thomas.

P.S. I shall be arranging a small intimate dinner soon, for a few handpicked friends of high distinction; would you care to join us for coffee and crackers afterwards, and to make a four at bridge.

We shall be simply *delighted* to see you, and *do* bring a bottle of Bulmer's best.

It will be a positive riot of glorious gaiety, with Mrs A.J.P Taylor as the guest of honour, in her furs, feathers and furbelows.

(Where are you Uncle Skunk? You are neglecting little me.)

On her visits she consulted a psychiatrist; it was the kind of thing that Wyn would recommend. Later Caitlin told Stuart Thomas that should this psychiatrist present a bill for fifty pounds 'for perfecting me', he needn't bother to pay it, since she remained imperfect, 'and, I am sorry to say, still *Caitlin Thomas*'.

The prescription for her malaise looked like being a further dose of abroad. There was nothing to stop her. The nightmare of her marriage was over, and she was free to run her own life. She didn't say the marriage had been a nightmare: on the contrary, she was ready to shout her grief and remorse from the house-tops. But the evidence suggests that at the end it tortured them both. If one believes her remarks in old age, she came to terms with that reality: 'Dylan's death was an enormous liberation for me. I had come into my own again.'

Having found her freedom by accident, she wished to retain it. This ruled out conventional solutions. Writing to David Gardner from the Boat House in February 1956, she played with the idea of domesticity, telling 'Darling Davey' that

> it is a lot easier and pleasanter in every way, living with you, and please believe I miss you terribly, and best of all we are so cosy in bed together: if only we need never get up into the icy morning to make that tyrannical tea; so why do I persecute us both with my vague aspiring ideas of something else that has got to be done: especially cruel to you who want nothing of these floating dreams, but just a warm body.
>
> Forgive my stupid dilly-dallyings [. . .] but never depend on me, and never leave me altogether: you are the only half grown up man who actually loves me, strange as it may seem, and I can't do without that yet.
>
> And in return I will look after you, make you stews, and keep you semi-clean and stinking a bit of booze and tobacco; and give you lots of children's, mother's and even a drop of flopsy's love. Your very sweet domesticated
>
> Caitlin

Her old illusion that she was a deserving cause, that if she desired something she was entitled to have it, won a new lease of life. In this mood, she was more intolerant than ever of inconveniences that most people have to take for granted. It magnified her troubles. If the pipes froze it was a personal affront. If the children howled she was uniquely burdened. After an unsatisfactory Christmas ('swamped in holiday humbuggery') Wyn Henderson was ill in hospital. 'I, needless to say, on my tragic Island of vain absorption, have seen fit to do nothing,' Caitlin wrote to a mutual friend, Jack Schwarz, a book dealer: 'not a syllable of sympathy'.

The *Fool* manuscript must have been completed during the winter. Wyn Henderson typed it, with 'Laugharne, 1956' at the end, and it was put in the queue behind *Leftover*. In retrospect it became part of the process of forgetting. The hysteria was dying down, though Caitlin hadn't stopped dramatising herself, and never would. She quoted her husband's phrase, 'There is an illumination about her, she shines', and said it was 'the best thing that has ever been said about me'. She didn't add that the phrase in all its theatricality came from Brinnin's book, having been reported to him by Reitell along with the other last words. 'It is a long time now since I shone,' she wrote; 'it is as well he can't see his limp, sodden, golden girl smouldering on a dung-heap.'

She piled on the self-pity. 'There is so little left to lose,' she wrote –

an old leather coat stolen from Bill McAlpine [. . .] now used for carrying coal, a tangle of bedraggled ties that were once his father's pride and a couple of Welsh flannel shirts, pink and blue which came down nearly to his ankles and which he had made specially for him in Carmarthen market to sleep in in the winter though he wore them by day as well.

Despite her contempt for Laugharne's 'small admonishing people' she managed to write about the place with a kind of respect, the 'indifferent estuary that reminds me irritatingly that it will be here long after I am gone'. Still, the need to be somewhere else ran through the book. Even America, home of betrayal, was rehabilitated:

One day I shall go to New York: the best city in the world; let a city be a city; not posing as a rural haven, like London, with a village pump [. . .] I want all hard angles, all continual noise, all steam-heating: what glorious luxury that is; all saloon bars, all rye on the rocks, all blaring talk, no solitude ever again, never to be alone any more for a split midnight whisper.

But she barely set foot in America after that. Europe was her continent, preferably a country with peasants in it. In 1956 Italy was in the air again. There was talk of Wyn Henderson going to Venice to join Peggy Guggenheim. The trustees* quite liked the idea of Caitlin leaving the country again. She might lose interest in moving the grave (the Vicar of Laugharne was being difficult), and once out of the country she would be less of a strain on the Trust's resources – exchange control, they innocently hoped, would save them from having to send her too much money.

A plan crystallised for the spring: Caitlin and the children, accompanied by Wyn, all paid for by the Trust, would sail away to Naples at the end of March, in time for Easter. It was when Brinnin's book would be published in Britain; perhaps Mrs Henderson was

* Daniel Jones had resigned the previous year. Wynford Vaughan Thomas, also of Swansea, the broadcaster, had replaced him.

getting her out of the way. By the time reviews of *Dylan Thomas in America* began to appear, Caitlin and party were in Positano, the resort on the Amalfi coast south of Naples. This she scathingly described to Daiken as an 'icy, touristy, chichi, snob fool's clip joint [. . .] neither fashionable nor primitive enough: no big names for Wyn, and no rough and toughs for me . . . who ever said it was *fun* to go abroad.'

Llewelyn and Aeron were soon flown back, preceded by letters and telegrams to Nicolette, Daiken and David Gardner, Caitlin's network for ensuring they were met at the airport and steered back to school with any new clothes they needed. D.H. Evans was the place to go for her daughter's summer hat, gloves and socks. 'I know it sounds too abominably awful,' Caitlin wrote to Nicolette, who was inclined to be nervous of her sister, 'but somebody has got to do it.'

Caitlin had better things on hand, such as the revising of *Leftover*, which might make her name if she could get it right. Wyn had thought of a place to spend the summer. The Bay of Naples has a famous island at either end, Capri in the east and Ischia in the west. Between Ischia and the mainland is Procida, an islet that saw few tourists then. It was primitive enough to appeal to Caitlin, but close enough to Ischia, which had associations with Auden and others, to suit Wyn. As well as artists, Ischia catered for male homosexuals, and Mrs Henderson always enjoyed their company.

They had not been long on Procida before Caitlin cheered up and spoke of finishing the book in no time. A journalist from London called on her and saw the manuscript lying on a table under a lemon tree (he kindly took three years off her age and reported a shape 'as lithe as a teenage girl's'). She had some extra dollars of her own, perhaps from Schwarz, the dealer, to whom she had sold the Dylan Thomas manuscripts in her possession, against the Trust's advice. Schwarz is said to have paid three hundred pounds, a fraction of what they would realise when the American collectors and institutions began to assemble their Thomas archives.

In June Caitlin was arranging for Wyn to fly back to London and see to domestic matters, including the children, who were to return with her for the summer. The Trust was helping her apply for resident status in Italy. She was feeling the first breath of affluence. That summer she covenanted to pay her mother a small regular income. Sales of Thomas's work were rising, bringing in royalties –

representing about one-tenth of the bookshop price – of two or three thousand pounds a year. This was at a time when most books cost less than a pound.* Caitlin would be able to live happily or at least comfortably ever after, enjoying security; always assuming that security was what she wanted.

For the first time in her life she was spending a summer in the climate she liked, by a warm blue sea. The island was poor, a place that the boats to Ischia paused at or passed by, a blur in the heat with a patch of tinted houses above the cliffs. Naples was an hour away. The Thomases shared a house with a friendly family that kept goats and chickens and grew fruit. Apricot trees provided the juice to mix with Caitlin's vodka. The rocks where they bathed were five minutes away. To Aeron, her mother was 'like a sun-worshipper, a sun-goddess', forever oiling her body between bouts of swimming – 'that was what seduced her, not the men. It was easy to make her happy'. The Italian children, dark-skinned, were delighted with these off-white strangers – Colm aged seven, Aeron thirteen, Llewelyn seventeen. They thought 'games' meant games of cards, until the Thomases introduced them to northern pleasures, hide-and-seek and sardines. In some ways it was a family holiday. In other ways it was not.

A letter from Caitlin to Nicolette (24 August 1956), replying to what sounded like a reminder that she ought to be working on her book, agreed entirely, adding that she was haunted by the ghost of their father, who never finished anything. But she had a problem, her ugly, much-bitten hands.

> I am going to be more painfully frank with you than I have ever been with anyone before, because the subject is such a sore one; it is something to do with my *hands*. Now please don't start laughing, because this is not a laughing matter, and it is ruining what is left of my wretched life. And that is one of the reasons I was so cross and disappointed with Ronnie [perhaps the psychiatrist], because he never got to the root of my trouble at all; which was not Dylan, as he automatically and stupidly presumed, but my *hands*: long before that. And it is getting worse every day; you have no conception of the hours I waste tearing at them, and they won't let me move, refuse to let me get on [. . .] The mental anguish that I endure in these increasingly frequent crises is unlike anything else, quite horrible,

* In 1955, *Under Milk Wood* (7th impression) cost eight shillings and sixpence (45 pence today). *Portrait of the Artist as a Young Dog* (3rd impression) ten shillings and sixpence, *Collected Poems* (ninth impression) twelve shillings and sixpence.

and dangerously near to the Bin door. I have always pooh-poohed my shows of madness before, but this is too buried, too low down, too organic, to be brushed off lightly. I could tolerate the disfigurement if I was achieving something, but to be humiliatingly atrophied between the desire to create some kind of music of my own, and the means of putting it down, is beyond intolerable [. . .]

But apart from cutting them off, which I long to do: but then how could I smoke, wash, drink, *Write*; or having them sealed in malleable plaster: I have seriously considered obtaining false hands; I can see no solution. I would give *all* my future, such as it is, to solve this problem; because it is the rot behind all my troubles, and removes devastatingly any small chance of happiness that I might have. So please *please* help me, if you can think of anything. I am not dramatising my ills now I swear: this is the plain, unvarnished, unpleasant truth. But no more, and forgive this awful long splurge, but I had to say it to somebody.

As well as the flattening heat, the dragging to chewed morsels of the children, I am hopelessly in love with an impossible young, beautiful, black creature from a forbidden world, doomed to tragic extermination. So imagine my plight; and the losing battle of my frantic maiden-aunt duty.

Perhaps her beautiful black creature – she meant dark-skinned – was the problem; perhaps he was part of the solution. Wyn Henderson, more interested in a lover's artistic provenance, saw him as a callous young Latin with designs on a buxom blonde who had money, and preferred to spend her time in the cafés of Forio d'Ischia. 'Mario', not his real name, spoke no English. As on Elba, Caitlin's infatuation was complete. Mario slept with her at the lodgings and was one of the family. One night he took Aeron out in his fishing boat by moonlight, but nothing improper happened. Looking back on it, Llewelyn says robustly that the close proximity of their mother's love affair 'didn't affect us. We didn't think about it.' Aeron says that now she doesn't *want* to think about it, and speaks of 'having had to suffer Mother's boy friends'. She adds that 'while most of us are working on guilt, that's not part of her emotional equipment'.

The three children returned to Britain in September, Colm going to Brigit in the New Forest, the others to school. Caitlin was still heavily engaged with Mario. She described him to Brigit, the sister she was closest to and most honest with, in the course of a self-critical letter that sought the root of her dissatisfactions – rather than blaming her hands for it, as if they were independent entities, as she had done to Nicolette.

I don't know what is the matter with me; I have got everything heart could desire: a private island to myself; an almost perfect climate so far, but I fear gales and winter agonies are on the way; a pleasant old house and garden over the sea, with sympathetic people; work to do of my own, if only I could do it, and nobody to bother me. And last, but not least, by any manner or means: a perfectly *ravishing* lover; but *really* my dear, the like of which has never been seen before or since; nor never will again by me. I hold my breath and wait for the unbelievable edifice to explode, which it frequently does, and I get blown and pounded in jealous smoke; which all adds to the hell of it.

In the meantime I am as molten putty; you have never seen anything like my abject subjection – quite some revelation for me; in his powerful brown hands. And I have not the courage to contemplate leaving him for England, where I have Welsh buggerall to go back to. I need only add that he is a complete, black, hairy animal with no impeding brains whatsoever; and you will understand why I have got it so badly. Only snag is his age: still in the impossible twenties [. . .] But am I content in this stimulating situation? Not a bit of it, not me, it would not be me if I was, would it? I have got this curse on me, it is no good, that won't let me enjoy things, that gnaws, rankles, grapples at me, and gives me no peace ever.

Howard Dark remained on her list. He got a postcard to say, 'Sun & the summer islands & love make very heady wine – perhaps a little flat Welsh beer is needed for the good of the soul! What do you think?' Visitors came or threatened to come from England. David Gardner was still keen on her, still being encouraged to persist. One of her letters to him from Procida said, 'I do need you *soon*'; a postscript added, 'Thanks for the proposal, but I think it is safer to stick to sin.'

Gardner decided it was time to join her. He travelled third-class to Naples, took the ferry – they tried to stop him going ashore at Procida, thinking he must have mistaken it for Ischia – and asked for Signora Thomas. She was less than delighted to see him, and pretended he was a journalist; a wise precaution, Mario being impulsive. After she went bathing with Gardner, the Italian tore her bathing suit apart. According to Caitlin, he had earlier burnt his fishing boat following a row, and she had to buy him a new one. Gardner had come at the wrong time. He pushed off to Ischia.

Caitlin followed soon afterwards. Another visitor was waiting for her with Mrs Henderson, a London publisher, Roger Lubbock of Putnam, who had read a typescript of *Leftover*, and had ideas for reshaping the book. Lubbock was in his thirties, relaxed and gentlemanly, an instant target for Caitlin gibes about stuffed shirts. For a while they were all together in Forio. It was October, and the season was over, the last tourists departing. Lubbock wanted a free hand to reorganise the book, and Caitlin agreed, not without misgivings.

There were regrettable incidents. At a dance, Caitlin used her teeth on Gardner's cheek. Later she went back to his hotel for the night. Early next morning someone was outside the door, hammering and shouting in Italian. Caitlin said it was Mario and warned Gardner to keep quiet. They left the hotel unobserved, but later that day, when Gardner was in Wyn's flat, Mario appeared at the window, and the visitor hid in a cupboard. By this time he had had enough. Caitlin was back with the Italian, and Gardner, dismayed to see this forthright woman reduced (it seemed to him) to 'cheating and crawling', departed for the north, drinking the chianti he had bought as a homecoming present *en route*. When he reached London he had a hangover and no money, and was no longer in love. To colleagues in television who asked what had happened to his face, he took pleasure in saying that Mrs Dylan Thomas bit it.

Wyn feared the 'barbarous impression' that Caitlin made. 'It is a great mistake to draw me out,' Caitlin wrote to Lubbock when he, too, was back in London, 'for what comes out is not what nice people want to see at all.' She resented the way he had taken her manuscript away with him, feeling 'cheated and wronged out of the book [. . .] which I feel now is more yours than mine'. A month later, in November, she was convinced it would all have to be rewritten, or thrown in the estuary at Laugharne, when they met in Britain to discuss the next stage.

I agree about London, it does not suit me, and would not be the best meeting place for us [. . .] Nor do I wish, why should I, to disgrace you socially, or soil the hem of your stuffed shirt: I know all about keeping artists in their place, which happens to be the gutter: haven't I attempted to do it for countless years, and as long as he was there, he was all right; but if only I knew I *was* a miserable artist, for to be miserable and not an artist is asking a little too much, even of Santa Caterina. Is this the end of a sentence or is it not: just a simple editing job: yours.

Her idiosyncratic use of colons and semi-colons to partition sentences gave them an awkwardness that reflected something in Caitlin's nature. She talked to Lubbock about her 'stilted agonies' as a writer, brushing aside his faith in her talent. Both letters and manuscripts were afflicted by the staccato punctuation, which sometimes obscured the meaning, and perhaps was meant to. It made her sentences look bad-tempered.

Lubbock also had the *Perfect Fool* manuscript, and Caitlin was planning other books. She had been keeping a diary of her life on Procida with a view to publication – Gardner glanced at it, finding rude remarks about himself and an account of a 'luminous evening' with Mario. Caitlin eventually called it *Year of Disgrace* and in 1957 tried to interest Lubbock, but he thought it was too much on the lines of *Leftover*, and would harm her reputation.

In October, 1956, with *Leftover*, *Fool* and *Disgrace* in varying states of completion, Caitlin and Wyn Henderson left Procida for Sicily in search of a fourth book. The inspiration (probably Henderson's) was the social reformer Danilo Dolci, who was making himself unpopular with both the authorities and the Mafia in western Sicily. Caitlin had some half-baked idea of carrying on where Dolci (who was then in prison) left off. Henderson decided their base should be Taormina, the steep-built resort on the east coast, a place that was classy and cultured in those days. Caitlin thought it a glorified Bournemouth. Nor were there expeditions into the hinterland in search of bandits. What happened, she told Lubbock, was that their money was 'devoured in tourist boredoms: frowning mounds of earnestly nude, too similar, crepitating Hun Bums; and visitors' frivolous trivialities'. Whatever all this meant, it went on for ten days, when Mario ('my black bastard') appeared, and carried her off, back to Procida. Wyn refused to travel with them. As Caitlin put it, 'Wyn would not speak to Signor Bruto, on a matter of beating-up principle', that is, he had been knocking Caitlin about, no doubt following all those visits from Englishmen. This violence Caitlin was apparently prepared to tolerate.

The Procida interlude ended in similar fashion to Elba's, with money short – despite remittances of £150 a month – and the sense of a departure delayed too long. Someone stole more than a hundred pounds in lire from her room. Henderson, who was beginning to act like a business manager, reported the theft to Stuart Thomas, adding mysteriously that ponces lived on the premises. She suspected Mario and was glad to get Caitlin away from him. But Caitlin didn't forget him.

Italy was where Caitlin went to escape from Britain; Britain was where she escaped back again. Her restlessness was like a disease. 'My blood is alive with poison,' she told Lubbock. At least on Procida she could drink unnoticed. In December 1956 she was no sooner back in London than the television programme *This Week*, short of a subject, decided to interview her about *Dylan Thomas in America*. Apparently drunk, she held on to a chair and said she was tired of questions about cheque books; they faded her out after less than a minute.

Once again she returned to Laugharne, where both Henderson and Lubbock stayed in January 1957, working together on the re-assembled *Leftover*. 'You baffle me,' she told Lubbock before he arrived, 'and that annoys me. Two Different bloody Worlds isn't in it.' Surviving typescript pages, heavily amended, show big rewrites taking place, with no indication of when. Caitlin says now that 'Lubbock rewrote it', but the details have vanished from everyone's memory. What emerged was certainly her book, stamped with her anger and self-absorption. Even if the editing process had made her acutely aware of her limitations, she was at last able to face the world with something of her own.

Leftover Life to Kill was published in May 1957 – books on the spring lists that year included Roger Fulford's *Votes for Women* and John Braine's *Room at the Top* – with suggestions of scandal that should have delighted Caitlin, though there is no evidence that it did. Reviewers used words like outrageous, comic, squalid and extra-ordinary, and in general showed her as a woman intent on indiscretion. To the *Times Literary Supplement* she was surrounded by 'an atmosphere of smouldering sexuality'.

To Louis MacNeice in the *New Statesman* it was a 'highly personal and often deeply moving document', produced by a 'lovable but spoilt child' – the 'lovable' sounded like MacNeice being kind to an old friend's widow. He did say that she exasperated him 'when she talks about either God or Death, both of whom are treated as nursery ogres who have picked upon this child beyond all others'; adding that her purple passages were a bad imitation of her husband's, and by the way there were too many semi-colons.

Extracts from *Leftover* had been serialised in the *Observer*, which

Augustus John's painting of a radiant but predatory Caitlin,
not long before she married Dylan Thomas in 1937. It is
probably the 'pink picture'. See page 72.

(above) Caitlin and
Dylan Thomas at
Blashford, soon after
their marriage in 1937.
'I am lost in love and
poetry,' wrote Thomas.

(right) The couple at
Laugharne, about
1938.

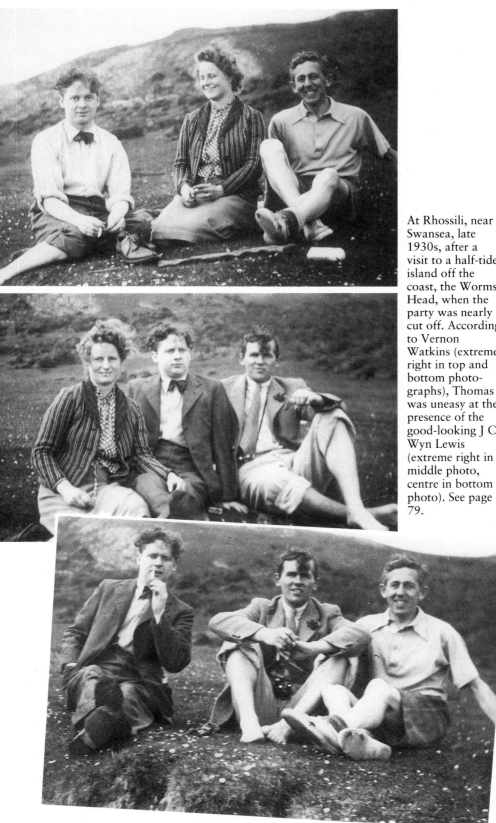

At Rhossili, near
Swansea, late
1930s, after a
visit to a half-tide
island off the
coast, the Worms
Head, when the
party was nearly
cut off. According
to Vernon
Watkins (extreme
right in top and
bottom photo-
graphs), Thomas
was uneasy at the
presence of the
good-looking J C
Wyn Lewis
(extreme right in
middle photo,
centre in bottom
photo). See page
79.

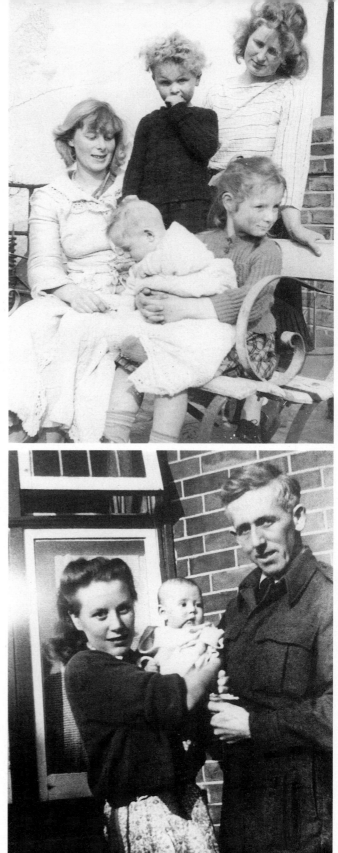

Families in wartime. Caitlin (on right) and her sister Nicolette, on the roof of the latter's house in Chelsea, 1942. Llewelyn Thomas sucks his thumb. Nicolette's daughter Emma holds her brother Esmond.

Vernon Watkins, poet and friend of Thomas since he was twenty, with Gwen Watkins and their first born son.

David Gardner, one of Caitlin's post-Dylan lovers, with her daughter Aeronwy (extreme right) and friends. (Inset) Caitlin then, the mid-1950s, in her early forties.

King Street, Hammersmith, 1955. Caitlin (on right of group) is about to leave for Ireland with Gardner in his snappy sports car. Cordelia and Harry Locke have come out to wave goodbye.

Giuseppe Fazio, Caitlin's companion since 1957, in a film-publicity still of the 1960s.

Wyn Henderson, Caitlin's friend and sometime manager, as a young woman and (lower picture) in later years.

(right) Caitlin's daughter Aeronwy, the notional subject of her mother's 1963 book, *Not Quite Posthumous Letter to My Daughter*.

Caitlin with Aeronwy's children, Huw and Hannah Thomas Ellis.

(right) Brigit Marnier, Caitlin's 'reliable' sister, who still lives in the New Forest. She lost an eye in a riding accident. (below) Two of the Dylan Thomas trustees, Stuart Thomas (on the right of group) and Michael Rush, with Llewelyn Thomas, Dylan's son, between them. September 1990.

Caitlin and Giuseppe at Syracuse, Sicily. May 1991.

Caitlin, aged seventy-seven, with her son by Giuseppe, Francesco Thomas Fazio, outside the house at Catania. May 1991.

concentrated on the chapters about Dylan Thomas. Some reviewers were disappointed, when they read the book, to find that most of it was about Caitlin. This school included the *Economist*, which deplored the absence of reticence and decency, and concluded that those who enjoyed Francis Bacon paintings, with their 'flayed, disintegrating images', might – just might – be able to 'relish the exhibitionism of Caitlin Thomas'. *The Times* dismissed it as 'a monument of egocentricity which must be without equal in our time'. *Punch* compared it favourably to the usual stuff produced by literary widows.

A literary magazine in South Wales even found a spiritual lesson in the book, a discovery that might not have been quite as alien to Caitlin as the reviewer supposed. The magazine was *Dock Leaves*, the writer its editor, a Roman Catholic, Raymond Garlick. He assumed, as most did, that *Leftover* was about the aftermath of a death, Dylan's, rather than about the continuation of a life, Caitlin's, that was haunted even before she was widowed. But his observation is unaffected:

> Reckless souls, seeking a way out of the prison of themselves, will sometimes find the way of abandon: to nature (the abandon of sinners) or to supernature (the abandon of saints): in both cases to an experience of love. That is why saints and sinners are so much less strange to each other than both are to the compromising, calculating, criticising souls between. And yet, paradoxically, abandon to nature proves unnatural: human nature desires more than nature can give, and so the soul is still tormented by itself. Such is the situation which this book records, though perhaps it would bewilder the author to see it stated in such terms.

Caitlin was not in Britain to read her reviews, having gone abroad again in February, as soon as the book revisions were disposed of. Now that she was an Italian resident, her visits to Britain had to be limited, or she would incur tax penalties. Wyn Henderson was left behind. At Caitlin's request ('she has become a real institution in the family') she received an allowance for keeping an eye on the children. After a short stay in Rome, Caitlin went to Anzio, on the coast thirty miles away, with vague ideas of looking for 'a country place'. Letters with Italian stamps kept arriving at Stuart Thomas's, usually wanting money. A postcard of a blonde on a beach, laughing and showing her teeth, announced that Caitlin had been about to post him a stern letter for not sending her a word of comfort, 'but now the money has come, so I am sending this ravishing lady instead'.

It was not like Caitlin to be unaccompanied, and Mario may have been in tow. Early in the spring, Wyn flew out with the children, and another family holiday got under way, this time on Sardinia. Mario was present, in rented rooms at Alghero, a coastal resort favoured by the British. The weather was cold, Caitlin and lover were quarrelling. Llewelyn remembers his mother rising to the circumstances with jokes. She wrote sharply in reply to a letter from Lubbock to say that 'I am not having a *jolly* time, but I still prefer my mudraking to your parody of over-parodied classy English.' She was suffering 'as nobody never suffered before, so what are you complaining about? And why such a spate of spite on poor, innocent, dark angel [Mario's] head?' Meanwhile Wyn wanted the Trust to hand over three thousand pounds for a house that Caitlin had found by the sea, complete with vines and olive trees, where they could settle and cultivate the land. The Trust preferred not to.

A month later the children had gone home, Caitlin was on Ischia, and the Mario affair was coming to a climax. She wrote to Lubbock, dealing first with the reception of *Leftover*. 'I still cannot connect the notorious monster of the newspapers,' she wrote, 'with my lonely strivings in an anonymous rut, and I am beginning to get cowardly cold feet at the thought of launching myself on the offended mercies of the Welsh people again.' She was doing no work. 'I am a dishrag: straccio: of negation.' Her real problem was 'Signor, child delinquent [Mario] whom I cannot successfully purge from my system; and I used to be so good at purging people out'. The phrase echoed her remark twenty years earlier to Rupert Shephard, about her determination to 'eradicate that bugbear' – Dylan Thomas – 'from my system'. Men were a taint to be removed; though they had their uses.

The passion in the letter was reserved for Mario. A book, it seemed, was just a book, but her young Italian, who turned out to be facing criminal charges involving her, was indispensable.

He has been banished from Ischia for a year on pain of arrest for living off a soft headed, hearted, daft foreign woman who needs, they aggressively presume, protecting from herself and himself. What the hell has it to do with them, and am I not grown up yet? Then a prison sentence hangs over his head for robbing money from me and beating me up from way back and I, it seems, am the only person [who] believes implicitly in his innocence. So he is confined to the reproachful torments of Procida and treated lower than a cur even before he is proved guilty. And I am not allowed to speak to him which I nevertheless ignore, let alone live with him. In the meantime he is planning an escape to England on an illegal ship with my aiding and abetting, but the chances don't look too favourable. I can hear your oh *dears* and oh *lords* at this frivolous concoction [at] such a distance, but I assure you there is nothing frivolous about a prison. And I could not stand to see him behind bars.

Caitlin decided to kill herself. She would go to the farthest point of Procida, jump from a rock and swim into nothingness. She remembers leaving a note for Wyn Henderson, and gliding through the tepid water. She knew all the time that she didn't mean to do it, that it was another of her gestures. In her words, 'I was so happy, I started swimming back.' But her love affair had made the island intolerable. Soon she was telling Stuart Thomas that she had to get out, regardless of tax penalties. Whether in the end she gave evidence for Mario, and whether he went to prison, is forgotten.

Her next appearance was in Ireland, a foreign country for tax purposes, holding court at the Falls Hotel. It was August 1957. Her income was comfortable, around two thousand pounds a year, although the high tax rates of the day made inroads. In the future she could spend only limited amounts of time in Britain. The Ennistymon party consisted of Caitlin, Wyn, Caitlin's mother, Brigit and assorted children. Yvonne did some weeding in what would have been her garden in a different world. Brigit, the out-of-doors person, took the boys bathing in the rain at Lahinch. Llewelyn had left school and his future was uncertain.

Money blew away like dust. On 2 August two hundred pounds was urgently needed because, as Henderson put it, 'we are a large party and do not wish to lose face'. All but Henderson were Macnamaras, back in the old country, where people remembered what a grand hospitable fellow Francis was, God bless him. A week later they desperately needed another hundred and fifty.

'Dear Nobody,' Caitlin wrote to Daiken, heading her letter 'Falls, Falling, Fallen'. She told him that 'Mother Melancholia is in full swing' and signed herself 'Your irredeemably lost Caitlin'. Behind the pose of humorous despair, the question of what to do with her life consumed Caitlin. 'My heart,' she told Lubbock, 'is unmentionably mutilated and I never want to see a pair of trousers again, especially not Italian ones.'

Lubbock had moved into the category of trusted friend. She wrote:

My life has come to a complete full stop. Like that. No parentheses, colons, semi-colons, three dots, or even dashes. No, no, nothing, nothing at all. Why am I being so nauseatingly literary, anybody would think I was a highly paid budding authoress, when really I dare not say what I am. Where does my next sentence begin is what I want to know from you. Unless I find work, I mean manual work, and who the hell would employ me at what?, I shall never write again. Not that it matters, but I can only do it that way: through a penitential task, not on my bum in front of blank paper.

After the party returned to Britain late in August, Wyn was all for floating off again; life in the entourage suited her. The Trust's accountants advised that Caitlin go back to Italy. She was defeated or tempted; probably tempted. This time the move had an air of finality. Florence Thomas, living temporarily with friends on the other side of Swansea, but soon to return to the Boat House, was told they would all be away for at least a year. It was to be Rome this time, and the ever obliging Wyn went on ahead to find them a flat.

Mably, the old dog, still cared for at the Boat House, was put down. Howard Dark saw to it after they had gone. Aeron can't have heard the shot, even if a gun was used, which is unlikely. But she can still hear it, echoing over the water.

12

Roman Holidays

Ever since adolescence, Caitlin had used alcohol as a means of enhancing her identity. During Thomas's lifetime she drank heavily, and after his death her role of brilliant widow required the resources of the bottle to see her through. Late in life she spoke admiringly of 'that Zelda woman who kept going into loony bins', meaning the wife of the alcoholic novelist, Scott Fitzgerald. Mrs Fitzgerald (1900–48) was variously diagnosed as a schizophrenic and a psychopath. Drink played a part in her earlier life. Herself a writer, she wanted to be a dancer when she was young, and at parties would whirl grimly on table-tops. Probably Caitlin liked to feel an affinity with artistic temperaments cracking under pressure.

Her move to Italy called for the strong colours and sharp edges of liquor. She was saying goodbye to Britain and settling in Rome – why, she wasn't sure. To help her make this transition into shadowland she took with her a louche acquaintance called Cliff Gordon who would happily drink with her kind of abandon – unlike Wyn Henderson, who was not a serious tippler. Gordon, who wrote and acted for the BBC in Wales when he was sober, had various party tricks, including trance-mediumship, in which state he claimed to have raised King Henry VIII, Jesus Christ and Dylan Thomas. He travelled to Rome with Caitlin and the three children in the second week of September 1957, and over the following weeks (with Henderson radiating disapproval) Cliff and Caitlin proceeded to pour drink into one another.

The apartment that Wyn Henderson had chosen was in the suburbs. It was smart but cramped; Caitlin called it 'a streamlined box' and liked to get away from it. In the mornings she rose late and lingered in the bathroom, anointing her skin, washing her hair, following her strict regime of exercises. There was no question of staying in it to write. In America, *Leftover* was published and talked about. *Time* magazine (14 October) called her 'an insolent, self-confessed sinner at the bar of society's judgment' and said that the book, though 'vulgar and shameless', was 'a beautifully written, classic portrayal of the romantic temperament'. Seymour Lawrence of *Atlantic Monthly*, joint publishers of the book, cabled her from Boston (18 October) to say, 'We think you are an important writer and we are eager to see your new manuscript.' None of this made any impression. Caitlin told Stuart Thomas (25 October) that she couldn't possibly write under 'these meaningless circumstances', in which 'nothing truly touches me, and I am racking my brains for a way out'.

The first sign of progress in her affairs had nothing to do with books or career or even freedom. She simply found another man.

One of Wyn's haunts was the Via Margutta, near the Piazza di Spagna where the English have always liked to go, a street of art galleries and dealers. She and Caitlin ate in a restaurant there. The whole pack of them were having dinner one evening when a well-built Italian with a neighbouring party caught Caitlin's eye. They exchanged pleasantries and he said she was drinking too much. This naturally made her want to fight him, a prospect that causd him to smile.

He was an attractive man, with thick eyebrows and slightly menacing features. Wyn, who spoke French to him to begin with, decided from the start that he might be a suitable companion – socially he was a cut above miners and fishermen – and he was invited back to their apartment in the Via Mogadiscio for cocktails the next day. His name was Giuseppe Fazio and he was a Sicilian of thirty-three, eleven years younger than Caitlin, employed in films. As a 'director's assistant' he had been around the studios for years, finding work in the happy days of the Fifties which reestablished the film industry in Rome following the War. His facility with languages – besides Spanish and some French he spoke German and a very fair English – made him useful to film companies employing international crews, and gave him the faintly cosmopolitan air that appealed to Wyn. What appealed to Caitlin was what she had seen in the restaurant, a fanciable man.

When he first saw them all, Fazio thought that Caitlin and the small, balding figure of Cliff Gordon were husband and wife, and Henderson – now amazingly stout, and referred to by Caitlin behind her back as 'Moby Dick' – was the grandmother. He was quickly introduced to Caitlin's way of life. An English couple who had been with Fazio at the restaurant, and who were also invited to cocktails, made a statement fifteen years later, as part of Caitlin's campaign to prove she had been an alcoholic. When they arrived, about seven in the evening, they found the remains of lunch still on the table, Wyn and the children sober, and Caitlin, Gordon and other guests drunk. Caitlin grew drunker by the minute. Later she tried to throw herself off the balcony, four or five floors up, but let herself be saved. After a while she tried again; this time Fazio came to the rescue.

The new man drank little. But he was not unwilling to be drawn into Caitlin's circle, on his own terms. Next day Wyn puffed round to his apartment and (so he remembers) announced, 'Caitlin very keen on you. Why don't you come over again?' Fazio turned out to be a man of action. He came over with great frequency. Soon he was sharing Caitlin's bed, warning her of the evils of drink, and giving her injections of Vitamin B12. There was an unfortunate encounter with Cliff Gordon, of whom he disapproved. Gordon was homosexual. He had narrowly escaped prison at a notorious Welsh trial some years earlier, when a circle of gay men in a small town was broken up by police with customary viciousness. Going down in the lift with Giuseppe at the Via Mogadiscio, he decided it would be a nice idea to give him a kiss. In no time he was flat on the floor with a broken arm. He is said to have got back into favour with the Italian, using what Caitlin called his 'killing imitations of Winston Churchill' (who was still the enemy, Giuseppe having been one of Mussolini's soldiers before he was captured by the British in Sicily); but it was not long before Gordon left for England.

'Joe', as Fazio was at first referred to, was regarded as a saviour. A story somehow got around that he had been a pilot in the Italian Air Force during the war (with exciting detail of how he was shot down in the desert), and that he was now, or at some time had been, flying civil airliners. Wyn Henderson, writing to Stuart Thomas, was anxious to stress what a paragon he was, big and strong, his paws, as she put it, well worth buttering with good meals to keep him happy. Wyn gave a rosy picture of life in Rome. Caitlin was having psychoanalysis and responding well, after a bad start when she abused the analyst and was sent home with a morphine injection. All she drank now was wine with meals. Parties were being given for her in palazzos. Money was the only blot. Detailed figures in Wyn's neat handwriting told fresh tales of woe, and the Trust obliged with a few more pounds a week.

Caitlin's letters described a different Rome, in which they attended 'a few sticky cocktail parties' and the analyst was 'less use than a dose of salts'. She saw time being frittered away; the usual forces beyond her control were responsible. Debts mounted up, and in between blaming Stuart Thomas she blamed Moby Dick for not managing things better. 'It is true that living is very expensive here,' she told Brigit, 'but it is principally a matter of bad management, and our money would be a fortune to most Italian families who would live like kings on it.' Llewelyn remained a problem, his future undecided, while the Trust tried to see if the American fund would pay for him to go to university there. Caitlin suggested an Italian university but he wasn't having that.

With the two younger children at school, she described lost days when she and Llewelyn got up as late as possible and drifted about the city. 'Here is Rome laid out in all its riches and beauty,' she told her mother, 'and it is no more than a dead leaf to me.'

But there was always the Sicilian. Amid long complaints to Brigit at the end of November she said:

Did I tell you we have a new member of the family, a certain Joe Fazio who has taken on bodily all the functions of husband and father, including driving a car for us. He is Sicilian, solid, and ugly, with a big heart and a great lot of patience, and his head, though excessively large, is not overburdened with intellectual inhibitions. He is the only person who could possibly put up with the neurotic bunch of us, and we can't do without him. Luckily no complications of *Love*, though good in bed, as I am still breaking my heart over my previous beautiful traitor whom I can't forget.

Hollywood was showing interest in a film about Caitlin and Dylan, and the producer David O. Selznick, who had just finished making *A Farewell to Arms* from the Hemingway novel, asked tentatively about Caitlin's willingness to work in Hollywood with a professional screen writer. Such ideas come and go in the film business, and this one was no exception, but Caitlin's lack of interest in furthering her career can't have helped.

Her attitude always implied mysterious difficulties to do with the conditions she lived under. At least her boredom and malaise were now being attributed to drink, and an attempt made to improve matters. Giuseppe saw it as his duty – and his opportunity – to cure her. He decided the right place was Catania, where he was born and brought up, and where he knew the assistant director of a clinic. Before Christmas they abandoned the flat and went south, minus Wyn and Aeron who returned to Britain, and from 2 January 1958 Caitlin was undergoing treatment. She remained there intermittently for ten weeks, at one point having insulin therapy to induce prolonged coma, a method more often used with schizophrenics. A woman who drank so heavily and behaved so irrationally might have appeared, by Italian standards, to be insane.

In a manuscript book supplied by Henderson she began to write again, this time the work called *Jug*, meaning a prison or place of incarceration. Once more she found it hard to write a connected narrative, being too easily sidetracked. But there were passages of angry autobiography where she struggled with her 'stubborn spirit', trying to make sense of herself in relation to the world in general, and to men in particular. A cold wind of inadequacy blows through the pages. Remembering her first days at school, when she was fourteen, she finds herself in her forties equally self-conscious and embarrassed in the company of strangers. 'I like to believe I am afraid to grow up in the sense of a proper woman, though I feel millions of years older than any proper woman in the world, in case I lose my keenly preserved child's evil perception.'

But such insights didn't make her an artist, as she recognised. A moment later she considers how useful the clinic would be to a real writer, rather than 'a pretend writer like me [. . .] There is nothing in my head except myself, and I am sick of it but can't get rid of it: I want to get on to something beyond my peevishly petulant vexations.'

Jug hinted at her dilemma, that she didn't much care for the kind of person she was, yet was reluctant to see herself altered into something else. After her sleep therapy she finds herself for a time in a state of 'unnatural selflessness', of 'giving up the egotistical ghost'. Nothing remains of 'my fiendish endeavours for right, justice, truth and all the old idealistic claptrap' – which always ended in failure, 'since I was unendowed with the accompanying requisites of sweet moderation, caution, common sense'. What else the original Caitlin (who was banished only temporarily by the insulin) consisted of is left vague, except that she frequently defines herself in relation to men. She feels that she must concentrate – 'half a life too late to be sure but I never gave up' – on 'the eternal problem of how to be a passive, submissive, yet fully fledged woman'.

Elsewhere she blames men for creating the problem in the first place, complaining at their

> superior status, treatment and increased privileges [. . .] this mortally wounded indignation of mine all began in Wales when my newly acquired shrimp of a husband was given a double helping of everything at 'dinner' by his trouser worshipping mother, and daddy's armchair [. . .]

Now aged forty-four, Caitlin was already thinking about the menopause and women's 'terrifying dread of middle age: when a sex-persecuted woman has got to recognise, whether she wants to or not [. . .] that she is not wanted any more'. Women's looks, unlike men's, 'disperse, like tasteless cabbage water, down the sink'. It is women who get 'the dirty extremity of the preordained unfair sexual bludgeoning hatchet'.

A decade or two later Caitlin might have adapted her rhetoric on feminist lines. *Jug* dealt firmly with men in a long passage about pony-riding when she was a girl. After describing the delights of galloping across Dorset, she went on:

> The great advantage of the communion between man and beast, or in this case girl and beast [. . .] is that she is not constrained to powder her nose, dress up, or put on a phoney feminine act for her beast; for he is blind to shiny faces, does not care what outlandish clothes she wears, is unaware of her unfashionable shape, and unmoved by her grotesque dimensions; so that he communicates directly, not with the outward swathings of her personality as in a human relationship, but with the immediate unswathed inner essence of her person. Thus approaching that closely guarded, cowering back room, with the natural ease of one belonging there, as his instinctive birthright. Whereas for a man to penetrate that far inside her bristling defences to her secreted self, might take arduous years of loving, confidence instilling wooing; and even then he might never get there at all. Most of them are content to remain on the borderland, and do not think it is worth the trouble, or are too morally frightened, of broaching more violent hazards: if they think at all. They prefer not to know, or to ignore,

that woman is a wild and violent animal; still like to bluff themselves with
the quaint outdated conceit that she is a sweet, soft, seductive thing solely
obsessed with his enjoyment.

   Not until the lid shoots crazily off her fermenting-for-compressed-years
frustrations, the cork pops fizzling sky high out of her bottled longings,
and she is meekly led, or driven fighting as her recalcitrant mood dictates,
to the soporific horrific slaughter house of the mind, where the offending
flutter of rebellion is steam-roller removed, is he forced to recognise that
perhaps she was not so blissfully serene at home after all.

The manuscript comes to a sudden end there, on page 69.

Wyn Henderson approved of the chastened Caitlin, who, she
hoped, would be happy from now on. A single glass of wine with each
meal was to be the new regime. Henderson was back in Taormina,
thirty miles along the coast from the less salubrious Catania, having
left Aeron at Dartington Hall, the progressive boarding school in the
west of England. She told David Higham of her satisfaction at seeing
Caitlin accept a submissive role, this being the true function of women,
though it hardly seemed to have been hers. Caitlin was apparently
basking in Joe's adoration. News on the Llewelyn front was not so
good. His relations with Giuseppe were cool. Caitlin's rows with him
'left us shaking', he says, 'but Mother would say, "Row? What row?"'
The English in general were not favourites among Sicilians. 'My
dream,' says Llewelyn, 'was somewhere like Watford.'

Caitlin was in Britain in the summer of 1958. She was at a dinner
party given by Lord Kemsley, then the proprietor of the *Sunday Times*,
in July. Augustus John was there, too. Now in his old age, he was
scraping the barrel for literary reminiscence, aided by Kemsley's
journalists, and Caitlin was probably invited in this connection; a
patronising article by him about Thomas and Caitlin appeared later
that year. John wrote to Leonard Russell, the newspaper's literary
editor:

> I thought Caitlin's favourite adjective was now firmly established in the
> language. But when I dined as a guest of Lord Kemsley, our host found it
> necessary to remove Dylan's wife a step or two down the table to my side
> (opposite Henry Moore) and I don't blame him. I was accustomed to her
> table manners though I never approved them.

Soon after, Caitlin and Giuseppe, together with Colm, were on a touring holiday, towing a caravan around Britain. For once Caitlin had money in the bank, having just received three thousand pounds in *Leftover* royalties from America; David Higham begged her not to spend it all at once. When they reached Carmarthenshire, Laugharne was interested to see that the scarlet woman was back. The caravan was there a few days, parked near the sea. Granny Thomas was visited at the Boat House, where, thanks to the Trust, she was now settled permanently, with Dolly Long to look after her.

Caitlin's life was too far removed to make much impact on her these days. 'Fancy,' Florence wrote to old friends the previous November, 'its 4 years today that Dylan was taken ill in New York & died bless him 4 years next Saturday, time flies it doesn't seem so long since he left Laugharne for the last time. Well soon we shall be having Christmas here, time flies when you are getting old.' Sometimes she signed herself, 'Florence Thomas, Dylan's Mam'.

The August that Caitlin and her foreign paramour descended on the Boat House, *Under Milk Wood* was due to be performed in the village. The visitors, however, left a week or two earlier. A newspaper reporter caught up with them in Buckinghamshire, where they were staying on a caravan site. Giuseppe ('a Sicilian air pilot') appeared in a scarlet dressing gown to say that 'This Catalina is very nervous, perhaps a little neurotic, you understand, but she is an artist. I think I have been very good for Catalina.' Then Caitlin came out, looking cross, having told Giuseppe to pretend he couldn't speak English. The reporter heard from her about *Jug*, and how she was 'leaving myself out as far as possible'. Presently the caravan moved on, other caravanners complaining about the noise at night.

In Laugharne, *Milk Wood* was the centrepiece of a festival week, with nightly performances. Villagers wondered what the fuss was about. But the Thomas Industry was stirring. The same week, Carmarthen county museum was exhibiting 'Dylan's only pair of cuff-links', as brought back from America, and Cliff Walk was given its tourist-trade name, Dylan's Walk.

Florence Thomas, the survivor, rarely left the Boat House. The visit by Caitlin and Giuseppe had distressed her; so had a scheme they had (but soon forgot) to buy another property in Laugharne, the Ferry House. 'I don't want them so near,' she wrote to Stuart Thomas, 'as I know what it will be like.' She was happiest dwelling on the past. The churchyard at Llanybri, across the estuary, contained many graves of obscure Williamses, her family. Distant cousins and great-nieces called on her sometimes from their farms in the backwoods that begin where Laugharne ends.

For the festival week she sent a message, welcoming 'lovers of my son's work'. But she was unwell, and little was seen of her. The last of four performances of *Milk Wood* was on the Saturday night, 16 August. Florence, as though conjuring up a sense of occasion, died in the Boat House the same day. One version had her passing away 'as the curtain came down on the final performance'. She was seventy-six, a kindly woman who stayed close to her 'respectable' origins, and would hear no wrong about Dylan. When her will was published, it showed an unexpected sense of humour. Caitlin received fur coat and fur cape, bed and table linen and a chest of drawers, for which she was no doubt duly grateful. She also got a vacuum cleaner and a carpet sweeper.

Caitlin had often insisted that she wanted to be close to 'ordinary lives'. In 1958, surrounded by such lives in Sicily, she thought to make a book of them. She had lost interest in *Jug*, now that she was no longer in one. In Catania she was among artisans and traders. Giuseppe's father, who died when he was a child, had been a miller. His mother kept a shop. The family owned property in the middle of the city, which, when Caitlin first went there, was in the process of being taken away from them by the municipality for redevelopment.

She and Giuseppe lived in an ugly new estate outside the city, a few rooms in a municipal dwelling given as compensation for a house in the condemned quarter. She began recording the lives of friends and neighbours.

> The method we employ [Caitlin wrote to Lubbock] is first to lure a prospective victim with flattering cajolery, domestic baits and sly bribery into the house; then to persuasively lead her on: it is inevitably a she because a he is too fraught with dangerous sexual implications; to pour out verbally her entire life story, with no reserves, into a tape recorder.

Dates and the order in which things happened were not a problem, 'helped no doubt by the Catholic habit of confession, unencumbered by inhibiting shame'. But because Italians in general and Sicilians in particular were clever improvisers, it was hard to tell the true from the false. Nor was Giuseppe interested in the book. He had to translate each story from Sicilian dialect into Italian, which Caitlin rendered into 'as near literal plebeian English as I know'. She began to realise that the people she wanted to interview were of no interest to a man who saw himself moving up the social ladder, and abandoned the project.

Forces were against her: bad luck, unreliable friends, the trustees, the dead hand of Francis Macnamara. She seemed always to be drifting into unlucky environments. A council estate on the outskirts of Catania sounded less than ideal – 'a three-room box in a hideous new estate for the lowest of the low people', she told Nicolette. It was a desert, she said, adding that 'Laugharne was a positive centre of the Beaux Arts in comparison'. But she had been just as dissatisfied in Rome.

Aeron and Colm were with her. A progressive school in England had turned out to be not what Aeron wanted. Soon after she went to Dartington Hall she wrote to her Aunt Nicolette, to whom she remained close, doing her best to list the virtues of the place, which had no rules, no uniforms, no exams and no competition. 'From one to four is utterly free, no lessons. Smashing. You may stay from school all day if you like. I began by doing just that. And am now utterly miserable because no one stops me and there is no point in doing it [. . .] in fact it's ghastly.' Nor was she keen on the nude bathing. A convent school in Catania suited her better. 'God knows what the school itself provides besides God,' wrote Caitlin. Llewelyn had been in America since the summer, and was now at Harvard, on a scholarship.*

Wyn Henderson was no longer on the scene, having returned to London after a quarrel. Giuseppe had taken her place. The Sicilian, like Giovanni Chiesa on Elba, but with more success, strove to make Caitlin behave like a respectable woman. Drunkenness was not the only vice to be cured. She was discouraged from going out by herself. The estate was within walking distance of the town centre, and Caitlin was a walker. Given the chance she would march through olive groves and along beaches, getting the physical exercise she craved as much as ever. Such behaviour was not only unladylike but dangerous, according to Giuseppe. An attractive woman by herself might give simple sons of the earth the wrong idea. Unaccompanied walks through olive

---

* It is said that Llewelyn's friends at university avoided the subject of Dylan Thomas, since he never mentioned his father's name.

groves were frowned on. The worst that happened was that boys threw stones at her and shouted insults. But it was a warning. To an extent she was a prisoner.

To Roger Lubbock she wrote early in 1959 about 'my rocky road to Marbletown', ending her letter with

> the saying of the week by the hallucinations of a freak: there is nothing so big as an artist creating, nothing so small as not. I go on the assumption that an artist is the direct offspring of his torture. Or what would it all be for?
>
> There is a lizard in the woodpile that runs up and down the walls, sidles into the sink, follows me into my bedroom: I am terrified of finding it wriggling inside my bed; in whom I whimsically put my superstitious faith for want of something better to put it in. I saved its life the other day when Signor Sadist was just about to asphyxiate it with a gigantic puff of flit. So I hope it brings me luck, nobody needs it more.

Life in Catania alternated with life on the road. Giuseppe liked cars and sometimes imported them from abroad. Bringing a Mercedes in from Austria in spring 1959, when Caitlin's presence was needed for the paperwork, saved some money. She managed to spend much of the notional profit. Where Giuseppe would have lived cheaply, treating the exercise as a commercial venture and driving non-stop between Sicily and the north, she insisted on comfortable hotels and delicious meals — it was her money, after all — and in Venice she naturally wanted to buy clothes. Stuart Thomas received a telegram asking for four hundred pounds.

Back in Catania, Caitlin wrote to thank him for it, adding, 'I never want to see a bleeding car again.' There were many caravan trips. A vast camping site south of Catania, packed with foreigners and especially with the Germans who are popular in Sicily, was a perpetual attraction, the sea on one side, Etna looming on the other — 'Giuseppe's famous Etna', in Caitlin's tart phrase, 'to which, in pride, virility and erupting boiling blood, all the Catanese liken themselves'.

Later in 1959 Caitlin's restlessness took them to Rome, where she seemed briefly happy, writing to her mother that Aeron, once a problem, was now a 'rock of comfort' who 'prays ceaselessly for the redemption of my soul'. Both the children were promptly placed in boarding schools there, and Aeron, as Caitlin informed the trustees, had to have money spent on her to keep up with her friends. 'There is no limit to the luxuries of these old-fashioned rich families that go to snob convents,' she explained. 'They call it giving up all for God, but it seems to me a very affluent Paradise. So don't be too horrified by the amount, and please do it as soon as possible.'

She and Giuseppe lived at the apartment of his brother Carmelo, a lawyer, pending some more permanent arrangement. Her income soon became insufficient for a capital city. 'I always prefer to be a monarch in a mud hole to a rat in a city gutter,' she told Stuart Thomas, and talked of meandering through Spain and Africa to the Canary Islands. Her travels, whether real or only contemplated, were like nervous spasms, serving no purpose except to release a tension. Cuba was another gleam in Caitlin's eye. The Canaries plan went so far as to become a short holiday in 1960. Not long afterwards she went to Canada, taking Aeron with her, 'to do a cretinous programme on television for a few dollars', returning via Boston, to see Llewelyn, and New York, to buy hats.

Her latest manuscript, unfinished, was another piece of auto-biography. Its working title, *Out of the Frying Pan, Into the Fire*, may hint at her feelings after two or three years of living with Giuseppe. They were close but quarrelsome. Caitlin still drank and fell into alcoholic rages. Giuseppe had rages of his own. Aeron saw him pull a tablecloth off the table, depositing the meal on the floor. As Llewelyn noted, emotional storms went over their mother; though, since she was involved in so many throughout her life, she can't have found them too disagreeable.

By 1960 she showed signs of being tired of Giuseppe. If marriage was ever considered, Caitlin dismissed the idea because it would have meant losing control of her money. Her unmarried condition was no great problem, being regarded in Italy, when it was noticed at all, as the kind of idiosyncrasy to be expected of a foreign woman with unladylike tendencies. Occasionally there were embarrassments. Staying in the mountains of the Abruzzi, where they later built a house, she found herself in the unusual position, for her, of being tactful – asking a correspondent, 'If you write me here, it will be more considerate of the proprieties, among these strait-jacketed mountaineers, to put: Signora Fazio, painful as it sounds. Or: at least: Presso Fazio.* As I am ignominiously known here.'

---

* The English style would be 'care of Fazio'.

In the summer of 1960 she decided or was persuaded to do what she had never done, abruptly end a steady relationship with a man. On their way back from Germany, after another of Giuseppe's car-buying expeditions, they had paused at a small resort on the coast, Castiglione della Pescaia, not far from Elba, which had a beach with pine trees. Above-average quarrels broke out. When Giuseppe left to spend a day or two in Rome, Caitlin, egged on by Llewelyn and Aeron, fled with her family. One version of the story says it was Wyn Henderson who appeared at the resort and did the egging on, but the older children have no memory of it.

They spent hours on a bus to Milan, in the opposite direction to Rome, and on arrival sent a telegram to Stuart Thomas. The solicitor with the mordant humour was an authority on cries for help. 'By order from Mrs Thomas we sended you the bild of all the merchandises that Mrs Thomas buy for the children' (a Rome department store) was unexceptional. When there was a landslide at the Boat House, or Wyn Henderson (at the time she was in favour) needed gold teeth from a Harley Street dentist, or one of Caitlin's relatives sought a few hundred pounds for chicken-farming, prompt application was made to Stuart Thomas. Caitlin telegrams saying things like STILL WITHOUT STITCH ON BACK IN KILLING COLD came regularly over the wires. This one said FAZIO BREAKUP RETURNING ENGLAND URGENTLY PLEASE CABLE MONTHLY MONEY IMMEDIATELY.

With no luggage and no passports for the two younger children, they flew to London as soon as funds arrived, and went on to Cambridge, because it was a town without associations that might lead Giuseppe to them. Wyn Henderson was there with them. Aeron, writing to her Aunt Nicolette, romanced it into a thriller ('dangerously exciting . . . *very* narrow escape') and said they had to stay in hiding because 'fear of discovery is too great'. She and Llewelyn were delighted with the coup. At the beginning of September they were all in Swansea, rendezvousing with Stuart Thomas, having 'beautiful meals and drinks' (said Caitlin), planning the future. There were various possibilities, all Giuseppe-free.

But a few weeks later the adventure came to a sudden end when Giuseppe found her in Wyn Henderson's flat in London. According to Caitlin, he tracked her down by telephoning Mrs Macnamara in Blashford and demanding her address.

I may say [Caitlin wrote to Brigit] I was keeping it from him on purpose, with original intention of leaving him for ever; but I was extremely grateful afterwards that terrorised mother, no doubt, gave him all the dope.

He had come all the way to England on a very small scraping together of resources to search me out, and finally, after tackling the paralysed family in Cambridge, pinned me down in Moby's flat where I had gone to see Llewelyn off to America.

I could hardly not be touched by the sight of him there in the large bulky flesh, and must confess, to the horror of my family who had helped manufacture the getaway, fell with great relief into his arms.

They were 'nipping back to Italy for a couple of months' hibernation', she added; 'which solid boredom I am hoping will give me a chance to get on with my ridiculous WORK.'

Her family assumed that she meant to be caught, and were either amused or furious. At about the same time as Giuseppe's descent she was found drunk in a London street and spent the night in a cell, being fined at Clerkenwell court next morning. A reporter who caught up with her in Cambridge a few days later saw 'a neat, pretty blonde', looking 'unspoilt and healthy'. Her 'swarthy Italian man-friend' sat in silence. Caitlin said she was an outcast, and slipped in a favourable mention for her *Frying Pan* book

Wyn Henderson, with her love of parties and the cultural high-life, was fading out of the story. Over the years she had been an influence of sorts, encouraging her friend to be an author, helping with the children, receiving in return certain material benefits – air tickets, rented apartments, beds in clinics – as well as a good measure of the cheerful contempt that Caitlin bestowed on her companions. She was more generous towards Caitlin. But once Giuseppe appeared, she effectively lost her role as minder. She had now converted to Roman Catholicism and taken up with a priest, Father Benet, a poet affiliated to a monastery, who later fell in love with her and left the Church. Caitlin claimed to be cross with her for not remaining in the apartment in Cambridge. 'As for her Catholic Faith,' she unkindly told Brigit, 'that is a bloody joke . . . Her excuse incidentally for deserting the roost was that her "Father Benet" priest had forbidden a Vestal Virgin, like herself, to remain in a house made immoral by Giuseppe and me. How much more hypocritical can one get?'

By October Caitlin was back in Catania. Far from hibernating and working, she was cursing fate again. Her pen had gone stale, the boredom was killing her, the danger of being attacked by the natives kept her cooped up in the flat. 'How right Eve was about the deadliness of peasants,' she wrote to Stuart Thomas. Furthermore she was stuck indoors with three men – Giuseppe, his brother and a friend with an 'insufferable guitar' – who talked about money all the time. The only solution, she had decided, was a boat. They already had their eye on one, a 45-foot fishing vessel with living quarters. They could cruise the Mediterranean and have room for the children when they were on holiday, and all they needed to start them off was a couple of thousand pounds. Stuart Thomas was unmoved, bringing a furious response from Caitlin that may have been an early sign of the wrath to come. 'Don't worry,' she wrote, 'I shall be in no hurry to unburden myself to you again [. . .] What have you got inside you anyhow? A fucking great Stone?'

She needed enemies to sharpen her claws on, and the solicitor, who could be assigned the part of drinking companion or bourgeois skinflint as it suited her, was temporarily made the villain. Yet to Nicolette, shortly before, she was dismissive of her own scheme, saying there was little chance of the cash, and that anyway boats reminded her of their father: 'The old Francis pattern keeps recurring devastatingly in my life, and I am now convinced I shall die very soon, as great a failure as himself.' In the same letter (14 November 1960) she declared herself to be in the middle of a 'suicidal nervous breakdown' and said she had abandoned the *Frying Pan* book, 'never again to worry my confused head with niggling words that won't come right'.

Caitlin was developing the embittered letter as an art form in much the same way that her husband had developed the begging letter; though with less practical purpose, since a percentage of his concoctions at least brought cheques. Her outbursts sounded more genuine than his worked-over persuasion. The style was plainer, the woman behind it uninterested in concealment. One of her themes was an inability to confront her everyday existence as others seemed to confront theirs. Boredom and ignorance haunted her. It was as if her upbringing or a natural arrogance or both had made it difficult for her to contemplate filling her life with the ordinariness that most people take for granted; in addition, she was unable to grasp what ordinary life consisted of, so that she couldn't participate in it, even if she wanted to. All this had been implicit in the 'vague young woman' of the 1930s who was so easily incorporated into Dylan Thomas's fantasies of innocence. At the back of her mind, too, were still traces of the old conviction that a special destiny awaited her; but this belief or superstition she kept hidden most of the time.

The 14 November letter to Nicolette addressed some of these matters. After describing how she wept all the time, Caitlin went on:

Giuseppe, I must admit, has been killingly kind; because in the eyes of the Sicilians, like the Welsh, the sick can't do wrong. But his conception of kindness is to tell me: to go and have a *nice long* rest; when it would be a lot better for me, I know, to be told: to go and dig in the fields. In fact, in this wild island of savage country, it is the country I miss most because I am never allowed into it. Believe it or not, it is true because of barbarian attacks . . . and, even more, because Giuseppe hates it anyhow. So I am deprived of my chief source of physical and spiritual wellbeing; being a born country lass.

Then he pumps me full of male hormones* to build up my strength, which strangely makes me weaker and more hysterical [. . .]

What I am really leading up to is:- Is there *anything* you can suggest that I might conceivably *do*, to ward off this awful stagnant rot that has got into my bones? Because, I swear, life, under these circumstances of inertia, is quite simply not worth living. Too unbearably futile.

It is not enough to say: the children need one as a symbol in the background, because the wretched symbol must have *something* to do as well. To show you the depths to which I have sunk, I assure you, I literally save up the washing up, turning out a cupboard or clearing a dump, as a treat for the future to give me a tiny sense of purpose.

Why is Brigit run off her feet, while I wear out my bum in the bed? What wouldn't I give to change with her? Yet I am considered lucky with a loving man, a loving family and a car to move in. So what is wrong? Only that I am trained to do nothing. That has been the great handicap with us, but you have managed to get over it, and your life is wonderfully full. Can you call yourself reasonably content? and can you please tell me how it is done. Limp love. Now enough of this paean of misery. Excuse me.

There were no further attempts to escape Giuseppe's clutches; the clutches were what Caitlin wanted. By early 1961 she had prised him away from Sicily and they were back in Rome, at his brother's apartment, but without Aeron and Colm, who were at school in

---

* Reading this years later, Caitlin said they were really 'vitamin and mineral pills'.

England. She embarked on another bout of metropolitan living, enjoying the comparative freedom of Rome. Cycling around the back streets she was safer and less conspicuous than walking through the Sicilian countryside, though she liked to think she was the only woman in the city on a bicycle. On good days she joked about herself as the 'wandering bloody Jew' who could never settle anywhere. For whatever reason – reluctance on her part, caution from the trustees – no suitable apartment was found until September 1962, and they remained crammed into Carmelo's quarters. They caravanned in Sicily and stayed by a mountain lake in the Abruzzi national park, where the nearby village of Scanno reminded her of Laugharne; it was here that she was prepared to be known as 'Signora Fazio'. On a trip to London in 1961 she saw another solicitor about Trust affairs, but decided to remain loyal to Stuart Thomas. On the same trip she contacted David Gardner, who was now directing television films, to propose he take a house in London ('the Trust will pay') that would provide a base for Llewelyn and Aeron. He declined, half hoping that she would talk him into it. For old times' sake they went to bed, a mistake, as he says, there being no spark. More experienced himself by now, he found Caitlin less shy at love-making than he remembered her, ready to take the initiative. She remarked mysteriously, 'You have to do this sort of thing in Italy.'

By 1961 Caitlin was again at work on a book, writing slowly and painfully over the next year or two (it was 'that bloody bastard book' before she had finished), determined this time to escape from the confines of autobiography. What hemmed her in was Dylan Thomas's life as well as her own, the dark comedy of poetry, alcohol and begging that she had subscribed to. Others were toying with the legend; the Thomas Industry was under way, incorporating her story into his. In America, Brinnin's friend Bill Read, Professor of English at Boston University, was planning an unauthorised 'pictorial biography' of Dylan Thomas. A Welsh academic, John Ackerman, had a critical biography, also unauthorised, in the works.

The trustees, anxious to commission the official Life, got off to a bad start by choosing Ruthven Todd, the British poet and old friend of Thomas. Todd was strong on reminiscence but shaky on research, and had little interest in doing any. His address was care of a bar in Majorca, where money was sent to get him started, without success. The Welsh climate and a weak chest seemed to be the trouble, and by

1962 the trustees, complaining they had been let down, began looking for someone else. Stuart Thomas sought the advice of Kingsley Amis. From America came the suggestion of Richard Ellmann, James Joyce's biographer. In the end they chose a client of David Higham, Constantine FitzGibbon, another friend of the subject. A novelist and the claimant to an Irish peerage, he remarked at first that 'I cannot see a full-length book in it.' A substantial offer changed his mind.

When Caitlin was consulted as a courtesy, she gave lukewarm approval – FitzGibbon was 'not too bad . . . that is to say he is a nice person but not such a good writer and only knew Dylan's superficial side: his social rakish raffish act'. She would have preferred John Davenport, who saw 'the anguish underneath as well as the froth on top', but who, she admitted, might be no more reliable than Ruthven Todd. Although her fears that FitzGibbon would write a superficial book were unfounded, she began referring to him in letters as 'C. Babboon'.

Her foothold in British life, insecure for years, was crumbling. Giuseppe had become a permanent fixture. Whatever his faults, he suited her, as she suited him, whatever hers. From time to time he still worked in films; in 1961, acting as a language adviser to the director of a Second World War movie starring David Niven, *The Best of Enemies*, he landed a part as a sergeant in the Italian army. Their property-owning plans, of which there were many, made some progress in 1962, when they bought a piece of land high in the Abruzzi, by the lake where they had stayed before, and, helped by several thousand pounds from the original American fund, began to build a house. That autumn, after a summer spent in the mountains away from the heat of Rome, they finally rented a furnished apartment of their own, in a new block in the 'American colony', 'just like all the other nice people's, full of false refinements that never work'. A long account to Nicolette joked about their awe at such grand surroundings. 'We sip our beer in terror out of crystal goblets,' wrote Caitlin. Colm was attending the American school near by. They had a Sicilian scullion who never wanted to go out.

It is the poor decadent old Lady [she was forty-eight] of the Establishment that I am worried about; waiting all day, in tranquil leisure, to be served. That is where the damage lies, where the rot sets in, where the vein slashing begins.

A few weeks later (15 October 1962) she was telling Nicolette how 'cracked and cracking with hate' she felt – 'those ignominious ignoble "Menepaws" must be on the way. What does one do to keep them under lock and key? Oh not to be a weeping woman!'

Her elder children added to her difficulties. Idiosyncracies on their part would hardly have been surprising, given their rigorously unorthodox upbringing. Caitlin's natural sense of antagonism flickered in their direction, while at the same time she sought their affection and wanted them near her. Pondering the future, when their education would be finished, in a 1961 letter to her mother, she said that 'I want them in Rome naturally'. This was not so easily arranged. By 1962 Llewelyn, aged twenty-three, had graduated from Harvard and found work as a copywriter with the J. Walter Thompson agency in London. Later that year he married Stuart Thomas's step-daughter, Rhiannon Edwards, who was Eve Thomas's daughter by a previous marriage. Aeron, Nicolette, Brigit and various cousins were there, but not Caitlin, who later wrote to Nicolette, thanking her for a description of the wedding, to say that 'I could see it all only too horribly distinctly . . . I felt both disgustingly jealous, and disgustingly smug: to be out of the orgiastic feast.'

Aeron was more susceptible, to begin with. After leaving school in Oxford she chose a nursing career, and started training at Queen Elizabeth Hospital in east London. She liked the work, but in a year or so Caitlin persuaded her that it was a mistake. Why not find a 'more civilised' post in Rome? A course of shorthand and typing was organised at the American business school, and Aeron went there in January 1963, aged nineteen. She regretted later that she had been swayed by the argument that nursing was beneath her. At the time she was still a Roman Catholic, and in Rome she lodged in a convent, rather than live at the family apartment. Aeron's feelings about the robust Giuseppe were equivocal. She once spoke of the period when he first joined them at their apartment in 1957, in the Wyn Henderson days – 'The doors were left open, and there he was, plonk in my mother's bed. My mother didn't have much sensitivity. I came from the same bohemian/artistic background, but I always felt that she and I were playing different tunes.' As Aeron (like Caitlin) acknowledged, Giuseppe the strong-man had another side, a capacity for succour and kindness when someone was ill. At least he was the right partner for an alcoholic.

While Caitlin was arranging Aeron's affairs, she was putting the finished touches to the new book, which, ironically for Aeron, turned out to be written in the form of a homily from mother to daughter. *Not Quite Posthumous Letter to My Daughter*, which was postponed from 1962 because revisions had to be made, didn't appear until the summer of 1963. By using the literary device of letters – or, rather, one long letter – from a parent, Caitlin had persuaded Putnam's, who made a success of *Leftover Life to Kill*, that she could break new ground. Near the beginning of *Not Quite* she described *Leftover* as a work she was ashamed to look at again, with its 'frightful, untidy, messy muck of writing'. But the first book was autobiography in a rage. The second, which she later tried to excuse as 'satire', had the faults of its predecessor with none of its merits.

Its tone was cold-hearted; the plain-speaking malevolent. The advice, which rambled on for 174 pages, boiled down to a suggestion that her daughter marry a rich man. (This was the precept – she had always complained – that Yvonne Macnamara gave her own daughters, encouraging them to think that wealthy husbands were the answer to life's problems.) Caitlin's mistake had been 'spreading [my] meat on the waters', in her peculiar phrase. 'Store it,' she advised, meaning virginity, 'till it is seductively high, and ready to fetch the most profitable price from the highest bidder.' Somehow the book managed to be both unfunny and impractical, with its artless vision of 'decrepit millionaires' and 'sugar daddies' from another age who were supposedly waiting to be won over by 'the symbols of femininity: bust, bum, legs, lips'. The kindest interpretation was that Caitlin, the disappointed wife and lover, wanted to revenge herself on men, and hoped Aeron would do it for her; the unkindest, that she was writing it for the money.

Occasionally passable aphorisms appeared: 'Never be so simple as to seek for happiness: it is not a bird that you can put in a cage.' But they were rare. The book was embarrassing. Aeron came to terms with it only by assuming it was addressed to a fictive daughter, not to herself. This helped neutralise (for example) Caitlin's comparison between her daughter and a thistle, and such sentences as, 'If you were the sensitive caring type, like your less omnipotent brothers, I should never dare take the responsibility of opening my woodpecking beak.'

The book was not well received, though in 1963 newspapers could still find mileage in pretending that its sexual advice was 'shocking', as

Caitlin must have hoped they would. 'Caitlin Thomas bares her soul as no woman has ever done' was another popular line. At least one newspaper interviewed her in Rome, to be told that her daughter was living in a convent 'under discipline so that she can't have any boy friends'. When Aeron finished her secretarial course, Mother would help her find the right man. 'Until then I will make sure she remains pure.'

All this was nonsense. Nor did Caitlin refer to a matter that would have enlivened the newspaper coverage no end, that at the time of writing, June 1963, the author of *Not Quite Posthumous Letter to My Daughter* had recently given birth to Giuseppe's son.

According to Caitlin's version later on she had asked a woman doctor in Rome if she was pregnant, only to be told it was a pseudo-pregnancy; this was about the time of her forty-ninth birthday in December 1962. When she found it was genuine, she took violent exercise, frequently rode a bicycle to a riding school – where she at once got on a horse – and even threw herself downstairs. At the time, writing to Brigit on 23 March 1963 to confide the 'dread secret', she said nothing about attempts to miscarry. When she learned of the pregnancy,

> I was filled with a secret pride: as *you* can imagine; mitigated by panic at the outcome of it all. On top of that I had the public-face shame to deal with: of being a gaped-at freak* in this woman-controlling country: of doing their functions at the right time in the right place. And quite obviously at this stage, my right place was the broom closet; breeding more brooms.

The event concentrated Caitlin's mind on her family, and in particular on Giuseppe. At least, she wrote, he had

> the ancient civilisation to fall back on and their beaten-down philosophy of resignation in all things: acceptance, patience. Not that he does not feel dullness, boredom; or fret and fume and shout against the obstacles that hold him down. But neither does he radically believe that anything can be

---

* Delivery at the age of forty-nine is rare, though seven or eight years short of the record. British statistics don't sub-divide the highest age-group, '45 and over', but a reasonable estimate is that each year about twenty-five women who are forty-nine and older give birth; say, one delivery in 24,000.

radically changed: in the material shape of life. It has always been this way, and always will be.

So, being unable to change fundamentals, he settled for temporary escape – an attitude that Caitlin seemed both to envy and deplore. It was easy for a man, she thought, 'the trousered God', coming and going as he pleased, usually in a fast-moving car, with interludes for food and sleep.

But I fear I am sinking into my fatal old sink pot of criminal abstractions; and must switch off at once. Too much time on my bum is my trouble. All I meant to say was that, in spite of all his Latinisms, Giuseppe is exceptionally good and kind: as an Englishman could never be [. . .] For, being born under the sign of Venus, there is nothing he does not know about the horrific intimacies of women. He knows a hell of a lot more than I ever heard of. So I must count myself very lucky in this respect, and in many other basic essential things as well with him: such as a Johnny that goes up when needed. Not to mention the small item of attachment: which I can never quite decide whether it is based more on loathing or love. Sometimes one is uppermost and sometimes the other. But the cord between us goes on just the same; even if it gets pretty ragged at times and jars against each other's edges. But then, I try to remember, I am not Lady Harmony in person myself: and perhaps we both deserve a gold medal for living with each other. He is up in the mountains now trying to finish the half-made house on no money . . .

The letter was barely sent when the child was born, on 29 March. He weighed two pounds, lived in an incubator and was almost despaired of. Caitlin told Brigit that the birth was two months premature; Stuart Thomas was told three months, softening him up for the bill he was going to get from the clinic. She called the child Francesco, after Francis Macnamara, the father she said she hated.

A mother again in her fiftieth year, Caitlin rejoiced, up to a point, but with no illusions that life would get any easier. Some violent domestic fracas was hinted at in a letter she wrote to Stuart Thomas that summer, about 'an accumulation of strains: of my book, of my baby, of my housing problems etc etc etc; coming to a bursting head'.

An article in the London *Sunday Times* about money pouring in to the Thomas estate stirred her up in other directions. They were all living with Giuseppe's brother again. She wrote to David Higham, demanding the trustees buy them an apartment; she also wanted to see the accounts. Caitlin liked a fight. It helped to pass the time.

13

Family Finance

Caitlin's campaign to make the Dylan Thomas Trust do as she wished – in particular, to send her more money when she wanted it – began in the mid-1960s, when she took legal action against the trustees. Presenting herself as impoverished and denied access to riches, she bombarded them with letters and writs, sprinkling her private correspondence with denunciations of the Trust in general and Stuart Thomas in particular. She engaged a robust solicitor and more than once gave him her power of attorney.

Conflicts are in the nature of trusts set up to manage money prudently, which is why miserly trustees (usually solicitors, an unpopular profession) are familiar characters in fiction. The reader's sympathy is with penniless unfortunates trying to get blood out of stones. Caitlin's contribution to the genre was her appetite for all-out warfare. The quarrels cut across friendships and enmeshed two of her children. Money drained into legal fees and costs. For years she was implacable. People who knew her, including members of her own family, recognised her old talent for upsetting those who crossed her path, and were not always as sympathetic as they might have been.

Royalties on Dylan Thomas's books and recordings made up the Trust's income, and in the financial year ending April 1964 contributed £12,500, with a further £1,000 coming from investments. Tax had to be paid, and about £11,000 was distributed to the family, Caitlin receiving £5,500 as her half-share. Only a very successful writer could hope to earn at such levels. Earnings were more evenly distributed among authors in those days; there were fewer millionaires, and more rank-and-file who scraped a living. At book-prices then, an author would have needed to sell about 40,000 copies in hard-cover and nearly half a million in paper to gross £12,500, making him a best-selling property who was substantially better off than, say, a High Court judge or a permanent under-secretary in Whitehall.*

These were not comparisons that Caitlin and Giuseppe were interested in. They knew that Dylan Thomas had become a celebrity of a sort, and found it hard to accept that a poet with a comparatively small body of work in print was at the modest end of the celebrity scale. Even when his publishers performed talented feats of presentation, there was not much beyond ninety-odd poems, one play (*Milk Wood*), one book of autobiographical stories (*Portrait of the Artist as a Young Dog*), one group of fantasies (the *Map of Love* stories), one unfinished novella (*Adventures in the Skin Trade*), a few dozen radio scripts and ultimately his letters. This was never the stuff of a financial empire, although the buoyant income that rose with inflation until it was not far below £100,000 gross in a good year attested to the power of Thomas's romantic legend.

The other obstacle in the way of anyone becoming rich on the proceeds was that the Trust's income was irrevocably divided, one-sixth to each of the three children and only one half to Caitlin. Nothing could be done about this, or about the exclusion from Trust benefits of her natural son by Giuseppe, unless the Trust could be broken; as it could be, in theory, when all the children had reached the age of twenty-five – this would be in 1974 – and all agreed to do so. Some of Caitlin's energies went in that direction, too.

By 1964, acrimony was in the air. 'You are my solicitor, not my dictator,' Caitlin told Stuart Thomas in May. She wanted to see the Trust accounts, which the trustees were not anxious to send her, in case she realised how much capital was being accumulated for her and the children, and tried to get her hands on it. The trustees were not much good at taking her into their confidence, though Stuart Thomas kept in touch with Llewelyn (who was now his son-in-law) and told him what was happening.

The strategy in the middle of 1964 was to suspend her monthly cheques, on the grounds that the Italian authorities might start

---

* In Thomas's case, the royalties included income from recordings of him reading verse, a lucrative source.

claiming income tax, and that anyway Caitlin was temporarily better off than usual because a play called *Dylan* was running in New York, and she was receiving personal royalties.* The trustees sent her a letter of friendly admonition, explaining that it was all for her own benefit, and that the money she wasn't getting was being put aside for a rainy day. 'David', 'Wynford' and 'Stuart' signed these good tidings, which were not perceived as such when they reached Italy. A more disarming approach might have worked, then and on other occasions. Caitlin responded to flattery from men. But the trustees kept their distance. The austere David Higham never sounded as if he understood her, any better than she understood him. Stuart Thomas, though the most convivial of men – and Caitlin's drinking companion when he and Eve met her in Italy or London, as they did on many occasions – wrote brief, terse letters or no letters at all when he was back in Wales. Wynford Vaughan Thomas, a charmer of women, might have been able to personify the Trust as both a friend and an adviser who wasn't prepared to put up with any nonsense; but he was too busy enjoying himself to take on such uncongenial work.

In 1965 the Trust was still having difficulty in finding all the money that was called for. The two older children had needs of their own. Caitlin and Giuseppe had their house in the mountains to finance, and they were now in the process of buying an apartment in Rome with a 'romantic vista'. It was true that money was still reaching her direct from *Dylan*, and that there was talk of selling the film rights. But Caitlin was convinced that the central income from the Trust should make them much better off than they were. In the meantime, the monthly payments had been resumed; Caitlin and trustees rubbed along as before.

Contention was never far away. It became acute in 1966 over the *Under Milk Wood* case, brought by Caitlin to recover the original manuscript. The Trust helped her prepare the action; but it was brought in her name and she had to pay the bills. Later there were complicated arguments about whether this situation should have been allowed to arise.

The case itself was simple enough. When Dylan Thomas was about to go to America for the last time, in October 1953, *Under Milk*

---

* The play, by Sidney Michaels, was based on Caitlin's *Leftover Life to Kill* and Brinnin's *Dylan Thomas in America*, and concerned the end of Thomas's life. In the Broadway production, which had a successful run, Caitlin was played by Kate Reid, Dylan by Alec Guinness.

Wood, the radio play that had been commissioned by the BBC, was more or less finished. He then lost the manuscript while out drinking in London. The first part of it was a true manuscript, a fair copy in Thomas's hand of earlier drafts; the remainder was a typescript, much altered. It was not the first time the play had gone missing. Thomas mislaid a rather less complete version in Cardiff earlier that year, when he read some of it to a university audience, and the English Society got it back for him. If someone had lit the fire with it at the Park Hotel – it was the only copy, contained in a 'battered, strapless briefcase whose handle is tied together with string' – that would have been the end of *Milk Wood*.

In October the loss mattered less because he had previously handed it over to the BBC producer in charge of the project, Douglas Cleverdon, and copies had been made between a Thursday and a Saturday, when the original was returned to Thomas, who lost it in Soho over the weekend. Perhaps he was unconsciously rejecting a work he knew to be a sideshow. In the event, Cleverdon took three typescripts to the air terminal in London and gave them to Thomas as he was leaving. There had already been performances in America. One more was given near the end of October, two weeks before Thomas died. Afterwards *Under Milk Wood* was acclaimed as a radio play and sold 25,000 copies in Britain in its first year as a book.

Few people knew what had happened to the original manuscript. But in June 1961 it came on the market, when it was sold by a Dorset book dealer to the Times Book Co. of London for £2,000. The trustees got to hear of it, and five years later the action finally came to court, the argument being that the manuscript belonged to Caitlin Thomas (or, as some might have said, to the trustees), and so had been improperly dealt in.

The source of the manuscript was Cleverdon, who in 1961 was raising money for the mortgage on a house; the Dorset bookseller gave him £1,620 for it. He said flatly that the manuscript was his to sell, having been given it by Thomas. This was greeted with amazement by the Thomas camp, who reviled the producer for exploiting the dead; some of them still do.

Cleverdon, an engaging pink-cheeked man, aged fifty when Thomas died, was the most distinguished of a handful of radio producers who would have been called 'men of letters' a few decades earlier. He was bookish, amusing and enjoyed the company of poets. At first he knew

Thomas as an actor, using him in Third Programme productions (he cast him as Satan in *Paradise Lost*), but from about 1950 their relationship revolved around the 'play for voices' that became *Under Milk Wood*. Without Cleverdon it might not have been written. The two were friendly without being close; Cleverdon was not a serious drinker, and used to talk about a painful evening in Laugharne, when he was on a visit to coax Thomas into writing more of the play, and supper kept being postponed for more rounds of beer at the pub.

After the script finally came into his hands, he had his secretary type it out on wax sheets to make stencilled copies. Before Thomas left for America four days later, the original had been returned to him and he had lost it. Cleverdon arrived at the air terminal on Monday with the BBC copies. They spoke briefly about the lost manuscript. Thomas (said Cleverdon) named some pubs in Soho where he might have left it, adding that if Cleverdon found it he could keep it.

The offer was irresistible. At the first pub the producer visited, the Helvetia in Old Compton Street, known as 'the Swiss', he was able to secure the manuscript. 'As a book collector,' he said later, 'I was naturally delighted to include this in my collection.' Shrewdness was in Cleverdon's nature. He never failed to extract a fee from the BBC, as he was entitled to do, when radio scripts that he had written before becoming a salaried employee were broadcast. The *Milk Wood* manuscript was valuable at all levels, though its literary and senti-mental aspects probably appealed to Cleverdon more than the financial, if only because no one could have foreseen the large sums that were later paid for Thomas's papers.

After news of the sale came out in 1961, enquiries were made by the trustees. A private detective found the former manager of the Helvetia, who had no memory of manuscripts. There was a story that a barmaid knew something. Stuart Thomas followed the trail to the village of Stiffkey, in Norfolk, in vain. He also went to Rome to see Caitlin, and Majorca to see Ruthven Todd, who recalled Thomas during his last days in New York lamenting the loss of the manuscript. Others joined the Caitlin camp with anti-Cleverdon stories. Cordelia Locke said that she once asked Thomas if *Under Milk Wood* was his life's work, to which he answered 'Yes'. The implication was that such a manuscript would never have been given away. Cleverdon had a counter-anecdote, about an evening at his house when Thomas read the almost-finished play to a small gathering. Everyone was spellbound except Caitlin, who waited till he had finished and said, 'Bloody potboiler!'

The advice from her counsel was that unless Cleverdon emerged in court as a witness of 'transparent and superlative honesty', the odds were against him. As well as Todd and Locke, her witnesses included Daniel Jones, who, as the trustee responsible for making literary decisions, worked with Cleverdon on the text of the play before its first broadcast in January 1954. Jones was adamant that the producer had never mentioned the manuscript.

The onus was on Cleverdon to prove that Thomas had made the gift. Luckily – or shrewdly – he had told people about it at the time. His secretary at the BBC, Elizabeth Fox, heard the story. So did the writer Maurice Cranston. Cleverdon even put it in a letter to David Higham in 1954, adding that 'all my most rabid book-collecting hackles rise at the thought of parting with it, and I think I can square it with my conscience to hold on to the actual script'. This letter was read out by Caitlin's counsel, who may have thought its tone damaging to Cleverdon.

Among those in court was Rupert Shephard, Caitlin's old admirer. He was now her brother-in-law, having married Nicolette, following the death of his first wife and of Nicolette's husband, Anthony Devas. In his eyes, Caitlin, who came over from Rome for the trial, had become unreal. 'The moment she arrives,' he wrote in his journal, 'everyone gathers in pubs, takes taxis & eats expensive meals.' At lunchtime she led her party from the law courts to a fish restaurant in the City. Margaret Taylor was there, along with Rupert, Nicolette, Esmond (Nicolette's elder son), Aeron and Colm. Caitlin had a brief row with the head waiter over the prawns, and insisted on paying for everyone. Like Dylan Thomas, she knew how to spend lavishly on her friends.

Rupert had no time for her now (or she for him, as some of her letters to Nicolette make painfully clear). All he saw in Caitlin was a middle-aged woman using the tactics that had served her better when she was young. 'She still has considerable looks,' he wrote, '& still a power to direct people & make them slave for her, but she looks as though she has had shock treatment & is not really there. She walks in a funny stiff doll-like way. Her hands are very gnarled and ugly.'

In court Shephard watched Cleverdon being 'smeared with every sort of unpleasant insinuation'. Eventually, though, the judge had no hesitation in finding that the producer had been truthful, not least because when he was telling Fox and Cranston the story of the gift, everyone assumed that Thomas would soon be back from America. 'It would have been absolutely stupid to have invented a lie in those circumstances,' said the judge, 'and Mr Cleverdon certainly is not a stupid person.' Daniel Jones, a clever and talented man, weary of being known as Dylan Thomas's friend – instead of in his own right as a composer – was embittered by the case, and had suspicions (he told Caitlin in a letter) that David Higham and Douglas Cleverdon had conspired to Cleverdon's advantage. But the fact was that the court believed Cleverdon, not Jones.

As for Caitlin, she had to pay the substantial costs of a case that, she alleged later, she should never have been allowed to bring. Her view of the trustees changed. Giuseppe was in London even before the *Milk Wood* case, armed with powers to appoint a solicitor who would investigate her affairs. No sooner did Giuseppe have the authority than Caitlin took it away again; but presently she gave a power of attorney for one year to a well-known London solicitor, Anthony Rubinstein, and life became more difficult for the trustees.

Over the years, Caitlin fought battles with them and won some victories, without disturbing the core of the 1953 settlement and a 1957 amendment to it. If her three children by Dylan Thomas had agreed, the Trust could have been broken, or amended to make her Italian son, Francesco, a beneficiary. But Llewelyn and Aeron declined to act. Ultimately they supported Stuart Thomas, seeing him and the Trust as a guarantee of the status quo.

In the meantime litigation or the threat of it became part of Caitlin's life, an outlet for her anger. What she sought was money, but the writs and denunciations were also part of the drama of herself that kept alive the story of Caitlin Macnamara, a woman unjustly wronged. When she sued the trustees for £9,000 in May 1966 – claiming 'wrongful conversion' over five of Thomas's letters that they had allowed *McCall's* magazine to publish in America – David Higham wrote a pained letter, calling her 'my dear' and finding her action hard to believe. This was to misunderstand the degree of her aversion to such bourgeois figures as literary agents and solicitors – Rubinstein himself came under the lash before she had finished – who never quite succeeded in their ideal function, to further her one-woman crusade against the world.

Mini-sagas developed within the overall drama. In one direction the Law Society examined the Trust accounts, at Caitlin's request, without finding more than minor breaches, soon rectified. In another, the Boat House became a matter of contention, especially when it grew famous and more valuable as the poet's last home, where pilgrims came. The Trust had bought it from Margaret Taylor in 1954 at the knock-down price of £1,300, but for tax reasons it had not been put in Caitlin's name, and she didn't become the owner until 1967, when the trustees' hand was forced. Serious discussions ensued about a gas cooker, some books, a chaise-longue and a baby chair that were now in Aeron's London flat. When Caitlin tried to sell the house itself in 1968, the London estate agents who were putting it up for auction were irritated to find that a piece of apparent mumbo-jumbo – by which a body called the Grand Jury of Laugharne Corporation had first refusal of the property – was legally enforceable, as though in a real *Milk Wood*. It was another six years before Caitlin disposed of the Boat House, to a school in Swansea that wanted it as a study centre.

She liked Rubinstein ('my precious Ruby') but in 1969 he fell temporarily out of favour, just as he was taking proceedings against the Trust. 'Please withdraw my case against Stuart Thomas,' she instructed him. 'Stop it. Forget it.' She had been persuaded by 'the persuasive clan of family and old friends' to transfer the power of attorney to her elder son. Llewelyn held this hot potato for a while. Relations with the Trust improved briefly, but the basis of confidence became eroded beyond repair. At a meeting in Rome in 1971, when Stuart Thomas produced the accounts for Caitlin, Giuseppe accused him of withholding money. The conversation grew 'heated and insulting'. Aeron calmed things down by insisting that the accounts were in order, and generally supporting Stuart Thomas. Soon Anthony Rubinstein was acting for Caitlin again and was issued with new powers of attorney, although he seems to have been replaced by another solicitor in 1972, only to be rehired in due course.

Whatever case Caitlin may have had for the better management of her affairs, her methods hardly advanced it. The Trust's income grew, which was just as well, given the legal bills she incurred. In 1973–4 net royalties (after deducting the agent's percentage) totalled more than £28,000, about half of this generated by British and Commonwealth sales, the rest coming mainly from America. Caitlin's share was £13,800.

None of it was ever enough. In 1975 she put her husband's letters to her up for auction, hoping to raise not less than £10,000. She owned something over thirty, other letters having been lost or stolen, and had managed to stop most of them being published in the past. The copyright permission was not hers to give or withhold, and since the majority had been photocopied and were in other hands, her only sanction was to argue that they were confidential, and threaten to cause trouble. This sufficed to keep them out of Thomas's *Selected Letters*, which FitzGibbon edited in 1966.*

In 1975 the sale at Sotheby's in London was preceded by a television interview in which Caitlin said, 'I need the money to live on, and I don't get enough money from my trustees. It's quite simple.' Reporters in Rome were told in the same week that five million copies of Thomas recordings had been sold in America, but 'because of my drinking history I have no idea how much Dylan's copyrights are worth'. This drinking history was an important part of her case against the Trust; she said she had signed away her rights when incapable due to alcoholism.

Accused of this in public, the trustees repudiated it in public, their solicitors calling them 'men of the highest integrity'. The long-suffering David Higham told the press that Caitlin had been trying to sue them for ten years – 'This has been going on and on. At intervals she's made it up and fallen into our arms, and then she's fallen out again. There's nothing to sue about.'

Over the years numerous affidavits had been assembled in support of Caitlin's case that she hadn't known what she was doing, packed with colourful detail about violence, melancholia and clinics. Long after Thomas's death, Cordelia Locke and Nicolette were being enlisted, among others, in vain attempts to prove that Caitlin had been 'irrational' at the time she signed her name.

Caitlin probably hoped in 1975 that selling the letters would help finance further operations against the Trust. But at Sotheby's, bidders were wary; the letters failed to reach their reserve, and were withdrawn at £2,100.

Such stories kept Caitlin in the news. The books she had written were forgotten. Her public role was that of litigant and troublemaker. In October 1978, when her husband had been dead twenty-five years,

---

* The Dylan-to-Caitlin letters were eventually sold privately in America.

she was invited to London to help mark the occasion. When newspapers reported that she was living in poverty and unable to travel, a radio station offered her a free air ticket and accommodation, together with a hundred pounds spending money. Caitlin's response was to ask for five hundred pounds. The offer was withdrawn. She sulked in Rome.

Caitlin consistently overstated her own case, insisting that she deserved better of life, and that only the hostility of Fate and its servants (such as the trustees) was to blame for her plight. She gave impersonations of hardship; predictably, many disbelieved her. Trouble was never far away, and the emotional storms that gathered around her proved too much for many of those who might have been her friends.

Blackness of spirit, relieved by frenzy, is supposed to be a Celtic characteristic; as is self-indulgence. Yet within herself the predicament was real. As Caitlin settled – or sank – into quiet desperation after the birth of her Italian child in 1963, struggling with alcohol, her muse more recalcitrant than ever, there were deeper conflicts in progress than those with the Trustees for the copyrights of the late Dylan Thomas.

14

Home Thoughts from Abroad

What Caitlin wanted more than anything was to tell the truth about herself for readers who would see her as an artist in her own right. *Leftover Life to Kill,* with its indifference to what others thought, was a book of revelations, set down in anger. She realised that to be taken seriously as a writer, new directions had to be explored. But they eluded her. *Nearly Posthumous Letter* she recognised as a disaster.

One of her problems was that she lived in the shadow of Dylan Thomas. No doubt this was one reason that other people's books with Dylan at their centre irritated her. John Brinnin, who had written the first, remained on her blacklist for years, and when his friend Bill Read told her that Brinnin had had some misfortune, she replied that her faith in divine providence was restored; 'the guiding hand certainly knew where to strike,' she wrote.

Constantine FitzGibbon, though he was an old friend, received no help with his life of Thomas, which appeared in 1965. 'I am in the throes of the C. Babboon book, which maddens me with its personal inaccuracies,' she wrote to Nicolette, 'but it is my fault as I would not collaborate.' When Aeron met a film-maker who was enthusiastic about getting the family to cooperate in a bio-pic, the project was dismissed as ridiculous. Caitlin told Nicolette it would have featured

> the entire harmonious Thomas entourage tripping in and out of the ancestral 'seat' and tripping up and down the rosy-strewn path, past the decaying-to-ashes hut of the Immortal Genius. But unfortunately malignant mother's presence was also required to which blarney baloney she did not consent, being sick of delving into the 'dead as a duck' past. So that put paid to that little venture.

After the birth of Francesco in 1963 she had embarked on a book called *Professional Baby*. Meeting difficulties a year or two later, she put the manuscript on one side while she discussed a scheme to prepare a selection of her letters for publication. Nicolette could make herself useful by editing them. As a writer, indeed as a sister, Nicolette often came in for sharp words. Her way of life was organised and indisputably bourgeois; she went to smart dinner parties, drank in moderation and drew veils of romance over the family history. Behind Nicolette's back, Caitlin laughed at her. She was 'my literary sister' or 'that nitwit' the 'Lady Mayoress of Chelsea'. But Caitlin could be insulting and intimate in the same breath. She needed Nicolette as one of her confessors.

The letters project came to nothing, and Caitlin finished *Professional Baby*. It went off to London, where a publisher's reader produced a scathing report which was thoughtfully sent on to the author. 'It could not have been more filthily or foully insulting,' she told Nicolette. 'He repeated gloatingly several times that [the book] was pretentious and cheap and cashing in on Dylan's name.' Friends in Rome told her to blame the alcohol rotting her blood, which was hardly more encouraging. She responded by going on a bender and breaking up Harry's Bar in the Via Veneto, after which she was put in a clinic. More than a year later she was still complaining to Nicolette about 'that bastard — ' (she knew his name), who

> did his job most efficiently of wiping me off the map. I can't think what else to do with myself instead. My interests and talents are dismally narrow; I can't help resentfully blaming our mother for never having taught any of us anything constructive, not even cooking as far as I am concerned, so that now that I have outgrown full-time boozing and whoring there is nothing to fall back on [. . .] I am driven to forcing myself to do spinal exercises based on functional organic actions, like shitting and fucking, locked alone in the confinement of the bathroom. A bit pathetic, is it not? . . . Does it not twang a strain out of your heartstrings . . .

Caitlin's letters tell her story in their own fashion, and one can see why she thought to publish them, but they also suggest what damaged her writing in general: that she was too honest for her own good. The artistry (as she knew, only too well) was lacking. Her indifference to what people thought worked both ways. To hear someone haunted by her failures, confessing her weaknesses, is unusual enough to command respect. To hear axes being ground and old obsessions aired, with the same indifference to what others may think, risks boring them.

From the middle of the 1960s, while the war with the trustees waxed and waned, Caitlin moved restlessly between the Roman apartment and the mountain villa, with occasional sorties to Sicily to keep Giuseppe happy, sifting through her life, seeking justifications for the past and ways of escape from the present. Her colourful accounts of age and decay made her sound at least ten years older than the truth – in 1965 she was in her early fifties, in December 1970 she was still only fifty-seven.

'Dying sister', she signed letters to Nicolette. She was 'a harassed aged hen'. She told Brigit she was 'a disorientated ant, with a matchstick on its back, crawling with fixed determination towards its last home through "No Woman's Land"'. To Aeron she wrote that she was 'constantly consumed with the futility of everything . . . Everything presumably meaning me and my futile life'.

Alcoholism was part of the problem, but she was afraid that because drinking was so integral to her nature, to give it up would mean becoming a different person. With help from Giuseppe she had periods of moderation, only to break out into uncontrolled drinking when she needed to assert herself. She was in a Rome clinic for a month in 1966 with 'chronic alcoholic excitement', and again at the end of 1967, when, 'dispirited, anorexic, very anaemic and rather depressed' – this was after the Harry's Bar fracas – she went into the Villa Electra for electric-shock treatment. In between she was back at the Catania clinic, writing to Aeron (3 March 1967):

> Yes, I am back in the old familiar 'potty' hole again, for a last desperate endeavour to pull together [the] cracked remains: which is not at all sure whether it wants to be pulled together again or not. Whether it wouldn't prefer to explode in one last loud bang out of the elephant's bum over Santa Agata* [. . .] I am really I think terrified of going back into the world, small as my world was, with no crustacean skin of drink to protect me. It is not even that I miss it. I only know I miss something I had before which I can very well do without. But it is the *force of habit* when I get back into my own surroundings that I am afraid of: to pass by the 'Jo-Jin' for instance,

* The Piazza del Duomo, in the centre of Catania, has the statue of an elephant, made of lava, facing the cathedral of St Agatha.

without a backward glance; or even harder to go inside and munch a squelching cake unswilled down . . . Then, if I don't drink at all, because I fear like most Celts I am the all or nothing type: we are not unfortunately gifted to sip gently one wineglass all evening; there is the very real peril of *shrinking* like Hemingway did to less than nothing.

The old rumour of suicide still had its potency. In the same letter to Aeron (who was apostrophised as 'my dearest female child', no doubt one of her mother's sly back-handers) Caitlin went from chatting about Giuseppe's health to say:

In parenthesis, would you state to me what you consider to be the most 'happy' manner of suicide [. . .] Bearing in mind that I suffer from vertigo and refuse to jump; also that the floating downwards drowned and bloated carcase does not attract me either, one wee bit: not to mention the last moment, change of mind, suffocating struggles in the water before- hand. On the other hand I feel that an overdose of pills: *what kind, how many*; is too banally easy-sounding. Nor am I a born self-ripper with the knife: at the first spot of Irish blood I would be OUT. So what remains: yes, the *gun*, I like that, but don't know how to handle it . . . Must learn: put in Memo – So you see it is not so easy as people *think*, unless they cease to think, to kill oneself. Can you please send me by return some helpful medical information on the subject: or a phial of dynamite to put up the arse when desperate.

When on a binge, Caitlin could be comprehensively insulting, a talent that went back to her youth. In February 1968 she was in the south of France, with Giuseppe, to meet the film actress Katharine Hepburn, who was filming *The Lion in Winter* at Arles. The trip was paid for by an American magazine – she has forgotten its name – which hoped to base an article on a conversation between the two women. Both of them had lived with alcoholics; Spencer Tracy, Hepburn's companion for nearly thirty years, had died in 1967.

'Though I am pretending *not* to be,' Caitlin wrote to Aeron, 'I am, in reality, petrified stiff – I can't think [. . .] *what*, in boggling imagination, we can possibly talk about . . . Best not to think, and trust in primitive instinct. For, as you know, of the ignoramus, I am Queen.' Her recollection is that 'They said, "Whatever you do, don't mention Spencer Tracy," so of course it was one of the first things I did mention.' She was aggressive and insulting. Dimly she remembers going into a bar and wrecking herself with Pernod. All she recalls of Katharine Hepburn is that the actress flinched.

The following year, 1969, there was an unfortunate incident in Rome when a small Fiat being driven by an Italian woman friend went the wrong way up a one-way street. Caitlin and Aeron were in the back. A policeman stopped the car. When Caitlin began to berate him, the friend explained hastily that her passengers were English. Nothing much would have happened, had Caitlin not insisted on getting out and continuing the conversation in the road. During the course of it she told the officer he was a brute and his uniform made her vomit; after this she hit him. Aeron left hurriedly ('I wasn't going to prison for my mother'), and so did the friend. Caitlin was taken off to a women's gaol, where she was 'put in a cell with a little woman who had tried to get away from a supermarket without paying. You had to brush the cell floor, and she helped me. I'd never brushed out a cell before.'

For someone who hated incarceration as much as she always insisted she did, Caitlin saw the inside of a remarkable number of cells and clinics with locked doors. This time she was imprisoned for some days. The fastidiousness that made her shrink from physical unsavouriness was well in evidence when she wrote to her mother soon afterwards, describing

the list of privations in my order of horror precedence.

1) Lack of any privacy. Even lavatory behind flimsy curtain in freezing soaking cell. 2 or 3 cell mates together in each cell.

2) Lack of any washing materials or face creams. 1 cold tap and tiny oblong of mirror by barred door to observe conduct of inmates from outside.

3) No sleepers, shit pills or calmers down of any sort. For those fortunate enough to have deposited a little money at the gate when *ushered* in:-

4) 2 packs of cigs per day, surprisingly generous.

5) 1 quarter bottle of wine from second day on: agonisingly inadequate; then they all jumped on one for a sip. It was the only thing I had the strength to refuse. All the rest of my property, including packages of clothes etc and food sent in from outside, was instantly robbed. Mostly by prostitutes and gypsies and I hadn't the guts left to lift a finger of protest [. . .]

6) Food was the usual army bean mush bash [. . .] I was incapable of forcing down a spoonful of the revolting muck [. . .]

7) Neither, as far as I was concerned, did *sex* enter into the picture.

Never been anything further from my mind ever, and, least of all, *then*. But apparently the long-timers are very bothered by the deficiency of it and would put it as a priority on their list. In the meantime they made up for it, made do, by having a screaming hot time with the fat as pigs nuns in charge with the big jangling keys, playing them up with obscene words and gestures which the cackling nuns obviously adored and egged them on for more . . . Shutting the eyes of propriety.

8) I was personally bothered a lot more by the complete lack of exercise for the paralysed, stinking like a cod-fish by now, body [. . .]

But one good thing that prison did do for me was to appreciate deliriously every breathing second after in the prison of my home.

The case was not proceeded with. The policeman is said to have been a Sicilian, who agreed to help another Sicilian's woman by telling the judge that he had not been hit, only pushed. A more important effect of the episode was that it became involved in Caitlin's decision to abandon the action that her solicitor, Rubinstein, was taking against Stuart Thomas. This was the occasion, already described, when she gave instructions to 'Stop it. Forget it'. Family and friends had persuaded her, 'playing on my sentiment in my weakest moment after final delivery from dark incarceration'.

The experience alarmed Caitlin, and this in turn may have encouraged her to enjoy herself while she could when she visited London three months later, in January 1970. Once again it was Rupert Shephard who saw her in action. Protective towards Nicolette, he knew how oppressive she found her sister. Caitlin arrived drunk one evening at the house in Chelsea, refusing food and demanding white wine. After making herself objectionable to one of the Devas sons and his wife, she started giving orders to Rupert, and became aggressive when he told her he wasn't a servant. 'N. slapped her face twice & later C. pushed N. backwards on to the floor.' As he hurried out to look for a taxi that would take her away, Shephard could hear the sound of breaking glass. Eventually Caitlin left, protesting and falling about the place, while her hosts 'mopped up a flood of gin, sherry, Dubonnet, tonic & soda. I shall be happy if I don't see the Peter Pan of all time again'.

A few days later she was back in Rome, 'more dead than alive', writing to Brigit about her excesses in London. These included at least one convivial session with Stuart Thomas, referred to as 'the "Stewbags" onslaught'. Various drugs had been prescribed for her, including Antabuse, which causes nausea if alcohol is drunk; Giuseppe, alternately friend and enemy in her letters, was overseeing the treatment.

While in Britain Caitlin had also visited Blashford, where Brigit, officially Brigit Marnier since 1944 – though no Mr Marnier was to be seen – continued as spartan and self-sufficient as ever. A riding accident years earlier had left her with an eye-patch, which added to the air of inscrutability. A painting or two by Augustus John could be seen; she was his lover for years. Writing from Rome now, Caitlin told Brigit how much she envied what she called 'your dog's life', and made unfavourable comparisons with herself:

So the proof is in the results: lucky you, and unhappy me. Chronically unhappy, I don't even know why. Nasty character never satisfied so permanently punishing itself. Got all the material benefits that a mature woman is supposed to want, so what the Hell *more* do I want. All that *you* have got with none of the material benefits . . . that out of date French commodity known as 'joie-de-vivre'.

For the first time Caitlin determined she would give up alcohol. She joined the branch of Alcoholics Anonymous where Americans went, describing herself as 'Caitlin, a writer'. 'Fingers tightly crossed,' she wrote in the summer, 'garlic clutched to my heart and festooning the windows against D.T. vampires' – she could have meant 'Dylan Thomas' or 'delirium tremens' – 'I believe I am beginning to get around the bend.' Near the end of the year she was writing to Brigit to say she was physically well but mentally empty —

Utterly empty of everything that was there before. That is all to the good. Along with utter disappearance, in sympathy, of all carnal appetites and creative impulse. Not happy. But less unhappy. Never talk now. Never laugh; but never did come to think of it. Latterly occasional tiny glimmer of satisfaction. Minute gleam of illumination.

In different mood Caitlin could sound less of a martyr and more her old self. Writing to Aeron in December 1970, she described her fifty-seventh birthday, when a mixed bag of Italians and AA members invited round for the evening failed to enjoy themselves:

For myself, crucified between these contrasting breeds of Latin and

American, it was decidedly sticky going ... And, having previously sneaked Silvana's glass of red wine in the kitchen, at a certain point I turned palpitating puce: delayed effects of Antabuse pill not having worn off yet, which added even more to my embarrassment [. . .] A thoroughly wasted evening, confirming flatly my growing conviction that it is useless for me to attempt any social life without drink; suffer too much [. . .]

My best birthday present was, needless to say, from myself: a most attractive, real, glossy, black 'Lapin': rabbits to you: coat, divided up by strips of Leopard all the way down. Really fetching. I also got an outsize leopard bag to match the strips, costing 50,000 lire. Altogether, at Eurosport, where I buy nearly all my sporting wardrobe, on the 500,000 lira level [about £400]. Not bad, for a start, was it: can't accuse me of meanness to myself, at least.

Slowly and painfully, Caitlin cut drink out of her life; there were occasional lapses, but she reached some kind of stability. She wrote essays for Alcoholics Anonymous, raking through her earlier years, looking for clues to what she was. Her father and his illusions made a useful scapegoat: 'failure has bred, in direct line, failure.' His bombastic manner, his untrustworthy charm, his neglect of wife and children, were all laid out for inspection. It was his fault that his three daughters were denied a proper education, 'with the result that my eldest sister married a poor artist, my middle sister never married at all and stayed at home to look after my mother, and I married a penniless and drunken poet'.

It wasn't much of an argument, but Caitlin was concerned only to protect herself against the unbearable thought that whatever she had come to, it might be her own doing. Better to blame Francis Macnamara, or, failing him, blame drink itself. She embarked on another book, called *Double Drink Story*, in which alcohol was the villain and explained everything about her and Dylan Thomas.

Alcoholics Anonymous had helped her stop drinking, but abstinence brought none of the serenity that she confidently awaited. Anxiety and boredom still plagued her, and the post-alcoholic world was crueller than its predecessor. Preparing for one of Giuseppe's caravan tours, she told Aeron that they thought of visiting Italian beauty spots, 'which, in all these years, I have shamefully seen so little of properly. Or only through the purple fingers of a beautiful winey curtain'. With wine, all countries were the same; without it they were 'frightfully clear and sharply different: hostile and unwelcoming'.

Her body continued to be washed, creamed, oiled, pummelled and kept in the best possible condition, using what she called 'my sacred essential paraphernalia'. Morning exercises were crucial, followed by olive-oiling herself from head to foot. When they were at the mountain villa her corporeal routines kept her inside till eleven o'clock, when she hurried out to bathe in the icy lake, or cycle '2 billion times' around it with 'Chico', her Italian son. Their apartment in Rome in the fashionable Via Salaria, where they moved in 1973, had a heated swimming pool near by, and Caitlin and Chico swam in it most days.

Exercise she found was the best therapy for alcoholism, 'seeking perpetual harmonious motion of the body', rather than endlessly talking through the problem with other alcoholics, 'the nearest they dare get to being drunk. Rather like the sexual "voyeur" who gets a second-hand kick out of watching a couple fucking.' Her bicycle still helped her exercise in Rome, and people still jeered, calling her a 'little cow', 'la vacchetta! la vacchetta!', while Chico, pedalling at her side, loyally shouted insults in return. 'Chico, of course,' she wrote to Brigit, 'is a pure gift from the sky – but it is a gift with fringe discomforts – that of [my] being such an ancient mother and trying not to put him to shame with one's great grotesque age. He explains me in the school as a crazy aunt.'*

While continuing to keep her body in shape, she had no illusions – was in fact anxious in her letters to emphasise blemishes and grey hairs. Always quick to cast a cold eye on her surroundings – and herself – Caitlin seemed to gain a feverish clarity of vision from the absence of drink. 'I think I have got *Cellulitis*,' she announced to Brigit,

> which means floppy folds of flabby flesh hanging off my backside, my thighs, down the backs of my legs and arms, and any other likely bits of my body it can conveniently hang off ... Constantly demoralising me, reminding me that I am done for – that I am nothing more than an old bag of flapping flesh. *Charming* – as Colm would say. Especially for people like us – essential body-users – it is an intolerable insult to one's last "amour propre". It is easy enough to accept one's brain as a bad job, but one's body – one's pride and joy – no, never – that is too much. Do you agree? [. . .]
>
> I still wear gloves to stop my nail-biting and flesh-tearing but I have

---

* Francis Thomas Fazio comments (1993): 'I was never *once* ashamed of my mother's age, and had no problems in saying she was my mother.'

found a way out of that one – I simply take them off, do what has got to be done, and put them back on again. Then Giuseppe wonders, baffled, why they refuse to grow properly . . . Although he is so cunning and suspicious about most things, he is surprisingly innocent about others. Poor bloody long-suffering bastard – all this gruelling time – with me. Can't help pitying him *sometimes*. Sometimes me.

Her gallery of horrors was kept up to date. Winter had always been a signal for despair, closing in on 'four individual lost souls' – Silvana, the Venetian housekeeper, made up the family – each of them 'alone and apart in their separate black boxes of desolation'. Brigit was assumed to be the one who understood the primitive fears that came round with the seasons: 'I expect like us you are about to cut your throat with the winter gloom descending.' Or, they were like 'mummified statues', kept together only by the child. Or, her wisdom tooth was poisoned, or she was close to death after swimming in 'that icy shit-filled lake in the mountains' (Caitlin's letters often had cloacal preoccupations), or she had a broken right arm caused by hitting Silvana over the head. Or there were dogs barking in the night and worse – she hated animals, and described for Brigit, who loved them, the dog problem when she was taking Chico to school from the Via Salaria apartment –

You can imagine my blind, handbag-swishing at them, *rage*! Then, to add insult to injury, the classy dogs are taken out from their enclosed palaces, at given intervals, solely in order to smear the pavements with their loathsome extra rich and juicy in this snob district – souvenirs of almost human SHIT. Unless one walks permanently with nose to the ground, zigzagging skilfully between their lavish excrement, one's squeamish feet inevitably land up squelching in the middle of it! *Charming* – to be among the 'Best People' at last, I must say. But that has always been Giuseppe's dream [. . .] to make *his* idea of a real lady out of me . . . Not mine. A losing battle I'm afraid and too late. I am the believer in the 'Low-Life' addict – like all of us *Artists* dear – *so* sensitive. In theory anyhow, as long as it doesn't get too close.

Her future as a writer was still something that Caitlin took seriously. A manuscript of *Double Drink Story* began to circulate. Wyn Henderson, advising from afar, didn't like it, and Caitlin was heard to complain of 'poison pen letters from my lifelong friend'. A few months later she reread Brinnin's book and was 'shattered all over again', this time to discover that it 'says everything – very well and very piercingly – that can be said. It makes my stupid manuscript look like a heap of stale turds [. . .] I am afraid Wyn was right – it is unqualified bullshit.' Predictably, she didn't take her own advice, and continued to pore over the manuscript.

Nicolette, whose family biography *Two Flamboyant Fathers* was well reviewed when it appeared in 1966, sent Caitlin another instalment of the Macnamara story, in manuscript form, in 1972, and received some harsh advice.* Caitlin's letter was one of her exhausters, thirteen large pages and a postscript, well over three thousand words. She began by chiding Nicolette for fearing negative reactions – 'You make me feel like a most unpleasant person, which I am doing my best not to be now: was I really as scathingly vile in the old days as your fear and trembling would suggest?' Then, moving on to passages in the manuscript about Brigit and herself, she told her sister that she was being far too tentative, and didn't understand what biography was about.

> Talk about bursting at the seams: it is only too obvious you are dying to say more, but dare not; and I am afraid the reader, as I was, will remain dissatisfied. As in 'Flamboyant Fathers' you hold out a fascinating titbit but withhold the joint of meat. That is alright as far as it goes, but it is not far enough [. . .] you [have] got to give the whole HOG or nothing. And to Hell with your, or other people's, feelings: if you are going to consider *them* you might as well forget it. A semi-biographical work, with the guts taken out, is of no use whatever in the final event. So just decide whether you wish to be nice and liked, or truthful and disliked . . .

Nicolette had used the word 'honey' in connection with Brigit. That wasn't good enough. 'The whole concept of honey is too soft and sweet to be associated with her. Her substance is more like molten lava pouring from a boiling benign volcano over the open wounds of mankind.' Caitlin was getting into her stride.

Now if you could allow yourself to apply to people the same force of

---

* The manuscript was never published in the form Caitlin saw. It may have ended up as *Susannah's Nightingales* (1978), a slim memoir about the French side of the family, which was Nicolette's last book.

unsuppressed passion that you allow yourself to apply to 'truffles' – and other manifestations of nature with which you are passionately familiar – that really *would* be something. But in dealing with people you are too fearfully self-conscious: you are walking on eggs which woe betide to you if you risk breaking their shells . . . And unfortunately for the reader people are incomparably more interesting than truffles!

It may be that you just don't know about people; who does, who knows even about themselves: I am sure I do not . . .

As for remarks in the manuscript about herself, Caitlin claimed to find 'a grudging admiration, one might say almost envy' in 'your very discreet little hesitant piece'. But Caitlin was no more indifferent to criticism than anyone else, and her advice earlier in the letter not to worry about hurting people's feelings was a general observation, not to be confused with particular references to herself. Thus she spotted in Nicolette's manuscript a 'nearly invisible sting in the tail', which would have left her 'utterly deflated', had there been anything left to deflate.

I don't quite understand why you decided I was *surprised* – trailing along after Dylan in that broke drunken world, what great projects could I make for myself? – not to win. And to win *what* exactly: the rat race to the ambiguous 'top'? In what does this ambiguous 'top' consist according to you? Is it a famous name for great things as opposed to, in my case, a famous name for infamous things? Is it quite simply what nearly everybody – inevitably including me – would like, and hardly anybody gets; genuine artistic recognition? For I don't imagine you would stoop to consider material gains. Besides, whatever material gains I ought to have by now by rights, as you may have gathered after our London fiasco,* [would] go into all the 'Big Boys' pockets – instead of mine. And even if by some miracle I did win my case, it would still not go into *my* pocket!

Well if this is what you want to hear, if it gives you any real satisfaction, here it is. I regard myself as the biggest misfit of the age who even now, at this impossibly late stage, has not found anything resembling a 'niche' for myself. I am not even sure that I want a fucking 'niche'. I am the eternal wandering tourist: always escaping and never getting anywhere. Could there be a worse fate than that? But, worse still, to feel that it is richly deserved . . .

---

* Caitlin's case against the trustees had been rebuffed earlier in 1972, and was never resumed with quite the old vigour.

Occasionally her bold front was weakened by nostalgia. In a letter – only one – to Aeron (1979) she wrote about missing her 'first life' with Dylan and its 'disreputable fun'. They were young, they were in love, they never stopped drinking; although her body may have been present in those days, she wrote, half the time her mind was not. She was ignorant of 'reality'.

Sometimes she confessed to Brigit that she longed for 'the green rainy pastures of England', but it was the past in relation to Brigit that she seemed to have in mind. 'I can see you now in your black forest,' she wrote, 'sitting beside your little red-glowing stove, and I wish I was there too.' Blashford as a place failed to arouse any sentiment, though on a trip to London she did revisit Barker's – the Kensington store, still agreeably old-fashioned in the 1970s – and found that it revived memories of her early childhood, when 'Granny Mac', the wife of Henry Vee, took her shopping.

It was ridiculous, she told Brigit, to find that she was homesick yet had nowhere to be homesick for. Sobriety made her aware that 'it is not the sun I want but the clouds and mists I was accustomed to in a life before this one. So long before, that I can barely recall it'. She had nothing good to say of her present condition.

I was really surprised and touched when you said: I would like to see you happy . . . Nobody has ever said that to me before and I think you are the only person that has ever noticed that I am unhappy. I think I have been unhappy for more years than I can remember – ever since I have been in Italy, more or less . . .

Yvonne Macnamara had died in 1973, at the age of eighty-seven. At almost the same time, Aeron married a Welshman, Trefor Ellis. Neither event brought Caitlin from Rome. She wrote to Nicolette, thanking her for her 'fascinating descriptions of two such very different events' (adding that she would show the wedding photographs to the neighbours, if only she had any), and hurried on to talk about alcoholism, before reining herself in:

There you are – you see – my daughter gets married – my mother dies – and all I can think about is the alcoholic implications for me in these dramatic situations. Sometimes I am convinced there is not a grain of love left – if there ever was any – in my whole burnt-up system. Burnt to a cinder by alcohol [. . .]

I don't know why you should think I had a hate relationship with my mother – I did not hate her. I disapproved – in retrospect – of her Lesbian set up – and in my childhood suffered from her indifference and neglect – of all of us. The good old story of deprived-of-mother-love and consequent resentment. Not to mention all the other educational things we were deprived of.

But – notwithstanding my act of rising above her death – I have been dreaming about her solidly every night since . . . So where's the logic?

Her relationship with her children grew no easier. Of the letters she wrote to them, only those to Aeron are available in any quantity. Llewelyn and Colm moved to Australia, and Caitlin saw little of them – 'my sons,' she wrote, 'are like passing spaceships.' Aeron – who has made no secret of her pride in having Dylan for a father, and who writes poetry of her own – was as determined as her brothers were to lead her own life. As a young woman she travelled widely, dabbled in Buddhism, as she had earlier dabbled in Roman Catholicism, and met Trefor when he was singing in America with a Welsh choir, and she was a guest artist, reading poetry. She had 'been with Italians for years, and it was refreshing to meet Welshmen. I thought, I'll marry one of those.'

Her mother's letters to her range from warm and loving to angry and sarcastic. The full emotional armoury was deployed over the years. 'I doubt sometimes if you possess a heart of your own, or you would not so mutilate your mother's' (1967) rubs shoulders with 'Nothing can kill my love for you' (1974). Hints that she will be dead soon are slipped in amid the gossip. In a letter to Brigit shortly before Aeron's marriage, Caitlin describes her as 'My Lolita, my volatile Ophelia carried down the current of the river with the weeds and her fish-eyes wide open; my too close, too cossetted, too loved Aeron'; her misdeed on that occasion was not to have given Caitlin her London address – 'Why, if I dropped down dead in the road or flung myself – unable to accept such total rejection – under a train – nobody would know where to find her to tell her the happy news.'

The affairs of the Trust drove a wedge between her and the two elder children, because they seemed too ready to side with Stuart Thomas. When Caitlin was busy fighting the trustees in the 1960s, she told Aeron it was 'imperative that you finally commit yourself one way or the other. In blunt words: for or against your mother [. . .] So consult your conscience scrupulously [. . .] Stick by your one and only

Mother.' They were unwilling to give the support she wanted. In 1973 Caitlin was complaining that 'nothing more has happened about my three big children providing for Francesco'. There were reasons for their reluctance, but she saw what they did as treachery.

Llewelyn didn't escape the wrath. In a 1978 letter to him,* Caitlin complained of 'being left, as I always am, in the pitch dark by you and by your pal Stuart Thomas'. It offended her that Llewelyn wouldn't talk about business matters, although 'according to my book of maybe old-fashioned rules, it is the solemn duty of the eldest son, in particular, to look after the welfare of his poor old dogsbody of a mum'. She spoke of her children's frequent generosity to her –

> So why, I ask myself, in the case of your half-brother, is there such a strong resistance from all of you – bar Colm – against letting him into the money fold too – for his little crust of bread as well [. . .] It is very odd, it is very strange, it is very Welsh – never committing yourself – it is not as I should wish you to be.

By the 1980s, Llewelyn had left advertising, his marriage had ended, and he was working as a landscape gardener in London. He still saw his mother from time to time, and went on practising detachment. On one of Caitlin's visits, Llewelyn and his woman friend arranged to take her out to dinner. At six in the evening, when they called at the flat in Kensington where she was staying, they found that she had already eaten. 'Caitlin, she no hungry,' said Silvana. 'We go to Dino's at five o'clock and have spaghetti and apple pie.'

With Aeron, the bond remained strong, subject to the frictions between a volatile mother and an independent-minded daughter. When Aeron was pregnant for the first time in 1975, her mother wrote cheerfully to suggest some names – Chloe for a girl, Daniel for a boy, 'unless of course you would prefer something very distinguished like – John Hamilton Stuart [Stuart Thomas's given names]? Or something reeking of Latin shores like – Giuseppe? I hope you can hear the bells pealing to warn you of a joke.' In the event it was a boy. It was named Huw Dylan. Caitlin said, 'How original.'

I first tried to meet Caitlin in about 1975, when I was at work on a biography of Dylan Thomas. She ignored my letters and remained a distant threat, but after the book was published in 1977, she wrote to

* The source is Caitlin. She often kept copies of her letters.

ask for a copy, and we began a correspondence. Her second communication was a postcard showing an arrangement, possibly symbolic, of a cat and some pink roses, with a characteristic message to say she was 'very disappointed there was no note of dedication for me'. Her third was 'a rather tame porno card from the mountains!' (two young women whose dresses disappeared, leaving them naked, when the card was tilted), hoping we might meet one day.

When Caitlin had read the biography, she wrote with some friendly remarks that culminated in a criticism – 'not enough emphasis on the booze, not only at the last but from the first: it ate up all our money and all our lives'. In a following letter (September 1977), she wrote about her and Dylan's naïveté in matters of drink and sex; how it rankled with her that he 'obtained both fame and escape, his two most desired ends, in one fell swoop – leaving me holding his babies'; how those children meant that Dylan was always with her, and were 'the greatest gift that Dylan has given to me'. It was in this letter, too, that she deliberately gave the game away by saying that the children, 'with their funny looks and big brains', were '*miraculously*' his, because they could so easily have been somebody else's.

One reason for her interest in me was that she hoped I might write something about the Trust and how it had treated her. I avoided this entanglement, and when we did meet, when she was visiting London in May 1978, the excuse was a magazine article to be called 'Portrait of a Marriage'. I went to her hotel in the Cromwell Road on a Saturday morning, and was surprised at how frail she was, her face deeply lined, with only the glassy blue eyes to light it up. Her aspect was sad more than anything else – sad but alert, with a brilliant green silk scarf and orange shirt as if to assert that she wasn't finished yet. Her hair was harshly blonde, probably tinted; the voice small and soft-vowelled; her hands invisible in white cotton gloves, which, she explained, stopped her picking at her fingers.

We talked in her bedroom, with a tape-recorder on the quilt. Was Silvana there at one point, hovering in the background? I think I would have remembered had Giuseppe been in the offing. Caitlin answered questions easily enough, although even then, aged sixty-four, her memories had blank spaces, or bore the marks of frequent repetition that suggest the experience itself has become second-hand, a photocopy of a photocopy. She spoke about Francis Macnamara ('a bad father, a bad writer, a bad everything'), about Dylan, men, drink and

America. Laugharne came briefly out of the mists – 'I don't know why it turned into such a sentimental dream, because in point of fact it's a pretty dull, awful little backwater. Apart from the rather beautiful estuary, the birds and so forth.' Old Mrs Thomas appeared hobbling on her two sticks – 'Typical Welsh woman, very kind, drove Dylan mad with all that chattering'. After Dylan's death, Caitlin came across a drawer at the Boat House filled with the letters that she, Caitlin, had written to him. 'Burn them,' said old Mrs Thomas, and they were burnt.

Was that a true story, or a story invented to conceal the fact that Dylan didn't bother to keep Caitlin's letters?

'When you get old,' she said, 'you do a frightful kind of summing-up.' She talked about her sisters:

> Our old age has completely turned the tables, because it's perfectly true, I was more or less the fighting and the vital one then, and I was usually the one who got the man that anyone was after. But now, Nicolette's done extremely well and got everything she wants, Brigit's quite happy where she is, and I'm the isolated, cut-off one, the solitary one, who's been left on the shelf. You know? So it's a sort of divine justice.

On the Monday we met for a second time at the hotel. This time Brigit was in the bar, with her eye-patch; so was Llewelyn – at thirty-nine the same age as Dylan when he died – with his daughter Jemima. His face was recognisably his father's. He had prospered as a writer with the J Walter Thompson agency, latterly in Australia, but would drop out of that world over the next decade. Caitlin and I went upstairs again and talked in the bedroom – more Dylan, drink, America, Laugharne.

> He liked to do the wild things in London, but then he always wanted the little hole to come back to, with the little woman at the sink and so forth, the mother figure. It was very ingrained in him, that pattern. I'm afraid I'm sounding rather acid and waspish. There was that very sweet side, that loving side of him. Everybody adored him. I wanted him, like most women, more privately for myself.

We came to the present. Caitlin said that after years of Alcoholics Anonymous she had been rendered 'nice and flat and crawling. I'm a worm now.' This was plainly untrue, though one or two things did seem to make her anxious. When the subject of Giuseppe Fazio came up, she described him guardedly as 'a typical Sicilian character', who was a lot calmer now than in the past. He had 'looked after me and really saved my life. I most certainly would be dead but for him.' That was all she wanted said about Giuseppe.

Difficulties with the *Double Drink* manuscript were sapping her confidence. Wyn Henderson had been scathing about it, quoting Oscar Wilde at her, the remark about a cynic knowing the price of everything and the value of nothing. 'I didn't like that,' said Caitlin. 'It was too near the truth.' Nicolette, she added, was the one who did the positive thinking – 'got immense confidence in herself, and though she writes a lot of rubbish, she's quite happy about it'. She looked distastefully at her gloves. 'To tell you the truth, there's nothing I'd like more than a large whisky after this.'

That sounded like a hint and we went out to lunch. But her choice was a hamburger restaurant in the Gloucester Road, and all she drank was Coca-Cola.

Life in Rome, or anywhere, was becoming more difficult. Caitlin wrote to Nicolette:

> Giuseppe is roughly ten years younger than me – and although this didn't matter so much when we were both more or less in our middle ages – we seemed on an equal sexual footing then – now that we are both in our advanced years the difference has become much more pronounced, apart from incompatibility of temperament, mind and nationality [and] since my sobriety of about seven years now the mere thought of repulsive sex makes me shudder! Also I feel at my age it is not dignified, so once and for all time *the iron curtain is down*. It may be due partly to my over-indulgence in the past that my rejection now of sex is so fanatical.

The Thomas Fazios were becoming more self-contained in their idiosyncrasies, as people do. 'Nobody asks us to their houses,' Caitlin told Nicolette. 'I do not wonder why, we are both difficult unaccommodating people, and a very ill-assorted couple.' By the end of the Seventies, Sicily was on the agenda as their next and last place of domicile – 'in the depths of the lava,' Caitlin wrote to Brigit, 'hidden away from the open sea – where [Giuseppe] has been trying all along to lure and ensnare us. And so, one door after another is closing in on us.'

To Giuseppe, whose roots were deep in the place, it was simply going home. His mother had left him a small property on the edge of Catania, where the fertile ground of the lava slopes is dotted with apartments, sheds, wasteland. The light railway that circles the base of Etna crosses the road half a mile away. It is high enough to feel the wind blowing in off the Mediterranean. The house – 'the shack', to Caitlin – was suitable for development.

When they left Rome, about the end of 1982, the alterations were still in progress, so they lived in an apartment at Acitrezza, a fishing village and summer resort on the coast to the north of Catania, while Giuseppe supervised the building works. The seascapes at Acitrezza are much admired. It is known as the 'Riviera di Ciclopi', its rocky islets supposedly the missiles hurled at Ulysses as he escaped from Polyphemus, one of the leading Cyclops. Caitlin wasn't much of a one for legends. Winter storms covered the promenade in stones. She enjoyed the fresh fish from the quays but complained at the smell of sewage that invaded the rooms. When warm weather came, the smell got worse, tourists began to arrive, and a nearby disco throbbed at night.

They moved to the house in June 1983: 'my black solitary confinement in Sicily', as Caitlin described it to Aeron. 'How painfully I miss you,' she wrote to her in 1984, after a visit to Britain, 'and what unspeakable pleasure your company gave me in London.' That year, too, she was in Ireland, staying for a month with Theodora FitzGibbon, who had formerly been married to Constantine FitzGibbon, Thomas's first biographer. Theodora, herself a writer (she specialised in cookery), was helping Caitlin rewrite the intractable *Double Drink Story*, about which publishers were not enthusiastic. The house was at Dalkey, the village along the coast from Dublin where Francis Macnamara had died.

The two women worked at the manuscript every morning; Caitlin said she was hypnotised by the ruthless way Theodora attacked her punctuation and sliced out whole pages. The setting was dramatic, rocks and boiling tides under the windows. Her room overlooked the bay. But nothing was right. 'All my yearning nostalgia for my wild Ireland of the past,' wrote Caitlin, 'was squashed flat by the cream of the Bourgeoisie enveloping me in their tidy surrounds.'

Stuart Thomas visited her there; so did I. Over dinner in a restaurant she picked at her food and smiled at the noisy conversation, not joining in. She didn't much enjoy her visit. Before leaving Ireland she made a last trip to Ennistymon and spent three nights at the Falls Hotel. Husband and son met her when she flew back to Rome, to stay in the mountains *en route* to Sicily. 'I was never so happy at seeing G. and F. at the barrier!!!' she wrote to Aeron. It might be hateful (and she said so, often enough, in her letters), but it was home.

15

Keeping On

Caitlin remained unreconciled both to old age and to the past; still cursing her failure to find a publisher for that damned *Double Drink Story*. She anticipated beds of nails and crowns of thorns, as befitted a 'martyred woman', the Santa-Caterina figure. As a rule she was at her best when expecting least of life.

In Catania, in 1991, she showed me a folder of essays and notes, most of them written as part of her Alcoholics Anonymous therapy, and insisted I read them all. Among them was a single sheet headed 'My Citations'. It was undated and contained three epigrams:

(1) In the shrivelled-up heart of a bastard lies the sought-after Golden Heart. Cunningly hidden in a patch of stinging nettles.
(2) I think Friends are a lot more important than Lovers. At least they do not stain the sheets . . .
(3) No, the sands are not golden; never have been. That is only another stretch of the tourist's imagination.

The essays included one on 'Our Substitute Father' – memories of Nora Summers, her mother's lover. Caitlin described Nora's visits to New Inn House and the locked doors behind which the women disappeared in the afternoons. The three sisters, believed Caitlin, all came under the influence of Mrs Summers.

In later life we suffered the results of such an unnatural upbringing . . . She taught us to despise all men as inferior beings – and although we were always in fierce opposition to her beliefs and opinions, nevertheless some of her negative attitudes must have persisted in us, because we all had great difficulties afterwards in adjusting to a normal relationship with a man.

Blaming others came easily to Caitlin. More than once I advanced the view that people brought things on themselves, but she wasn't listening. In another essay she blamed her father for deep flaws in her character. It was he who gave her a mistrust of men in general. 'He was an unhappy man. Just as I also, underneath all that same play-acting showing-off stuff, hidden underneath my dog-eared hearthrug, am an unhappy woman.'

In our conversations I waited to hear something magnanimous about Dylan Thomas, just a word now and then. Her voice did soften occasionally. 'I can't imagine why I ever went with Dylan, really, because there was nothing beautiful about him. I was very fond of him. Only I don't quite understand what the attraction was.' But in old age, attacking him seemed to make her feel better. Sitting in the big wood-floored living room – Giuseppe glancing darkly at a black-and-white television, Silvana in the adjacent kitchen rattling pans – she cursed the poet and tried to remember how she felt.

> It's all very mystifying to me. I can't make out whether I was in love with him or not. One side of me thinks he was the most bloody awful crook in the world. I didn't realise how mean and how deceitful he was, what a scoundrel, a low-down bastard, treading on my innocence.

At my request she wrote a few pages about her love life. Francis put them on his computer and printed them out. Her theme, inevitably, was how unsatisfactory it had been. She watched while I read the essay, smoking a cigarette she had cadged from Giuseppe, holding it awkwardly as if she had just learned the habit.

> There are many ways to sabotage love and sex and with Dylan they were all there: poor confidence, lies, unsatisfactory sex, constant betrayals, lack of trust, fights, booze, never having enough money and so on. I answered all this with reproaches, fights, blackmail and going to bed with lower class men (working class, peasants, miners, builders). I preferred the lower class men to the 'civilised' ones because their bodies were better looking, they did their job instinctively better and one didn't have to make a polite little speech when it was all over.
> With most of my men, sex intercourse always lasted so little and I was

always left high and dry. I was more interested in sex than Dylan; I think he liked being cuddled and cosseted, and in a woman he was always looking for the image of his mother.

I wanted to ask if she had thought like that half a century earlier, or had merely come to believe it with hindsight, after reading too many books on the subject. But the question seemed pointless, not to say insulting. She could only give me the answers that were available.

For all her denunciation, Caitlin has clung to the belief that Thomas needed her, that the letters he wrote were expressions of a genuine devotion. Her bitten fingers did their maximum bleeding when she spoke of the letters she had kept 'to comfort myself that at one time he did love me'. No doubt he did. He certainly depended on her; a fatal dependence, as it turned out.

Six months after returning from Catania, I found a poem by Caitlin among the Dylan Thomas papers of the University of Texas at Austin. It is copied out neatly in her own hand, undated but almost certainly written towards the end of the marriage. In this – more clearly than in her books and manuscripts, more perceptively than in the bitterness of old age – she described the condition to which life with the poet had driven her, which helped ruin them both. She called it 'Self Portrait'.

Is this me,
This carping crock,
Am I come,
The giant Christian,
The giant idealist
And the giantly ambitious,
To this poor forlornity
Of the ordinary woman's
Song drowning
Floundering on two levels,
One, the constant admonishing,
With the voice common
To countless sad admonishers;
The other, the half submerged,
Once wild, vain groaning
Of the broken sea horse.
The noose has dropped
On my prancing mane;

Can this tame nag
Be hagridden me?

She signed it 'Catnag Thomas'. I was going to send her a copy, but thought better of it.

Postscript

Francesco Thomas Fazio, Caitlin's youngest son, has written this brief account of his mother in her eightieth year:

How terribly sad it is for a son to see, day by day, the progressive mental and physical deterioration of his mother. One loves that person, but love alone, however big, can't stop her going to pieces. Because of increasing infirmity, it is only natural that she depends on me, on my companionship, enormously.

Old age, pain, suffering, the many privations of her life (such as no swimming, no dancing, no riding, no nature walks, no friendly contacts any more) consume her thoughts. The feeling of being in limbo, of living a succession of wasted days, of being trapped and having 'let herself go', is daily intoxicating her brain. The most she complains about is loneliness. But I know she is also too strong to cry in front of me.

Mine is not merely love but also loyalty to an infirm parent, a sense of duty and attachment. She needs continual care, especially at night, and it's in my role of 'night sitter' that we have the most revealing conversations. These are the moments she enjoys, when she tells me that old age is sad, not because with it end the joys of life, but because, day after day, every hope perishes. Perhaps I'm the only person who sees in her smile the happiness of hearing my footsteps coming back late at night after my dancing class.

This is what she herself says:

'Old age has taken away most of my beauty, the elasticity of my body and brain, my memory, my freedom to visit open spaces. Above all it's a reminder that one is no longer desirable to everyone. What

244

hasn't been taken away is my sense of humour, my witty remarks (shared with Francis), my wisdom that's come out of suffering, and the love and respect I have for people who – with difficulty – are still close to me.'

Only in this late stage of life can my mother more deeply appreciate the best way of handling her children: she can now give real love because she can concentrate more on them (the previous vain desires such as booze and sex only distracted her from being a continuously responsible mother to all her children).

She is surely cantankerous, unstable in her reactions (she suddenly passes from devoted and loving actions to bursts of fighting Macnamara rage). A happy medium does not exist. If one is having a relaxed moment and Caitlin *wants* to provoke a row (although the rest of the company tries its best to keep it down), one can be sure that Mrs Hyde will come out! But I know that within a short time she will bring out her tightly held-in natural qualities, her genuine loving kindness.

Notes

The location of written material is indicated as follows:

ATE   Aeronwy Thomas (Ellis)
BM   Brigit Marnier
CTP   Caitlin Thomas Papers – unsorted and unlisted material that she has accumulated over the years
Delaware   University of Delaware Library
Harvard   Harvard University Library
NDP   Nicolette Devas's papers, owned by her estate
NLW   The National Library of Wales at Aberystwyth
Shephard ms Unpublished ms autobiography, property of Rupert Shephard's estate
Texas   Harry Ransom Humanities Research Center, University of Texas at Austin

Other abbreviations:

Fool   *Am I the Perfect Fool?*, unpublished typescript by Caitlin Thomas, in the possession of Roger Lubbock
Jug   Unpublished manuscript by Caitlin Thomas, in her possession
Leftover   Caitlin Thomas, *Leftover Life to Kill* (Putnam, 1957)
Story   *The Story of a Woman*, unpublished manuscript by Caitlin Thomas. NDP
TFF   *Two Flamboyant Fathers* by Nicolette Devas

'In conversation' means in conversation with the author unless otherwise stated.

It would be impractical to note every occasion when I am drawing on my conversations with Caitlin between 1978 and 1991. They are identified only where it seems necessary. In general, where a source is not given for something attributed to her, it can be assumed it comes from a conversation.

Source-material about Dylan Thomas is given only when it differs from or is additional to that identified in my biography (revised edition, Penguin Books, 1992). His letters, except where indicated, can be found in the *Collected Letters* (Paladin, 1987).

The whereabouts of certain material is not indicated, in order to respect confidences.

1 Under the Volcano

2   C to Aeron: 19.3.83. ATE
4–5   C to the author: 30.11.90
5   'Carved-in-adamant marble': *Am I the Perfect Fool?* How this came to be written is described in Chapter 11. The typescript was given to Roger Lubbock in 1957 and rediscovered by him in 1992

2 Fathers and Mothers

9   *Time After Time*: Deutsch, 1983
10   The Macnamara family: in a paper on 'The Macnamaras of Doolin & Ennistymon', Michael MacMahon says they are 'among the oldest families in Ireland and can trace their lineage back almost to the dawn of authentic history'
10   Rents of £10,000 a year: Colm Hayes, 'The Macnamara Estate in 1863', *Ennistymon Parish Magazine*, 1991. Hayes said (in conversation) that the accounts book on which he based the article was 'rescued' by a relative
10   The 'illegitimacy' story: Francis Macnamara to Yvonne Majolier, 7.6.07. NDP
11   'That so-called Macnamara': quoted in Larry Healy, 'The Cattle Drive from Doolin', *Ennistymon Parish Magazine*, 1991
11   The ambush: *Clare Champion*, 6.12.19, 13.12.19, 3.1.20, 31.1.20, 6.3.20

11	Compensation: Henry Vee claimed £1,000 for personal injuries and was awarded £250
11	Letter from IRA: quoted in Michael MacMahon, op cit
12	'Macnamaraland': Romilly John, *The Seventh Child. A Retrospect* (Cape, 1975). Francis even designed banknotes for his republic
13	Francis the conqueror; the owl story; sailing: *TFF*
13	*Marionettes*: published by Elkin Mathews, Vigo Street. The *Irish Independent* thought Macnamara 'a real poet'. The London *Times* found 'little poetic emotion or arresting music'
14	Macnamara's ideas; clouds and underclothes: from letters to his wife in NDP
14	'Poet' as a profession: Oliver St John Gogarty, *It Isn't This Time of Year at All!* (MacGibbon & Kee, 1954)
14	Yvonne confides in Brigit: conversations with Brigit, South Gorley, 1992
15	Dismissing servants: Brenda Aherne, in conversation, Ennistymon, 1992
15	Francis in the cottages: Paddy Shannon, in conversation, Fisher Street, 1992
15	John on the 'forgotten people': *Horizon*, October 1941, quoted in Michael Holroyd, *Augustus John*, Vol. 2 (Heinemann, 1974)
15 et seq	Macnamara photograph albums: NDP
15–16	Francis to Yvonne: written on headed paper, 'Coole Park, Gort, Co. Galway', Lady Gregory's home, and a centre of Irish writing, and postmarked (probably) 22.7.14. NDP
16	Francis to Augustus John: Augustus John Papers. NLW
17	Nora Summers the artist: the Summers family has a water-colour by her of 'Coole Lake', dated 21 August 1915, and signed N. Munro Summers
17	Augustus John to Dorelia: John Papers. NLW
17	Balzac's book: Honoré de Balzac, *The Physiology of Marriage, or Meditations of an eclectic philosopher on happiness and unhappiness in marriage*, translated with an introduction by Francis Macnamara (The Casanova Society, 1925)
18	Euphemia Lamb: information from M. Holroyd, op cit;

Keith Clements, *Henry Lamb. The artist and his friends* (Redcliffe, Bristol, 1985); telephone conversation with Lady Pansy Lamb

19   Planning the divorce: NDP

19   Romilly on Francis: *The Seventh Child*, op cit

21   *Form of Diary*: published by the Pushkin Press, one of various titles used at different times by the idiosyncratic publisher John Rodker (d. 1955). Rodker was also behind the Casanova Society, which published Francis Macnamara's Balzac translation

21 ff   Erica Saye: conversations with Joan Rodker and Susan Watson, London, 1992; 'A Romance in E Flat Minor', by Michael Holroyd, in *People*, ed Susan Hill (for Oxfam, 1983)

24   *Gallant Ladies*: the publisher, in 1943, was John Rodker's Pushkin Press. Macnamara wrote a preface to this, too, with a novel defence of pornography. He argued that the sexual antics in the book were Brantôme's way of demonstrating a system of natural eugenics, in which the potent get to mate with the beautiful

3 Children of the Forest

26 ff   Blashford childhood: Conversations with C. and Brigit; Nicolette in *Two Flamboyant Fathers* and *Susannah's Nightingales* (Collins, 1978)

26   'Common': 'Common was our mother's favourite expression for complete contempt', C. in 'Negative Attitudes: where and when did they begin?', essay written for Alcoholics Anonymous

27   Yvonne and Nora: conversations with C. and Brigit. Nicolette knew about the sexual relationship, but left it out of her family biographies

28   Nicolette's novel: *Bonfire* (Chatto, 1958). Rupert Shephard, her second husband, told me that 'Vera' in the novel was meant to be Nora; in conversation, London, 1991

28   *Story of a Woman*: written in two 'exercise books'. (1) has 'Caitlin Part I' on the cover and inside a variety of titles: 'The Story of a Woman', 'Life with a Poet' and 'A History of Women'. Nicolette has added a glossary identifying some of

the characters. Pages are numbered 1–112, with some misnumberings. (2) is 'Caitlin Part II,' with the title 'Nine Months Labour (Part two)'. Pages are numbered 113–63. Nicolette has added, 'Given to me 1947'. The assorted titles suggest that Caitlin's original intention was to include her life with Dylan Thomas, and later volumes may exist, or have existed. The manuscript conceals as much as it reveals. It must have been sent to Nicolette to help her write about the family. NDP

28   C. to Brigit: 3.2.70
29   Nicolette's libel insurance: Nicolette in conversation, 1976: 'I was very frightened and I did take out a libel insurance, and the only person I was afraid of was my sister.' I tried to include this morsel in my biography of Thomas, but was told by the publisher's lawyer to delete it, lest it upset Caitlin by suggesting she was litigious
30   'Pink pudding': *Double Drink Story*, unpublished ms
30   Nicolette on C.: *TFF*
31   Six hundred pounds in trust: NDP
31 fn   Nicolette on the fantasies: *TFF*
31   Three surviving letters: 10.10.28, 17.3.29, 9.3.30. NDP
32   C.'s misery at school: 'Negative Attitudes' essay, op cit
34   Caspar John's biographer: Rebecca John, *Caspar John* (Collins, 1987)
34   Dorelia on Brigit: John papers. NLW
34   Caspar's letter: Rebecca John
34   William Townsend's journals: held at University College Library, London
35   Tonks on Lopez: Rupert Shephard, in conversation
36   'Set apart': *Fool*
36   Running away: C.; *Story*; an anonymous friend
36   The poky room: *Story*
36   C. to Nicolette: 10.12.65. NDP

4 Encounters with Artists

40   C. to Nicolette: ibid
40   Nicolette on John: in conversation, 1976
40   Pamela Glendower: in a telephone conversation, 1992
40   John to C.: on Fryern Court paper, undated. Sexual hygiene

is enjoined with the words 'Keep the fun clean also your quim'. NLW

40   Nude drawings of C: four in number, at the National Museum of Wales, Cardiff. They can be seen only with special permission. Cardiff has the 'striped cardigan' painting on display, and two unfinished oils in the basement. In 1972 the museum bought 1,150 of Augustus John's drawings, paintings and bronzes from the Dorelia John estate for £4,000. Special permission is needed to see any of them

41   Chiquita's seduction: Holroyd, op cit. The grunting and snorting is what Caitlin recalled, too

41   Unnamed witness: in a letter, 21.7.92. If Caitlin was seduced by John when she was fifteen or sixteen, the fact that she was 'going out with men' when at dancing school is irrelevant, since that came later. But it is the account as given.

42   'An old stag': Holroyd, op cit, Vol. 2

43   'Fabulous Courtesan': letter to the author, 30.6.91

44   At Dun Aengus: *TFF*

44   Caitlin's rage: letter to the author, 5.9.91

44   An unfortunate name: Francis to Yvonne, 17.6.28, the year after they were divorced. He added that his daughter's character still baffled him. NDP

44   Francis in the bath: *TFF*

45   Caitlin on the stage: her memories of the period have been confused for decades. *Story* has some general background. *Aladdin* she remembered, together with Playfair's name. The Mander & Mitchenson Theatre Collection found the programme. The pantomime ran from 22.12.31 to 16.1.32.

45 ff   Caitlin in Ireland: conversations in and around Ennistymon with Brenda Aherne, Dan Garrihy, Tony Garrihy, Noreen Garrihy, Jim Blackwell, Gus O'Connor, Colm Hayes, Paddy Shannon and others; *Story*

46   The Englishman in love: Rupert Shephard

48   'Road into the sky': 'Finito' ms – see fn to p 49

48   C. at empty Ennistymon: letter to the author, 5.9.91

49   Nicolette on Francis: *TFF*

49   Francis and the hookers: Frank Gilliland, 'The Galway

Hooker', in *Yachting Monthly*, Vol. XXVII–II, 1919

49 fn   'Finito' ms: Texas

52   C. to her mother: from 5 Upper Ely Place, Dublin, 10.3.35. NDP

52   Gyrating senselessly: *Story*

52   Twenty years later: *Fool*

52   'I do intend': letter of 10.3.35, op cit

53   Dancing at Fryern Court: *Story*

53   T.S. Eliot: Shephard ms

53   Euphemia Lamb: *Story*

54   Legas: the name is presumably false. In conversation Caitlin thinks he may have been called 'Segall'. So did Rupert Shephard. One or two Segalls could have been painting in Paris at the time, but the name is common, and Caitlin's Segall is untraced

54   Three in a bed: Brigit, in conversation

5 The Poet from Wales

56   The last revival: in 1904–06. The miner was Evan Roberts. It was a sensation in Wales; little known anywhere else

57   The Wheatsheaf: Julian Maclaren-Ross describes it (little changed) as it was during the Second World War, in 'Fitzrovian Nights', reprinted in his *Memoirs of the Forties* (Penguin, 1984)

58   Cameron's poem: 'The Dirty Little Accuser', in his *Collected Poems* (Hogarth Press, 1967)

58–9   Havelock Ellis's sexual habits: he was a devotee of uro-lagnia, a morbid interest in watching others (in his case, women) urinate

59   Veronica Sibthorp: Augustus John's letter to Caitlin (p 40), the only one known, is with the Veronica Sibthorp papers acquired by the National Library of Wales in the 1980s. Probably Caitlin left it behind in 1937 when she and Dylan vacated Oriental Cottage

60   Letter to magazine editor: John Johnson, assistant editor of *Life and Letters Today*, 15.7.36

60–61   Richard Hughes: biog. information, Meic Stephens, *The*

Oxford Companion to the Literature of Wales (Oxford, 1986); Lance Sieveking, *The Eye of the Beholder* (Hulton Press, 1957)

61   Thomas to Hawkins: 21.8.36

62   Shephard on C.: Shephard ms

63 ff   C.'s letters to Shephard: Rupert Shephard estate

63   'I nearly forgot him': C. interviewed in Rome for BBC Wales TV, 19.2.77

63–4   Francis's visitors: conversations in Ennistymon, 1991

6 Warring Absences

68–9   Letters to Coleman: University of Delaware Library. Not in Thomas's *Collected Letters*

69   'One day I shall sleep with her': presumably Dylan and Caitlin went to bed immediately they met, as alleged. Just conceivably, they did not.

69   Gascoyne's journal: David Gascoyne, *Collected Journals* (Skoob Books Publishing, 1991)

71   Donald Hall: *Their Ancient Glittering Eyes* (Ticknor & Fields, US, 1992)

73   'My rapacious vanity': C. to Aeron, 25.10.79

73   'A most lovable character': Yvonne to Bill Read, 23.6.64. Texas

74   Double helpings for Dylan: *Jug*

74   Augustus John to wife: undated. NLW

74   Varnish cracking: Thomas to Henry Treece, 1.9.38

75   'Rabelaisian appetites': *Fool*

75   'A lonely donkey': ibid

75   'Nursemaid' and 'maestro': ibid

75   Killing romance: ibid

76   In the double bed: Gwen Watkins, *Portrait of a Friend* (Gomer Press, 1983)

76   Ethel Ross: in conversation, Swansea, 1975

76   'Deadly serious': *Fool*

76–7   Professor Barone's manual: Gwen Watkins, op cit

78–9   C., Dylan and infidelity: the three passages quoted are from *Fool*

79   On Worms Head: Gwen Watkins, op cit and in conversation, 1992. J.C. Wyn Lewis was less than delighted in recent years to find himself cast as an object of Dylan Thomas's jealousy, since, as he points out, he hardly knew the couple, and there were never any grounds for it

80   Explaining to Hawkins: 14.8.39

80   Statements about infidelity: Thomas's editors have been inhibited in the past by uncertainty about how Caitlin would take to their assumption that there was something to be jealous of. Matthew C. Altman (Bay City, Michigan) makes some interesting speculations about the poems in an unpublished paper, *Dylan Thomas' Poetic Reactions to Caitlin's Infidelities* (1992)

80fn   Under the eyelid: *Fool*, in a passage dealing with infidelity

82   A kick in the face: *Fool*; and the incident is remembered in Laugharne

83   Told to Tremlett: in *Caitlin. Life with Dylan Thomas* (Secker, 1986)

7 Trial by Marriage

85   'I should be served': *Fool*

85–6   Lorna Wilmott's journal: Rupert Shephard estate

86 ff   The Glock affair: Sir William confirms the essentials of C.'s account. In conversation, Wallingford, 1992

87   The creamy dress: 'The importance of clothes and appearance', some notes by C., May 1991

88fn   'On a Wedding Anniversary': the inferior 1941 version could almost be read as a poem about the general effects of war – such as separation – on a marriage. Only as rewritten, four years later, does it crystallise into what Thomas presumably meant it to be all along, a metaphor for his badly damaged marriage, with phrases like 'Death strikes their house,' and 'The windows pour into their heart/And the doors burn in their brain.'

90   C. to Frances Hughes: Lilly Library, Indiana University

91   C. to Brigit: the first of the letter's six pages is missing. BM

92   Lindsay on C.'s temper: letter to the author from Jack Lindsay, 22.3.75

92   Thomas to C.: undated, probably 1943
92   Pamela Glendower: in a telephone conversation, 1992
93   Vera on the Thomases: in conversation, East Anglia, 1975
94   Theodore FitzGibbon on clothes: *With Love* (Pan Books, 1983)
94   The pink dress: *TFF*
94   Devas's painting at the Tate: it is not on public display, and has to be seen by arrangement
94   The writing of *Story*: one of the ms books has the address '55 Oakley Street', in Chelsea. Theodora FitzGibbon (who was not yet called FitzGibbon) lived in 'the top half of a house in Oakley Street' in about 1941. *With Love*, op cit
94   'Lucky wooden ones': *Fool*
95   The wrong train: *Portrait of a Friend*, op cit
95   Chinese restaurant; Marx Bros film: Gwen Watkins, in conversation, Oxford, 1992
95   Gwen Watkins on C.'s side: *Portrait of a Friend*, op cit
95   'Small mortal Dylan': *Fool*
97   A.J.P. Taylor and Thomas: the historian made his views clear in his autobiography, *A Personal History* (Coronet, 1984)
97   'Like going to bed with a god': Caitlin's story, not reliable
97   Elisabeth Lutyens: in conversation, London, 1975
97–8   At Puck Fair: Caitlin gives an unrewarding account in *Fool*
98   'Tried in the scales': Monk Gibbon in the *Irish Times*, February? 1979, reviewing Nicolette Devas, *Susannah's Nightingales*
98   'Put the goat out': Dan Garrihy, in conversation
98   'I am ashamed to say': *Fool*
99   Men's 'goggling eyes': *Double Drink Story*, unpublished ms
100   'Beautiful Giovanni': *Leftover*, written after C. revisited Elba
100   Taylor's autobiography: *A Personal History*, op cit
100   Cordelia Saleeby: technically she was still Mrs Sewell in 1948, Mr Sewell having been her second husband; she married Harry Locke later
101   Cordelia Locke on Caitlin: (to 'spotted handkerchief'), typescript recollections of the Thomases at South Leigh, with Thomas papers, Texas; thereafter, in conversation, 1975

102	Larkin to Amis: 21.11.85, *Selected Letters of Philip Larkin*, ed Anthony Thwaite (Faber, 1992)
102	Cordelia Locke on the Thomases: in conversation
103	C. to Brigit: BM
103	Dylan's accident: Cordelia Locke, typescript at Texas, op cit
104	What the Boat House cost Mrs Taylor: the information is in a letter she wrote after Thomas's death. Later she denied having spent so much, in order not to offend her estranged husband, A.J.P. Taylor
104	C. to Davenport: 4.3.49. NLW. The references to a woman and blouses are from a conversation, not the letter
104	'Between him and death': *Fool*

8 Boat House Blues

107	C.'s 'decrepitude': C. to Brigit, 14.5.49. BM
107–8	C.'s clothes; C. in the pub: Dai and Lou Thomas, and other conversations in Laugharne
108	Law and order in Laugharne: conversations with former police officers and delinquents
110	'When Dylan was on his long trips': in conversation, 1978
110–11	Brinnin on C.'s letter: John Malcolm Brinnin, *Dylan Thomas in America* (Ace Books, 1957, but first published by Atlantic-Little, Brown, Boston, 1955)
111	'Lovely' and 'beautiful' letters: Thomas to C., about 11.3.50 and 18.4.50
111	'Beyond endurance': C. to Oscar Williams, 30.3.51. Harvard.
112	'Sucked dry': *Fool*
112	Love letter in May: 7.5.50
112	Telling Margaret Taylor: letter dated 18.6.50
112	Jane Dark: in conversation, Laugharne, 1992
113	C. to 'Mrs Oscar Williams': 14.7.50. Harvard
113	C. to Brinnin: 14.7.50. Delaware
113	Sniffing suspiciously; finding letters: *Fool*
113–14	At Pennard: Gwen Watkins, op cit, and in conversation
114	'I gazed suicidally': *Fool*

115   'Baby weakness': ibid
115   'Deadly entanglement': ibid
116   The rat-hold: ibid
116   C. to R.L.F.: seven letters. Royal Literary Fund
116–17 C. to Davenports: 30.1.51. NLW
117–18 C. to Brigit: 27.2.51. BM
118   David Wright on C.: in a letter, 27.2.93
119   C. to Oscar Williams: 30.3.51. Harvard
119 ff Brinnin at Laugharne: *Dylan Thomas in America*, op cit
120   The later lover: David Gardner
120   Elisabeth Lutyens: she described the Laugharne visit in her autobiographical *A Goldfish Bowl* (Cassell, 1972). In conversation (1975), but not in the book, Lutyens said the row was about M.
121   Taking C.'s part: *A Goldfish Bowl*, op cit
122 ff C. on Dolly Long, and the Camden episode: *Fool*
122   Orchard Park, and other memories of Dolly Long: Sheila Morgan (Dolly's niece), in conversation, Laugharne, 1992

9 Breaking Point

125   C's ill-humour: Brinnin, op cit
126   'Pissing their pants': C. interviewed in Rome for BBC Wales television, 19.2.77
126   Posthumous accusations: *Fool*
126   At Cambridge, Mass.: Brinnin, op cit
126–7   At Maya Deren's: Howard Moss, in conversation, New York, 1975
127   Thomas dressed to kill: *Fool*
127   The thousand-dollar story: Brinnin, op cit; *Fool*
128   Markson's story: in conversation, New York, 1975
128   Rose Slivka: in conversation, New York, 1975
128   Mike Watkins: in conversation, New York, 1975
128   Unhappy Caitlin: Charles W. Mann, in a letter to the author, 9.7.75
129   Joint postcard: NLW
129   At Salt Lake City: Olive Ghiselin, 'Dylan', *Alumnus* magazine, University of Utah, Fall 1967; Marjorie Adix, an account (untitled) of Thomas in Utah, *Encounter*, c. 1954.

129	The telegram: Delaware
129	Thomas weeps: Barbara Holdridge, in conversation, New York, 1975
129	Marianne Mantell: in conversation, New York, 1975
130	C. to Brinnin: 10.5.52, misdated by about a week. Delaware
130	C. to Lougee: 7.6.52. Gabriel Pustel
132–3	Donald Hall: *Their Ancient Glittering Eyes*, op cit
134	What Thomas knew: one of his doodles, on the back of a worksheet, shows a lighthouse with the rays blacked out and the caption 'Darkhouse', perhaps a pun on the name of Howard Dark
135	'What I miss with Dylan': 12.2.54, C. to David Gardner, who owns all her letters to him
135	C. to Oscar Williams: 9.2.53, misdated 1952. Harvard
135	C. to Brinnin: undated. Delaware
135	'Affected ass': Reitell, telephone conversation, 1975
135–6	'Agree to anything': ibid
136	Thomas sends money: the $250 and the encyclopedia are mentioned in an unpublished letter from New York, 7.5.53, still in Caitlin's possession. It is in the style of his other letters, reiterating the awfulness of America and the depths of his love
136	Watkins at Laugharne: Gwen Watkins, op cit. The friend was Francis Dufau-Labeyrie, who had translated some of Thomas's prose into French
137–8	David Gardner: in telephone conversations when he was in Australia; his tape-recorded reminiscences; later in conversation, London, 1992
138	Haircut and trousers: Jane Dark, in conversation
139	C. in London: Cordelia Locke, in conversation
139	Not a 'doormat wife': *Fool*
140–41	C. to Thomas: Delaware

10 A Life of Her Own

143–4	Telegram to Williams: Harvard
144 ff	C. in New York: Rose Slivka and David Lougee, in conversation; Ruthven Todd, 'Dylan Thomas: a personal

account' (unpublished), National Library of Scotland; Brinnin, op cit

144   'He died before he left': *Fool*

145   'Drabs of wet nurses': C. to Brinnin, undated. A kinder view of Reitell is suggested by a one-page fragment of another letter from C. to Brinnin, which asks about the post-mortem on Thomas and continues, 'Tell Reitell thank you for her letter, it's all I wanted to know. I'm sure she is' – at which point the page ends

146fn   Medical bills: Delaware, with Brinnin's papers

146   'Familiar hands': *Fool*

146–7   With Rose Slivka: *Leftover*, where she is 'my little valiant Rose'

147   Llewelyn: in conversation, Cork City, 1992

148   'Raffish Londoners': *Leftover*

148   Conceiving the Trust: various recollections; David Higham, *Literary Gent* (Cape, 1978). Apparently no documents about the setting up of the Trust have survived

148   Affidavits: CTP

149   Dancing in the street: Sheila Morgan; Ethel Ross, both in conversation

150   Hospital notes: CTP

150   C. to Gardner: 'PM – 3.12.53'. The letter is headed 'Holloway Jail' (the clinic was Holloway Sanatorium) and 'Eternity'

150   C. to Lougee: 6.12.53. Gabriel Pustel

150   Ruth Witt-Diamant letter: 8.12.53, to 'Dearest Kitten'. CTP

151   C. to Brinnin: 19.12.53. Delaware

151   C. to Lougee: Gabriel Pustel

151   Memories of Ireland: *Story*

151   In Paris: ibid

152   Nightmares: C. to Daiken, 6.2.54. Texas

152   Colm's Granny: C. to Daiken, 29.1.54. Texas

152   C. and Florence Thomas: *Fool*

153   C. to Higham: 16.3.54

153   Eight pounds a week: Stuart Thomas to C., 15.1.54

153   C. to Daiken: 12.2.54. Texas

153   Five hundred pounds a year: David Higham to Stuart Thomas, 19.3.54

153	FitzGibbon declines: letter to trustees, 15.9.62
154	C. to Stuart Thomas: Trust files
155	C. to Daiken: 17.6.54. Texas
155	'They wanted a saint': *Fool*
155	C. to Nicolette: NDP
155	Havoc in Swansea: anon
155–6	To Gardner, 'never had a good person': envelope postmarked 14.3.54
156	Other letters to Gardner: 5.4.54, 31.5.54
156–7	C. to Nicolette: NDP
158	'Ceaselessly making beds': *Fool*
158–9	'Not yours': 22.1.54. Trust files
159	Date of birth: ibid
159	'If not for my sake': 21.8.54. Trust files
159	'Incapable state': 28.5.54. Trust files
159	The pressed plants: Sheila Morgan has the book
160	C. to Brinnin: 16.8.54. Delaware
160	'Told to write': to Brinnin, 8.2.54. Delaware
160	Booda and Howard Dark: anon
160	To Daiken, about M. Taylor: 12.2.54. Texas

11 Love Stories

163	C. to Daiken: card, postmarked 27.10.54. Texas
163	C. to Brinnin's mother: postcard, undated. Delaware
164	C. to Thomas: 3.11.54, 15.12.54. Trust files
165	John on *Leftover*: his *Finishing Touches*, ed Daniel George (Cape, 1964)
166	The deleted sentence: in a typescript of *Leftover*, described as 'bearing [Caitlin's] more or less final autograph revision', NLW. The title page has a curious dedication, in Caitlin's hand, 'To Giuseppi, and my Pino, and all the Peppinos in the world'. The book as published was undedicated. The typescript is said to have been found in Italy by a member of Nicolette's family. NLW bought it in 1981
167	'Destitute': 27.2.55
167	C. to Daiken: 4.3.55. Texas
168	Chiesa to the Trust: 9.3.55

Notes

183   Henderson 'an institution': C. to Stuart Thomas, 8.2.57
184   To Lubbock, not jolly: 'My dear, dear Roger', 4.4.57
184   Three thousand pounds for a house: Henderson to Trust, 2.4.57
184   To Lubbock, getting cold feet: 'Dearissimo Roger', 8.6.57
185   Having to get out: C. to Stuart Thomas, 27.6.57
185   'Dear Nobody': 1.8.57. Texas
185–6 C. to Lubbock: from the Falls Hotel, 16.8.57

12 Roman Holidays

187   Cliff Gordon the medium: information from Pamela Glendower, who knew him
188–9 C. meets Giuseppe: his account, in conversation
189   The English couple's statement: made in Rome, 16.3.72. CTP
189   Welsh trial: at Abergavenny, 1942
189   In the lift: letter to the author from C., 5.9.91, and in conversation
189   Henderson to Thomas: 11.10.57
190   Sticky parties: C. to Stuart Thomas, 25.10.57. Trust files
190   Dose of salts: C. to her mother, 15.10.57. NDP
190   C. to Brigit: 28.11.57. NDP
190   Selznick's interest: David Higham to C., 25.11.57, to say that Selznick's story editor in New York, David Weiss, suggested a 'very dramatic movie' could be made about 'Dylan Thomas and his wife'. Higham thought she could make $10,000 out of it if she was lucky
191   *Jug* ms: CTP
193   Patronising article: 'Dylan Thomas and Company', *Sunday Times*, 28.9.58. John told Russell that he was glad to have been able to write favourably about Thomas, adding that he hoped Lord Kemsley (the newspaper's proprietor) would be pleased
193   John to Russell: 9.7.58. NLW
194   Florence Thomas to friends: 4.11.57, to Nell and Bert Trick, formerly friends of Dylan. Ohio State University Libraries

263

194   At the caravan site: *Sunday Dispatch*, 10.8.58; *Sketch*, 11.8.58. The *Dispatch* quoted Giuseppe saying (with a grin), 'Do you know what they tell me in Laugharne? They say if I am not out of the town in three days I will be dead. I asked them, how do you mean dead? They jerked their thumb and said, "In the cemetery with Dylan".'

194   Florence to Thomas: 8.8.58. Trust files

195   Lost interest in *Jug*: to Lubbock, 20.12.58

195   'The method we employ': ibid

196   C. to Nicolette: 16.1.59. NDP

196   Aeron to Nicolette: undated. NDP

196   'God knows': C. to Stuart Thomas, 29.4.59. Trust files

197   Stones and insults: Aeron, in conversation

197   C. to Lubbock: this is the letter of 20.12.58, which she was still writing in January 1959. Some of her letters to Lubbock were very long. This one was sixteen pages, about three thousand words

197   Importing a car, 1959: C. to Stuart Thomas, 29.4.59. Trust files

197   'Famous Etna': postcard, C. to Nicolette, 26.6.62. NDP

197   'Rock of comfort': C. to her mother, 9.10.59. NDP

198   'Snob convents': 19.9.59. Trust files

198   'Monarch in a mud hole': 17.11.59. Trust files

198   'Cretinous programme': undated postcard, C. to Stuart Thomas. Trust files

198   Being tactful: C. to Stuart Thomas, 25.8.62. Trust files

199   Wyn Henderson: Stuart Thomas, writing to Higham 31.8.60, reported that Henderson appeared on the scene in Italy, and brought the children back to England. Trust files

199   Aeron to Nicolette: undated. NDP

199   'Beautiful meals': C. to Thomas, thanking him, 28.9.60. Trust files

200   C. to Brigit, 30.9.60. BM

200   Night in cell: *Sunday Dispatch*, 25.9.60, the 'neat, pretty blonde' article; Caitlin was fined seven shillings and sixpence (thirty-eight pence). She referred to it in her letter of 28.9.60 to Stuart Thomas as 'my disaster on that fatal night, which gave me a terrible shaking up, and a bitter loathing for the British bulging law'

200   Wyn and Fr. Benet: Susan Watson, Wyn Henderson's daughter, in conversation
201   C. to Thomas, 'How right': 8.10.60. Trust files
201   C. to Thomas, 'Don't worry': 27.11.60. Trust files
201–2   C. to Nicolette: NDP
203   Bicycle; 'wandering Jew': C. to her mother, 14.2.61. NDP
203   Remaining loyal: C. to Stuart Thomas, 24.11.61. Trust files
203   'Bastard book': 21.9.62. NDP
204   C. on FitzGibbon: to Stuart Thomas, 1.4.63. Trust files
204   C. to Nicolette, the apartment: 21.9.62
205   C. to Nicolette, the 'Menepaws': NDP
205   C. to Nicolette, the wedding: 21.9.62
207   Interview in Rome: *People*, 9.6.63
207   C. to Brigit: NDP, where the only version is a typescript copy, probably made by Nicolette for family distribution. The letter that followed, 1.4.63, with details of the birth, is similarly in typescript only
208   Softening him up: 1.4.63, written from a private clinic. 'It was a question of deciding between the unpaid slaughter house, or this; so I decided my slaughter house days were over'
208   'Accumulation of strains': 12.7.63. Trust files
208–9   C. to Higham: received 18.11.63. Trust files

13 Family Finance

212   Trustees to Caitlin: 27.7.64. CTP, which has many documents relating to the Trust, and is among the sources used in this chapter
213 ff Cleverdon, biographical information: personal recollections, and research for a BBC radio documentary, *A Natural for Radio*, that I wrote about him in 1990, three years after his death
214   Lamenting in New York: Todd's argument, soundly based as far as it went, was that Thomas knew the value of his manuscripts and was always selling them. He claimed that Thomas wrote out two poems in New York for the editor

Tambimuttu to sell, using headed paper from London hotels (supplied by Tambimuttu) to suggest that the manuscripts were genuine originals. Todd to Stuart Thomas, 14.3.62. Trust files

14 Home Thoughts from Abroad

226–7	Fifty-seventh birthday: C. to Aeron, 12.12.70. ATE
227	C.'s essays: CTP
227	Italian beauty spots: C. to Aeron, 9.6.71. ATE
228	Morning routines: C. to Aeron, 25.10.79. ATE
228	Perpetual motion; like voyeurs: C. to Brigit, 22.1.73. BM
228	The bicycle; the crazy aunt: C. to Brigit, 12.5.75. BM
228	Cellulitis: C. to Brigit, 8.11.71. BM
229	'Four lost souls': to Aeron, 10.11.68. ATE
229	'Winter gloom': C. to Brigit, 20.11.70. BM
229	Statues, tooth, lake and broken arm: from three letters to Brigit (1975–6) and one to Aeron (1973)
229	Dog problem: to Brigit, 22.1.73. BM
229	Poison pen letters: to Brigit, 23.10.74. BM
230	Rereading Brinnin: C. to Brigit, 24.1.75. BM
230	Long letter to Nicolette: 1.5.72. NDP
232	Life with Dylan: C. to Aeron, 25.10.79. ATE
232	'Green pastures': C. to Brigit, 8.11.71. BM
232	'Black forest': C. to Brigit, 14.2.77. BM
232	Visiting Barker's: C. to Brigit, 22.1.73. BM
232	Homesick; unhappy: C. to Brigit, 13.3.77. BM
232–3	A death and a wedding: C. to Nicolette, 19.6.73. NDP
233	C. to Aeron, 1967 and 1974: 16.11.67, 22.10.74. ATE
233	'My Lolita': 22.1.73. ATE
233	'In blunt words': C. to Aeron, 18.6.66. ATE
234	'My three big children': C. to Aeron, 14.12.73. ATE
234	C. to Llewelyn: 20.11.78. CTP
234	Suggesting names: C. to Aeron, 7.2.75. ATE
235	'Portrait of a Marriage': *Observer* magazine, 5.11.78. A strike interfered with newspaper production that weekend. Few people read it.
237	C. to Nicolette: 20.9.77. NDP
237	The Sicily agenda: C. to Brigit, 3.3.79. BM
238	'All my nostalgia': C. to Aeron, 17.5.85. ATE
239	'Never so happy': C. to Aeron, ibid

Index

Index

Ghiselin, Olive, 129

Glendower, Pamela, on A. John's habits, 40; in bed with Thomas, 92

Glock, Sir William, brief affair with C., 86ff

Gogarty, Oliver St John, 17, 63

Golem, The (film), 69

Gordon, Cliff, drinking friend of C., 187; upsets Giuseppe, 189

Greenwich Village, 128, 140, 144

Gribben, Vera, 62; C.'s dancing mistress, 51; plans Grand Tour, 52; in Paris, 53; C. derides, 54

Group Theatre, 53, 62

Groveley Manor (Bournemouth), C.'s school, 31, 32

Guggenheim, Peggy, 68, 172, 175

Hall, Donald, 71, 132–3

Hall, Marguerite Radclyffe, 27

Hammersmith (London), 12, 13, 15, 58, 91, 94, 139, 140, 141, 143, 146, 149, 151, 168

Hansford Johnson, Pamela, 57, 59, 68fn

Hardy, Thomas, 20

Harmsworth, Desmond, 172

Harvard University, 196, 205

Hawkins, Desmond, 61, 72, 80

Helvetia, the (the 'Swiss' pub), 214

Hemingway, Ernest, 190, 223

Henderson, Wyn, 23, 68, 172fn, 175, 183, 186, 191, 193, 205; biog., 58; young Thomas's lover, 58; C.'s intimate, 59; organises C.'s wedding, 72; C.'s 'manager', 172, 181, 189–90; helps C. with *Leftover*, 174, 182; travels with C., Positano, 176, Procida, 176–7, Ischia, 178, Sicily, 181, Sardinia, 184, Ischia again, 184–5, Ireland 185; in Rome with C., 187, encourages Giuseppe, 188–9; out of favour, 196, 200; and the Cambridge episode, 199–200; scorns *Double Drink Story*, 229–230, 237

Hepburn, Katharine, 223–4

Herbert, A. P., 91

High Wind in Jamaica, A (Richard Hughes), 60

Higham, David, 84, 133, 194, 204, 208; a Thomas trustee, 148, 212; C.'s literary agent, 170; and *Under Milk Wood* lawsuit, 215, 216; C. letters to *quoted*, 153, 169

Holroyd, Michael, 38, 39, 42

'Homage to Dylan Thomas' (Globe Theatre), 154fn

Houdini, 137, 139

Housman, Laurence, 20

Howard-Stepney, Marged, 131, 132, 133, 134

Hughes, Frances, 61; C. letter to *quoted*, 90

Hughes, Richard, 60–1, 85, 104; houses the Thomases, 89

Idlewild airport (New York), 143

'I make this in a warring absence' (poem by Dylan Thomas), expresses sexual jealousy, 79–80

'In Country Sleep' (poem by Dylan Thomas), 99

'In the white giant's thigh' (poem by Dylan Thomas), 116, 131

'Into her lying down head' (poem by Dylan Thomas), expresses sexual jealousy, 80–81

IRA (Irish Republican Army), threatens H. V. Macnamara, 11

Ireland, 2, 9–16 *passim*, 35, 69, 75–6, 136, 153; C. visits in early 1930s, 45–52, 151, in 1937, 62–7, in 1946, 97–8, in 1955, 168–9, in 1957, 185–6, in 1983, 238–9; C.'s nostalgia for, 5, 48, 168, 238; C. contemplates residence in, 153; Thomas's sobriquet for C., 62

Ischia, 176–184 *passim*

Janes, Alfred ('Fred'), painter, 60–1, 149; one of the 'Swansea gang', 113

John, Augustus, 15, 18, 20, 22, 24, 36, 38, 43, 53, 66, 94, 150, 157, 193; 'father of C.' story, 3, 42, 71–2, 138; sleeps with C.'s mother, 14, 42, and aunt, 17; affair with C., 3, 34, 39–42, 55, 58, 59–61 *passim*, 78; recalled by C. as an 'old goat', 40; his sexual appetites, 14, 39ff; admired by F. Macnamara, 2, 14, but thinks F. Macnamara 'a queer fish', 17; Brigit's lover, 34, 226; paints C., 40, 42, 72; visits Thomases, 74; may figure in Thomas poem, 81; on C. and Elba, 165; letter to C. *quoted*, 40, 72

John, Caspar, 38, 157; C.'s passion for, 32–4, 36–7, 41–2, 53, 75; Brigit's lover, 34

John, Dorelia, 17, 24, 34

John family (Augustus John's), 18, 27, 28, 29, 32, 42, 53; C. derides, 40

John, Romilly, memories of F. Macnamara, 19

John, Vivien, 72; C.'s friend, 32, and dancing companion, 35ff, 42–3

Johnson, Lilian, F. Macnamara's mistress, 22, from Aran, 24

Johnson, Pat, F. Macnamara's natural daughter, 24

Jones, Dr Daniel, 113, 120, 136, 151, 155; Thomas's intimate, 76; at Thomas's funeral, 148; a Thomas trustee, 148, wary of C., 154, resigns, 175fn; in *Under Milk Wood* case, 215, embittered, 216

271

Caitlin

Ringwood (Hampshire), 26
Rio Marina (Elba), Thomases visit (1947), 100;
    C. visits (1954), 161, 162–8 *passim*
River Crest Sanitarium, 146fn
Roethke, Theodore, 136
Rome, 1, 4, 7, 75, 132, 154, 183, 188, 196,
    197, 199, 202ff, 212, 214, 215, 217ff,
    226, 228, 229, 232ff; C. first lives there,
    187; C.'s 'lost days' in, 190; C. in clinics
    there, 221, 222, in prison, 224
Room at the Top (John Braine), 182
Ross, Ethel, 76
Royal Literary Fund, 116, 119
Rubenstein, Anthony, 225; C. gives power of
    attorney, 216, 217
Russell, Leonard, 193

St Agatha's cathedral (Catania), 222fn
St Asaph (Wales), 138
Saleeby, Cordelia. *See* Locke, Cordelia
Salisbury, 90
Salt Lake City, 129
San Esidio, 8
San Francisco, 110, 111, 129, 150
Sardinia, 184
Savage Club (London), 113, 136
Saye, Erica. *See* Cotterill, Erica
Scharwz, Jack, 176; C. letter to *quoted*, 174
'Segall'. *See* 'Legas'
Selznick, David O., 190
Shaw, George Bernard, 21
Shephard, Rupert, 69, 98, 184; useful admirer,
    62, 'Uncle Ruggles', 63; at Falls Hotel
    with C., 66–7; at Laugharne, 85–6; paints
    C., 67, 85; second marriage to Nicolette
    Devas, 215; disenchanted with C., 225; C.
    letters to *quoted* 63, 64, 65–6
Sibthorp, Veronica, 59, 70, 71
Sicily, 1, 4, 99, 181, 195, 197, 202, 222; C.'s
    final move to, 237ff. *See also* Catania
Silvana, C.'s housekeeper, 1, 2, 227, 229, 234,
    235, 241
Silver Tassie, The (Sean O'Casey), 43
Sinn Fein (Irish nationalists), 10
Sitwell, Edith, 20, 154fn; reviews *Dylan
    Thomas in America*, 169–70
Slivka, Dave, 128, 144
Slivka, Rose, 144ff; C.'s American friend, 128
Society of Authors, 98
Sotheby's, 218
South Leigh (Oxfordshire), Thomases live at,
    100ff
Spencer, Stanley, 21
Stiffkey (Norfolk), 214
Strand Films, 89, 93
Stravinsky, Igor, 136, 137, 138

Summers, Gerald, 17, 21, 27; biog., 18
Summers, Nora, 17, 18, 21, 26, 29, 34, 35, 39,
    53; lesbian relationship with C.'s mother,
    19, 27, 41, 233; C.'s dislike of, 28, 30, her
    'substitute father', 240
Summers, Vincent, 27, 29
Sunday Express, 153
Sunday Times, 193, 208
Susannah's Nightingales (Nicolette Devas), 230
    fn
Swansea, 55, 56, 59, 60, 61, 69, 87, 93, 95,
    106, 113, 120, 136, 148, 149, 186, 199,
    217; C. stays there, 72, 75, 76, 88, makes
    scenes there, 155; town centre bombed,
    89; its cheerful provincialism, 154
Swinburne, Algernon, 85
Synge, J. M., 14

Talsarn (Wales), 91fn, 93
Tambimuttu, J. Meary, 94
Tanning, Dorothea, 128
Taormina (Sicily), 181, 193
Taylor, A. J. P., 100, 102, 151; long-suffering,
    97
Taylor, Margaret, 103, 112, 143, 151, 173;
    Thomas's patron, 97, 99, 100, 102, 104,
    122, 131, 132, 133; and Caitlin, 114,
    117fn, 123; buys Boat House, 104, sells it
    to Thomas Trust, 158, 217; C.'s
    'poisonous panegyric' to, 160
This Week (TV), 182
Thomas, Aeronwy ('Aeron', C.'s daughter), 2,
    6, 96, 97, 98, 108, 122, 186, 191, 203;
    birth, 92–3; at school, 159, 193, 196, 197,
    202; career, 205; marriage, 232; first
    child, 234; witnesses quarrels, 133, 137;
    proud of her father, 233; and the Trust,
    216, 217, 233–4; on her mother, 159,
    177, 205; their close bond, 234; on C.'s
    men friends, 178, 205; C on 'my volatile
    Ophelia', 233, and other perceptions, 3, 4,
    167, 197, 220, 238; reluctant subject of
    *Not Quite Posthumous Letter to My
    Daughter* 206–7; her mother's confidant,
    eg on drink, 222–3, suicide, 223, life with
    Dylan Thomas, 232; on Giuseppe Fazio,
    198, 205; and the Cambridge episode,
    199; and the Rome policeman incident,
    224; and Aunt Nicolette, 147, 159, 176,
    199. C. letters to *quoted*, 2, 73, 221, 222,
    223, 226–7, 228, 229, 232, 233, 234, 238,
    239
Thomas, Caitlin, her old age in Sicily, 1–8
    passim; enjoying mischief, 2, devouring
    victims, 3; her regrets, 5, her hapless
    husband, 5–6; Santa Caterina's will, 7–8;

274